MARIANNE MOORE

Elizabeth Phillips

Frederick Ungar Publishing Co.
New York

To Eva, Mary Louise and John

Library of Congress Cataloging in Publication Data

Phillips, Elizabeth, 1919–
  Marianne Moore.

  Bibliography: p.
  Includes index.
  1. Moore, Marianne, 1887–1972—Criticism and interpretation. I. Title.
PS3525.05616Z75   811'.52   81–71399
ISBN 0–8044–2698–8   AACR2

Acknowledgments

Quotations from *Collected Poems* by Marianne Moore, copyright © 1935, 1941, 1944, 1951 by Marianne Moore, copyrights © renewed 1963 by Marianne Moore and T. S. Eliot; 1969, 1972 by Marianne Moore, and 1979 by Lawrence E. Brinn and Louise Crane, reprinted with permission of Macmillan Publishing Co., Inc., and Faber and Faber, Ltd.

Selections from *The Complete Poems of Marianne Moore*, copyright © 1952, 1953, 1954, © 1956, 1957, 1958, 1959, 1960, 1961, 1962, 1963, 1964, 1965, 1966, 1967, 1968, 1969, 1970 by Marianne Moore, copyright © renewed 1980, 1981 by Lawrence E. Brinn and Louise Crane, executors of the estate of Marianne Moore. Some of these poems appeared originally in *The New Yorker*. From *Predilections* by Marianne Moore, copyright © 1925, 1931, 1936, 1941, 1942, 1943, 1944, 1949, 1955 by Marianne Moore, copyright © renewed 1964, 1969, 1970, 1972 by Marianne Moore. From *A Marianne Moore Reader*, copyright © 1961 by Marianne Moore, copyright © 1931, 1934, 1935, 1941, 1944, 1946, 1948, 1949, 1951–1960 by Marianne Moore, copyright © 1956, 1958 by The Curtis Publishing Company, copyright © renewed 1974 by Lawrence E. Brinn and Louise Crane, executors of the estate of Marianne Moore. From *The Fables of La Fontaine*, translated by Marianne Moore, copyright 1952, 1953, 1954 © 1964 by Marianne Moore, copyright © renewed 1981 by Lawrence E. Brinn and Louise Crane, executors of the estate of Marianne Moore. From *Tell Me, Tell Me* by

I acknowledge here, too, a trying out of Marianne Moore's poems by seminar students in the fall of 1979 at Wake Forest University, an R. J. Reynolds leave of absence in the spring of 1980, and a grant from the University's Research and Publication Fund in the summer of 1981. I am, finally, grateful also to Marguerite Young, Donald Hall, Nancy Cotton, Mildred Garris, Philip Winsor, Patricia B. Giles, Margaret Seelbinder, Rob Ulery, Julian Bueno, Edwin Wilson, Robert Shorter, and Henry Stroupe for their help in my work on Moore. The readings—or misreadings—of the poetry are my own.

Contents

	Chronology	ix
1	*Marianne Moore*	1
2	*The Art of Singular Forms*	21
3	*Art Is Always Actually Personal*	69
4	*The Spiritual Forces*	115
5	*In the Public Garden*	155
6	*Conclusion:* Piercing Glances into the Life of Things	227
	Notes	232
	Bibliography	244
	Index	248

Chronology

1887   Marianne Craig Moore is born November 15 in Kirkwood, Missouri.

1894   Family moves to Carlisle, Pennsylvania.

1896   Begins preparatory education at Metzger Institute, Carlisle.

1905   Finishes high school; enters Bryn Mawr College.

1909   Receives A. B. degree; enrolls at Carlisle Commercial College.

1910   Completes business course.

1911   First of visits with her mother to England and Paris during summer. Begins teaching commercial subjects at United States Industrial Indian School, Carlisle.

1915   First poems—seventeen in all—appear in *Egoist* (London), *Poetry* (Chicago), and *Others* (New York).

1916   Moves to Chatham, New Jersey, where her mother and she keep house for her brother, John Warner Moore, pastor of Ogden Memorial Church.

1918   Moves with her mother to New York City; works as secretary and private tutor in a girls' school.

1921   Publication of *Poems* by Egoist Press. Takes part-time job in Hudson Park branch of New York Public Library.

1924   Dial Press publishes *Observations;* awards her $2,000 in recognition of "unusual literary value."

1925   Becomes acting editor of *The Dial* magazine.

1926   Assumes job as editor of *The Dial.*

1928   First poem to be translated, "A Grave," appears in *Anthologie de la nouvelle poésie.*

1929   *The Dial* ceases publication; she and her mother move to Brooklyn; devotes full time to writing.

1935   Brings out *Selected Poems.*

1945   Receives Guggenheim Fellowship.

1947   Is elected to National Institute of Arts and Letters. Mother dies.

1949   Wilson College confers Litt. D., first of sixteen honorary degrees from American colleges and universities.

1951 *Collected Poems* is published; receives Pulitzer Prize and National Book Award.

1953 Visiting lecturer at Bryn Mawr College, which gives her M. Carey Thomas award. *Collected Poems* wins Bollingen Prize. Brooklyn's Youth United for a Better Tomorrow selects her for Youth Oscar; *Woman's Home Companion* chooses her as one of six most successful women of the year.

1954 *Gedichte,* a bilingual edition of poems, published in Germany. Translation of the *Fables of La Fontaine,* for which she receives the Croix de Chevalier des Arts et Lettres, is published.

1955 *Predilections,* selected essays and reviews, is published. Is elected member of American Academy of Arts and Letters.

1961 *A Marianne Moore Reader* appears in paperback.

1962 National Institute of Arts and Letters observes her seventy-fifth birthday; Brandeis University awards her prize and medal for outstanding achievement in poetry.

1964 *Festschrift for Marianne Moore's Seventy-Seventh Birthday by Various Hands,* and *Omaggio a Marianne Moore* are published.

1966 Moves to Manhattan.

1967 *Complete Poems* is published. Receives Edward MacDowell Medal and Poetry Society of America's Gold Medal.

1968 Wins National Medal for Literature; throws out first baseball of season at Yankee Stadium.

1969 Is named "Senior Citizen of the Year" at New York Conference on the Aging; receives honorary degree, her last, from Harvard University.

1970 Publishes final poem, "A Magician's Retreat"; becomes semi-invalid.

1972 Dies February 5.

1981 *The Complete Poems of Marianne Moore,* definitive edition, with the author's final revisions, published.

1

Marianne Moore

People who knew Marianne Moore thought she grew taller when she talked, and those who had never seen her but knew her poetry were apt to think she was taller than her actual height of five feet three and one-half inches. She liked to be inconspicuous but look well, an attitude analogous to her aim of writing verse that was not ostentatious in its techniques but was attractive down to the smallest details. She had a distaste for looking in the mirror, "possibly"—although she wasn't sure why—because she had "a deep-seated feeling that the act is too frivolous,"[1] and yet, wearing an elegant black velvet tricorne by which she was known for the last twenty-five years of her life, she once served as a model in a New York sidewalk showing of hats. Ladies of her generation wore hats long after they went out of fashion.

She was a lady with interests ladies were supposed to spurn—tools, technology, mechanics, mechanisms, acrobatics, baseball, boxing; she made bookcases and other small pieces of furniture from orange crates and scrap lumber; she never made a pie. "Cook and sew enough of the time and you feel degraded," she said,[2] but she could cook—meat and eggs and vegetables. She admired "soldierliness," gallantry, and monasticism. She read *The New York Times* every day, the Bible almost every day,[3] the encyclopedias and new poetry and scientific journals or anything else that turned up to take her fancy. She did not drink coffee or alcohol, but said that if she were to drink whiskey she would take it straight.[4] She recommended carrot juice to increase vigor, and she liked fruits and stone-ground whole-meal bread.

As a young woman, she had reddish brown hair that she wore in braids wound as a low crown on her

2

narrow head. She had buttermilk skin. Her pale blue eyes "seemed to gather the light into them," but they could "gleam with mockery," be piercing or studious, and appear grey. Her smile was described as cool, warm, enigmatic, hale, or sly. Her figure was slender. She moved about swiftly, and her gestures were quick.

So was her wit. Once when a friend called to say that he had found a little gold bracelet she had worried about losing because it had been her mother's, she said, "I am so elated I could jump out the window, and jump back in again."[5] Writing for her was an act of intellectual self-preservation.[6]

She liked horses, dogs that barked, and small animals, but she thought that to keep pets or flowers was to be a slave to them. The subjects of the paintings, drawings, and etchings in her apartment were "preponderantly animals—elephants, kangaroos, alligators, chickens, mice, hermit crabs, and very nearly all the rest."[7] She referred to them as "our ancestors."

When she was a girl, she rode polo ponies; in her seventies she was still playing tennis and "could place the ball where they ain't."[8] The poems are often like that. She also enjoyed sailing—"when a ship is tacking, you know," she said, "the sails take a beautiful slant."[9] When she traveled by plane, she wanted to sit close to the window—"and if the plane flies below the clouds, you can see the fields, meadows, and so on . . . the conciseness of things in miniature."[10] And she liked "the senseless unarrangement of wild things."[11] Her poems have qualities in common with these pleasures.

In a self-portrait that reads like a spoof of a "know who you are" test prepared for a popular magazine, Marianne Moore's answers are succinct. She wrote:

Line of work: writing.
But what would you really rather do? The same.
Mainspring: Be of use—doing some kind of work that I
would enjoy doing even if I were not paid for it.[12]

The comments are by a poet, a writer, who is reported
to have left an estate of $450,000 when she died at the
age of 84. By the usual measures of success, now called
"job satisfaction," she was a fortunate woman.

Eschewing "prettified poetry," she also had "a
way of deprecating romantic notions about the profes-
sion" of writing, and "no patience whatever with the
tradition of starving for art's sake."[13] Yet she knew
one would make sacrifices for it. She also knew that
money sullied one's motives. She refused to sell the
manuscript of a poem that had been printed in *The New
Yorker*, but was willing to give the original to the man
who wanted it: "I thought it wouldn't be exactly fitting
to be paid twice for the same poem."[14] She did not like
to buy bargains, either, because she did not feel "com-
fortable exploiting a store."[15] She was thought to be
a trifle eccentric. She may have had her quixotic
tongue in her cheek.

As she prepared for the forthcoming translation
of *The Fables of La Fontaine*, she was reported to have
worried about the literary quality and the "details of
typography, paper, and binding"—"almost everything, in fact, except the remuneration she was to receive" for the work. She did "the whole thing over
completely four times," which took nine years, and
she worked at it "practically all the time" from six
o'clock in the morning on into the evenings.[16] As a
young poet, she did not submit anything that was not
"extorted" from her, but she had, on the other hand,
"offered a thing, submitted it thirty-five times. Not

simultaneously, of course." She was, she added, "very tenacious."[17]

In her self-portrait, however, when she came to the topic of "the terrible temptation," she wrote "to subside and not persevere." Discouragement, she once said, was a kind of temptation.[18] Another was to be lazy. Having taken along manuscripts to complete at a summer camp on Black Lake, New York, for instance, she noted, "I would rather observe the wild animals and the herbage than do my work."[19] The letters she wrote from the camp abound, typically, in "comic descriptions of people and their houses, their furniture, the food served to guests at parties," and "the vivid expressions of the caretaker."[20] She made her poems and her small fortune by being what critics called "the world's greatest living observer." Like most writers, she worked when she was not working, and she wrote with discrimination about what occurred to her. As she said of the skilled athlete, "when experience has lent confidence, opportunity seems like destiny."[21] She rarely subsided. She was an ordinary, extraordinary woman.

Of her education as a poet, she thought that the most important influence on her style was ethical, and she linked the statement with the advice of her brother, John Warner Moore, who "once said of a florid piece of description, 'Starve it down and make it run.' "[22] An observer of vices and virtues as well as of animals and herbage, she was, as Wallace Stevens said of her, "a moral force in light blue."[23] Anything less than the truth would have seemed to her too weak, and the words had to be true to the surface and the depth of experience, not embellishments of it.

Moore's authority with language was gained, as Jean Garrigue suggested of her and Emily Dickinson,

"by an insistent kind of self-schooling."[24] Moore also shared with Dickinson the fact that her primary education took place at home. Emily's mother, however, "did not care for thought"; Mary Warner Moore did. "My mother who first instructed us—my brother and me—in French and music (the piano) when we were very small had a passion for books."[25] Living together until Mary Moore's death, mother and daughter also traveled together, read together, and discussed ideas together. T. S. Eliot spoke of the help that Mrs. Moore, as "an acute and ruthless critic," had been in the daughter's literary career.[26] Moore noted, in her foreword to the translation of La Fontaine's *Fables*, that she learned verbal decorum, impatience with imprecision, and dislike, if not avoidance, of "the wish for the deed" from her mother.[27] A steadfast Presbyterian "who also had a high opinion of the Quakers," Mrs. Moore distrusted "mere vocativeness" and said a different grace "often in poetic form before every meal." Her son said of her that she "had faith in the providence and goodness of God, and matters of honor were more important to her than food."[28] She fought vigorously for causes in which she believed, particularly woman's suffrage and prevention of cruelty to animals. She marched in parades; she stopped in the street to speak to drivers who were mistreating their horses.[29] "And," the poet recalled, "we stood for the National Anthem. My mother insisted that we stand for it—'The Star-Spangled Banner' on the radio," and if the children sat down too early, they had to get up again.[30] Moore often made changes in her verse to please her mother. She was, the daughter told Donald Hall, "really" a literary woman but, never conscious of being expert, never wrote poetry. "She advantaged me more . . . when she remarked

under crushing disappointment, *Sursum corda:* I will rejoice evermore."[31]

Mary Warner Moore (1862–1947) was educated at the Mary Institute in St. Louis. In 1885, she married John Milton Moore, a graduate in engineering at Stevens Institute. They moved to Newton, Massachusetts, where—with his brother as consulting engineer and against his father's better judgment—he put up a plant to manufacture a smokeless furnace. Upon the failure of the design and financial loss, he suffered a nervous breakdown and returned to his family in Portsmouth, Ohio, where his father, William Moore, was a well-to-do iron founder. From an old New England family that had settled in Ohio immediately after the Revolution, William Moore was a river pilot and shipowner before the Civil War. He was also the brother of "Captain Bixby," the steamboat pilot under whom Mark Twain was an apprentice on the Mississippi. Among his forebears was Clement Moore, author of "A Visit from St. Nicholas." William Moore was "bookishly inclined," owned an enormous library, and read the *Encyclopaedia Britannica* from A through Z during the last years of his life.[32] Marianne cherished a pale gold pin "with a rosette (French-set) of small diamonds at the center— the clasp curled into a halftwist, so secure it needs no safety catch"—that he had bought in New Orleans. He had said, she was told, "I'll never get my money out of the Confederacy; I might as well buy diamonds."[33] She never saw her father, who was institutionalized before her birth. He never recovered from his failure. "My mother," the daughter said, "lost him early."[34]

Marianne was born at the house of her maternal grandfather, the Rev. Dr. John Riddle Warner, who was pastor of the Presbyterian Church in Kirkwood, a town outside St. Louis. He went there in 1867 from

Gettysburg, Pennsylvania, where he served churches
during the Civil War and where his wife, Jennie Craig
Warner, had died three months after the Battle of
Gettysburg, in 1863.[35] From him there were memories
of his playing the flageolet for Mary to dance to when
she was a child, his regard for "serious" books, such
as Gibbon's *Decline and Fall of the Roman Empire,*[36] and
his tolerance of sectarian differences.[37] His grand-
daughter remembered him too as "a most affectionate
person."[38] She, her brother, who was seventeen
months older than she, and her mother lived with him
until his death in 1894, when Marianne was seven.
They moved then to Carlisle, Pennsylvania, because
her mother had a good friend there. The poet thought
that she was too young for the vicissitudes in her life
to have been very upsetting. "Journeys," she said, "always followed funerals." When the Moores started for
Pittsburgh, she asked her mother, "Is this a funeral?"[39]

Living on a small inheritance, the family was frequently in strained circumstances. In 1900, Mary
Moore took a job as a teacher of English at Metzger
Institute for Girls, where Marianne had begun her
preparatory work four years earlier, when she was
nine. To Marianne, teachers were "very, very" important, especially one who taught German and drawing
—"made us think we liked teasels and milkweed pods,
jointed grasses, and twigs with buds that had died on
the stem." Marianne received, she said, a prize or two
at the county fair. She considered being an artist, always did a little painting ("accurate") in water colors
for fun, and liked drafting. She often copied drawings
by Leonardo da Vinci, who was her favorite person in
history. She also studied piano for years and won
prizes—"one for faithfulness in practice." Her mother

owned a Steinway on which she had set an example of practicing ten hours a day when she was young. And Mary Moore saw to it that her daughter had voice lessons, "not because I had a good voice but because I didn't."[40] The poet's musical tastes were for snare drums and trumpets. She was also fond of Bach, Pachelbel, and Stravinsky. In the autumn of 1968, she narrated a performance of Stravinsky's *The Flood.* One feels that very little of the child's education was wasted.

"I experienced society vicariously," she wrote; "my brother was not introspective, or brooding, or too diffident, and abounded in invitations." There was not, she said, "a shred of sadism in his nature," and "cynicism was foreign to him." He set an example of the "capacity for suffering in silence."[41] She relied throughout her life on his advice, even in politics; she learned much from him as she followed his duties or travels and often visited him at his stations during the years he was chaplain in the navy. Through him she also experienced World War I and World War II vicariously. She wrote repeatedly to him about her poems, her discouragement, frustrations, and accomplishments.[42] She referred more than once to his saying to her, as if he were both guardian of her conscience and protector, "Sometimes you have to have paws and teeth and know when to use them."[43] That too was crucial to her education as a poet.

It was her brother to whom she also confessed minor irritations if her mother became domineering, as she could be. There was not, however, any profound or prolonged disloyalty to the needs of any of them. They were a close family with a patrician sense of respect for themselves and one another. The personal history of the mother and the children surely

bears on Moore's never having married, her "obsession" as she called it, with security,[44] and her acceptance of what critics have too easily termed the narrow
range of experience in the poems.

The final illness and death of Mary Moore in 1947
was an ordeal, perhaps the greatest of many in her
life, for the poet. Her grief was intense: "The thing
must be admitted, I don't care for books that weren't
worked on by her."[45] It was inevitable that Marianne
Moore would be considered, as she once said mock-
ingly, a case of arrested development. One of the
poet's friends, Louise Bogan, remarked in 1944 that
even though Moore was a "saint" she followed her
mother's lead strings. Bogan, describing the poet
when she was in her mid-seventies, wrote that she had
"the soul of a little boy," was "wonderful as always,"
had "really worked out her public persona—half ped-
ant and half child," looked very old, and yet was "still
bright-eyed."[46] There were, of course, other kinds of
tributes. "We've all been given courage," May Swenson wrote of Moore, "by her beautiful daring, her
abundance, her naturalness that is as cunning, curious
and splendid as Nature's own. . . . Especially we *women
poets,* as we are called, are grateful and lucky in pos-
sessing the . . . indelible example of her work and
life."[47] Moore herself was, without disallowing her im-
maturities, meticulous in her loyalties not only to her
mother but also to everyone for whose gifts she felt
genuine gratitude.

By her own account, one of the principal forma-
tive influences in her development was the family of
Louise Jackson Norcross and Dr. George Norcross,
pastor of the Second Presbyterian Church in Carlisle.
Three of the Norcross daughters were graduates of

Bryn Mawr College, "and such was their attraction, scholastically and aesthetically," Moore said, "that I could not have imagined attending any other college." They had "an unfanatical, innate love of books, music and 'art,' " not only of the traditional masters such as Rembrandt and Giotto but also of Turner, not only of Dante and Blake but also of Trollope, the Rossettis, George Meredith, and Ruskin, all of whom were "household companions of the family and their friends." Because "we were constantly discussing authors," the poet observed, "when I entered Bryn Mawr, the College seemed to me in disappointing contrast—almost benighted."[48]

College was, for the first two years, a very painful experience; Moore was lonely and homesick. Having been, in her words, "hand-reared," she missed the individual attention, was not prepared to take enough responsibility, and did not know how to work.[49] She was "too immature" for English.[50] She liked to tell that she could elect nothing but courses in biology— "the professors in that department were very humane, also exacting, detailed and pertinacious"; they "made biology and its toil, a pleasure and like poetry, 'a quest.' " She did "fairly well" in Latin, but failed Italian twice; she had taken the course because she thought it would enable her to read Dante; the professor, not Dante, intimidated her. She chose a course in "torts" with a visiting law professor from Columbia because "he was compassion itself," "a relief from some of the more ferocious instructors." She seemed, she commented, "to need very humane handling, mothering by everyone—the case all my life, I think."[51]

She remembered that one professor created "an appetite for philosophy and for dialectic as on

occasion he took a few students walking under tall
sycamores by a brook,"[52] an experience that probably stimulated a late poem, "The Sycamore" (1955).
She paid tribute to the vocal president of the college,
Martha Carey Thomas, for her "diction and un-
stereotyped thinking," her combat with forces "knit by
the injustices of convention," and her sense of the
objectives of education that would free the mind.
Moore, reviewing a biography of Thomas, concentrated on her character and accomplishments rather than
on her prejudices. She was "one who was for women
an impassioned emancipator."[53] And Bryn Mawr was,
happily, not a finishing school.

The student who spent much of her time in the
biology laboratory also became a member of the staff
of the college literary magazine, to which she contributed stories and poems even after she left Bryn
Mawr. Having enrolled in 1909– at the Carlisle Commercial College, she completed course the next year.
After travel with her mother in England and France
during the summer of 1911, the twenty-four-year-old
Moore took her first job, at the United States Industrial Indian School in Carlisle. She coached the boys in
field sports, fixed the typewriters, and taught stenog-
raphy, typing, commercial law, commercial English,
and bookkeeping. She would rather have sat by the fire
and read. She continued to write poems, and in 1915
two of them appeared in the issue of the London
magazine, the *Egoist,* which also carried a chapter of
James Joyce's *A Portrait of the Artist as a Young Man.*
Moore's poems were "To the Soul of 'Progress' "
(later titled "To Military Progress"), reminiscent of
Stephen Crane's astringent style and ironic metaphors, although the rhymes were neat; and "To a Man
Working His Way Through a Crowd," awkwardly in

praise of the lynx eye of Gordon Craig, critic and revolutionary theorist of theatrical design, about whom she wrote "The most propulsive thing you say,/ Is that one need not know the way,/ To be arriving." Thereafter, additional poems were printed in *Poetry* (Chicago) and *Others* (New York) as well as in the *Egoist* during that year. Moore's first volume of verse, titled *Poems*, came out in 1921; the publication, at the Egoist Press, had been arranged by Hilda Doolittle (H.D.) and Winifred Ellerman (Bryher) without the author's knowledge.

In the meantime, Warner Moore had completed his studies at the Yale Divinity School, been ordained as a Presbyterian minister, and appointed the pastor of the Ogden Memorial Church in Chatham, New Jersey. In 1916, his mother and sister—"two chameleons," Marianne said[54]—moved to Chatham to be his housekeepers. The next year, after his training as a reserve officer, he joined the navy as chaplain and went immediately on convoy duty. He also became engaged to be married. Marianne, who had gone for a five-day visit to New York in the winter of 1915, moved with her mother in 1918 to a basement apartment at St. Luke's Place in Greenwich Village, where they lived until 1929, when they moved to Cumberland Street in Brooklyn to be near Warner and his family after he was stationed at the Navy Yard there. Even though he had a change of assignment within a couple of years, mother and daughter stayed in Brooklyn. After Mary Moore died, the poet lived there alone ("solitude," she said, "is the cure for loneliness"[55]) until she moved in 1966 to Manhattan because it was no longer safe on Cumberland Street. Having suffered a series of strokes and a heart ailment, she retired from public life in 1970.

From 1915 to 1970, Moore's major decisions were related to her desire to write—anything. Before she went to Chatham she tried to get work on newspapers in Philadelphia and Boston. When she and her mother left Chatham, the young poet felt emancipated. In New York, she took a job as a private tutor and secretary at a school for girls; more importantly, she made friends with other young writers, artists, and fledgling critics of the arts who gathered at parties to propel themselves on the way without knowing where they would arrive. And trapped by fortuities, in Moore's phrase, she demonstrated how unpredictable the materials of poetry can be. "Yes," she said in "Novices," " 'the authors are wonderful people, particularly those that write the most,' " quoting from another writer's autobiography.

Going less frequently to parties than to the Hudson Park branch of the New York Public Library, she was in 1921 offered a job as an assistant there, and took it for half-days so that she would have time to read and write. Some of her "elegant English friends" later looked on the tasks such as charging out books as menial work[56]; by 1924, however, she had poems enough to assemble from among them the volume *Observations* that the Dial Press published and chose for a $2,000 award in recognition of "unusual literary value." It was the first of many prizes, grants, and honors she was to receive for her work.

In 1925, she joined the staff of *The Dial* magazine as acting editor; in 1926, she was appointed editor. The magazine, taking its name from *The Dial* founded in 1850 with Margaret Fuller as its first and Emerson as its second editor, was reestablished in 1880 by Francis F. Browne. Bought by Scofield Thayer and Dr. James Sibley Watson in 1920, the fortnightly concen-

trated on the arts—writing, painting, sculpture, music, and film. Moore's catholic interests and openness to many tastes made her admirably suited to her job as editor. *The Dial*'s contributors included William Butler Yeats, Paul Valéry, Thomas Mann, Maxim Gorky, Ford Madox Ford, D. H. Lawrence, Ezra Pound, T. S. Eliot, H. D., William Carlos Williams, Wallace Stevens, e. e. cummings, Wyndham Lewis, Padraic Colum, Ortega y Gasset, Edmund Wilson, Paul Rosenfeld, Ivor Winters, and Kenneth Burke. Among the pictures, "as intensives on the texts," were reproductions of work by Henri Rousseau, Seurat, Picasso, Max Weber, Charles Sheeler, Georgia O'Keeffe, John Marin, Chirico, Brancusi, Lachaise, and Cocteau. Moore wrote reviews or comments and learned much professionally in the halcyon years she devoted to the publication, but there was no time for her own verse. It was decided out of chivalry to her, she said,[57] to discontinue in the summer of 1929 what had become a distinguished cosmopolitan magazine. She was sufficiently well-known that she could begin a career as an independent reviewer of books and writer of occasional articles, but more important, she could resume the writing of poetry. She continued to work as a free-lance writer until 1970, except for brief periods of teaching composition at Cummington School in Massachusetts or lecturing at Bryn Mawr, Vassar, Harvard, and the University of California.

Urged by friends, especially T. S. Eliot, Moore brought out *Selected Poems* in 1936. Almost five hundred remaindered copies were sold to Gotham Book Mart for thirty cents a piece; she and her mother "pounced" on two, then four, then twenty copies for themselves or presents to friends. "To have had the book printed," the poet wrote, "is the main thing, &

all will be well if I can manage to produce some first-rate stuff."[58] The *Collected Poems* appeared in 1951. Along with James Jones's *From Here to Eternity*, an "army" novel, which had sold 250,000 copies, and Rachel Carson's *The Sea Around Us*, an ecological study, which had sold 180,000 copies, Moore's book had sold "close to 5000" by 1952 when the three books won the National Book Awards. In her acceptance speech, Moore made the famous pronouncement that her work is called poetry because there is no other category in which to put it.[59] In 1953, she received the prestigious Bollingen Prize for Poetry. As May Swenson said of her in retrospect, Moore devised her own contests, made her own rules, and, at the point least expected, disconcertingly reversed them, so as to demonstrate that "it is not the acquisition of any one thing that is able to adorn" either poetry or life.

She has, of course, had her detractors, sometimes for the wrong reasons. The verse has been said to be too abstract and cerebral; it is neither, although it can be perplexing. Her minor work as a translator has been less controversial. Collaborating with Elizabeth Mayer on the first English translation of prose by Adalbert Stifter, she brought out *Rock Crystal* (1945), "in practically glacial style" said to read like the original. When Moore's version of Charles Perrault's fairy tales *Puss in Boots*, *The Sleeping Beauty*, and *Cinderella* appeared in 1963, they were praised because she retained the spirit and courtly style of the French, although one critic thought it unfortunate that she also retained the "gruesome ogre-ending" of *The Sleeping Beauty*. Her La Fontaine was more ambitious and received much attention both from those who commended and those who berated the liberties she took

with the *Fables;* French critics liked the subtleties of her rhythms and verse forms for the work.

She has, more recently, been decried as an insufficiently militant feminist, but she knew what a bundle of barbed wire the issue of women's rights was, and she also knew how to disentangle it. Commenting on Eliot's *Sweeney Agonistes* in 1933, she wrote, "There is, as the author intended, an effect of Aristophanic melodrama about this London flat in which the visitors play with the idea of South Sea languor and luxury—work annihilated, personality negatived and conscience suppressed: a monkey at hand to milk the goat and pass the cocktails—woman in the cannibal pot or at hand to serve."[60] Reviewing Pound's poetry in 1931, she noted: "and, apropos of 'feminolatry,' is not the view of woman expressed in the Cantos older-fashioned than that of Siam and Abyssinia? knowledge of the femaleness of *chaos,* of the *octopus,* of *Our mulberry leaf, woman,* appertaining more to Turkey than to Roger Ascham [tutor in Latin and Greek for Queen Elizabeth I]?"[61] Since Moore was, as a critic, accustomed to selecting for praise what she approved and overlooking many faults to make her points, she can best be measured by her remarks in 1946 on Paul Rosenfeld's "republicanism of respect for that *ignis fatuus,* liberty; a vision of spiritual fitness without visa; of 'inner healing' for white America's black victims," and his sense of the value of " 'woman,' as Margaret Naumberg, Gertrude Stein, my timid self, and many another have testified."[62] She also said, in 1963, that women had been discovered by society, that every woman she knew seemed to take increased responsibility in civic affairs, and that "aggressive women" were "a hazard to the availability of women for heightened civilization."[63] Kathleen Raine wrote that she

would never forget Moore's modest disclaimer: "Yes, I know they did say I was the best woman poet in this country; but you see . . . that means nothing, just nothing at all; because here in America not more than two, or perhaps three, women have even *tried* to write poetry."[64]

Although she rarely wrote poetry for a mass audience, she came to be a subject of copy for magazines with editors who thought readers would find her an exceptional person. "An Afternoon with Marianne Moore (1946)," by Marguerite Young, was the first of several pieces to be published in magazines with wide circulation. The flamboyant Cecil Beaton was asked by *Vogue*, in which Young's article appeared, to photograph the poet and her mother at their Brooklyn apartment. They were gracious; the photograph was filled with sunlight shining on the pewter tea-and-coffee service used as properties for the elegant ladies, but when the cropped picture appeared, two startled faces stared out of the shadows. People in the neighborhood said the Moore women looked like two old witches, and Marianne Moore threatened, according to Young, to sue *Vogue* for making fun of them.[65] Beaton took her to lunch and convinced her that it was all right. Having just won a prize for a slogan she had submitted in a contest at a dance studio, she invited him to go for a tango lesson. He, in turn, designed the three-cornered hat (she was later reported to have had dozens in that shape) and the great cape in which she was so frequently photographed as she became a newsworthy woman about town.

Upon her death, the New York Times News Service said of her, "Miss Moore, the personality, was more extensively known than Miss Moore, the poet."[66] Invited to a reception by the city's mayor in

Gracie Mansion not long after the publication of *The Complete Poems* for her eightieth birthday in 1967, for instance, she was introduced to Andrei Voznesensky, the Russian poet, and spontaneously recited to the guests some of his verses, which she had read in translation. The next year, 1968, she threw out the first baseball of the season (she kept her pitch low) at Yankee Stadium; in 1969, she was named "Senior Citizen of the Year" at the New York Governor's Conference on Aging and was awarded the last of sixteen honorary degrees, one from Harvard University. During those years, she also received the Edward MacDowell Medal "for outstanding contribution to letters," the Poetry Society of America's Gold Medal for Distinguished Achievement, and the National Medal for Literature.

Following her death in Manhattan on February 5, 1972, funeral rites were held for her on February 8 at Lafayette Presbyterian Church, which she had faithfully attended for the thirty-seven years she had lived in Brooklyn. The closing prayer was one that the poet had written twenty-five years earlier for the funeral of her mother.[67] A simple noon service for interment of her ashes in the Warner family plot at Evergreen Cemetery, in Gettysburg, on April 7, was conducted by her brother. A service was also held in her memory in February at the Protestant church in Venice, and Ezra Pound, who was to die nine months later, read her poem, "What Are Years?"[68] She and Pound were the longest lived of the modernist generation of American poets.

It is appropriate that Pound, with an unerring critical sense of the best verse by his contemporaries, chose "What Are Years?" as an elegy for her. If all else in her work is forgotten, she will surely be remembered for one of the great poems of consolation in the

English language. Yet, as Winthrop Sargeant observed also appropriately in the memorable profile of
Marianne Moore when she was seventy years old, "not
withstanding her lifelong dedication to the art" of poetry, she thought of it "as a luxury—or, at any rate, a
nonessential—when weighed against the really serious aspects of life"—for her, mortality and eternity.

2

The Art of Singular Forms

I

Marianne Moore came of age during the period of modernism, in which writers, following the example of the European artists, were incorrigibly experimental. Although she said in 1966 that she could hardly be called avant garde, she was one of the American poets, including H. D., Ezra Pound, T. S. Eliot, and William Carlos Williams, who fifty years earlier had begun to experiment radically and to risk new conceptions of form in their work. Whether their angles of vision were oblique or acute, whether their strategies were parallel or at odds, they fought stubbornly for the right to be themselves. Speaking her own mind, Moore was also able to remain free of the rivalries, for instance, between Williams and Eliot, that seem in retrospect to have stimulated rather than damaged the development of American poetry. She not only active-ly supported and enjoyed the support of both of them, along with that of Pound and H. D., but she was also appreciative of the qualities of two other Olympians, Wallace Stevens and Robert Frost, who experimented within the traditional forms of verse. She had both critical courage and politesse; she believed, as she said about the aims of *The Dial* magazine, which she edited from 1925 to 1929, in "encouraging a tolerance for fresh experiments and opening the way for them."

When she was introduced to the new movement in painting, for example, she was happily naive and receptive. During her senior year at Bryn Mawr (1908–1909), she had taken a course in English prose writers with Georgiana Goddard King, a lecturer in compara-tive literature and the history of art, an acquaintance of Gertrude Stein since the 1890s, and "one of the first

art historians in America to recognize the importance of Picasso and other modern French painters."[1] King had visited the studio in Paris where Gertrude and Leo Stein were bringing together a unique collection of work from Picasso's blue period (1901–1904) and the cubist paintings subsequent to that period.

Among Moore's first objectives on a trip to New York in December of 1915 was a visit to "291," the gallery of Alfred Stieglitz, the preeminent American photographer about whom she had also heard from the Bryn Mawr teacher. Moore went, she thought, to see some of the new photography, but she reported to her brother that "Mr. Stieglitz . . . has a magnificent thing of the sea in dark blue and some paintings of mountains by a man named Hartley also some Picabias and Picassos. . . ."[2] It was the paintings that especially interested her. Stieglitz invited her to come back, and after her move to New York in 1918 she went often to see the work he exhibited. In a tribute to him later, she said he "was not exactly a theologian but a godly man"; she agreed with him that "a thing is remembered, not for its shadows but itself." His gallery, she said, was "an American Acropolis . . . with a stove in it, a kind of eagle's perch of selectiveness, and like the ardor of fire in its completeness."

The spirit of "291" was to foster liberty and to encourage the enemies of convention. For Marsden Hartley, who called himself "the painter from Maine," it was "the largest small room of its kind in the world," and the people who gathered there found a sense of common effort similar to that in the Steins's Parisian studio. In the early nineteen-hundreds, up to 1912, Hartley was painting his native mountains "with an impressionistic breadth, and the yellows and crimsons of his autumn were laid against the bulk of his hills

with bold square touches; his gnarled cloud shapes
bore witness to his admiration" for what he spoke of
as "the immanent in things." He was to become one
of the pioneers and leaders of American modernism,
which meant to him "a fresh relationship to the
courses of the sun and to the living swing of the
earth."[3] Francis Picabia, the French painter, was at the
time, like Picasso, in a cubist period (examples had
been shown by Stieglitz in the New York Armory Show
of 1913). The cubists, bringing together in the same
plane visual elements normally separated into different relational planes on the flat canvas, shattered the
received concepts of pictorial representation and the
illusion of classic, one-point perspective. The breaking of images, the initiation of shifting or multiple
perspectives, the introduction of contradictory evidence within a design, the flash and counterthrust of
angular shapes or lines, and a free approach to color
were dynamic. Once the breach with the familiar
modes of seeing was effected, artists—still closely ob-
servant of the tensions and rhythms of daily life—
became cognizant of hitherto unsuspected possibilities of freedom in the interpretation of reality and the
extraction of its essence or inner meanings. And once
the excitement of change grasped the imaginative intelligence of a young writer like Marianne Moore, she
could hardly be indifferent to the implications for
verse. Her mention of "a magnificent thing of the sea
in dark blue" and Hartley's early work at the same
time that she noted the Picabias and Picassos suggests
the quality of mind affirmed in her poems: openly
independent in the search for images and structures
that have vitality, whether they are traditional or revolutionary, recognized or avant garde.

Because tolerance and receptivity raise questions

of criteria, Moore based her eclecticism on a principle that she applied to the art of any period or school: "Form is synonymous with content—must be." She observed that Louis Dudek, a contemporary Canadian poet and editor, was "surely right in saying, 'The art of poetry is the art of singular forms.'" Such a view allows for appreciation of many kinds of literary expression that can be judged by conceptual procedures and their efficacy. A response to the singularity of form not only increases enjoyment of the abundance that the twentieth century has inherited and wishes to preserve from past cultures; a judgment of the relation of form and content in art also requires disciplined, knowledgeable attention to both the individual work on its own terms and to the great variety of art, old or new. In reading Moore, one recognizes the remarkable range of predilections, the surety of the voice, the rigorous uses of tradition, and the originality of the poems.

II

The integrations of form and content in Moore's poems are noticeably various. Even after one has learned to expect characteristic imagery and mannerisms or a return to themes and attitudes that preoccupied her, the poems can be almost bewilderingly innovative. The inevitable variations of the minute particulars that she apprehends mean changes of structure, surrender to different influences, and a reconstitution of them in individual modes. She hardly ever repeats herself in the design of the poems.

No two of her poems, for instance, look alike on the page in the sense that the sonnets in Shakespeare's

sequence do. In the beginning of her career, she was especially attentive to the typographical arrangements combined with other factors that affect the formal qualities of verse. The influence of modernism does not account altogether for Moore's experiments with visual design, but the new art as well as previous interests gave her ideas for singular forms. Like Apollinaire, who as a young member of the French futuristes and cubistes circles had begun work in 1914 on his "pictorial typography" or *calligrammes* (1918), she had literary models. For Apollinaire, there were the poems of Mallarmé; for Moore, there were those of George Herbert and Thomas Hardy, both of whom she appreciated. As a former teacher of commercial subjects, she was also influenced by the use of the typewriter in the symmetrics of her "spacialist" verse.

"To a Chameleon"—printed first with the cumbersome title "You Are Like the Realistic Product of an Idealistic Search for Gold at the Foot of the Rainbow" (1916)—is the most obvious example of Moore's "pictorial typography." In the final version, for which she redistributed the lines on the page, she achieved what Apollinaire called "visual lyricism":

> Hid by the august foliage and fruit of the grape-vine
>   twine
>   your anatomy
>   round the pruned and polished stem,
>   Chameleon.
>   Fire laid upon
>   an emerald as long as
>   the Dark King's massy
>   one,
> could not snap the spectrum up for food as you
>   have done.

It takes little imagination to delight in the imagery, the rhythms, the caesuras, the inconspicuous light rhymes and the firmer ones, the verbal surprise of "snap," the kinetics, the sense of the observer's eyes darting in and out to see the "hidden" chameleon quickly absorbing, reflecting, and flashing green light, or even the kinesthetic arrangement of the lines. Skillful as the poem is, however, it is marred by the obtrusive word, "massy." A fastidious poet, Moore admitted that she fussed over the least detail; in writing, she said, "it is my principle that nothing is too much trouble." Perhaps that is why she withdrew "To a Chameleon" from the time of its republication in 1924 (when she changed the title and rearranged the lines) until 1960, after which she permitted it to be printed several times. Too good to sacrifice, it and "The Fish" (1918) are among the poems responsible for association of Moore's verse with the seminal movement of the Imagists in the pre–World War I period.[4]

Moore correctly insisted that she was not one of the Imagists. They, of course, had no monopoly on a tenet essential to their poetry: language "should endeavor to arrest you, and to make you see a physical thing, and prevent your gliding through an abstract process." On that basis alone, however, they could claim Moore's work. She said simply, "I like to describe things."

She was a fine descriptive poet whose keen sense of the visual and shifting images is perfected in "The Fish." The initial perspective is that of an observer looking down into the sea as she stands on the coast. The words of the title, "The Fish," run over to the opening lines:

> wade
> through black jade.

The typography is not mimetic, as it was for "Chameleon"; spacing, on first glance, is more jagged and seems to contradict the expectations of the movement of fish. The space between the lines, between the verb "wade" and the phrase "through black jade" (preceded by the use of the title as the subject of the poem's first verb), prevents one from darting through inattentively. The almost startling image depicts the slow motion of the fish and the stillness of the water, its resistance, color, sheen, and polish. Both literal and figurative, the image is not only powerful in itself, but prepares the reader for the poem's final subject—the "defiant edifice." The eyes move down to see crow-blue mussel shells: "one keeps / adjusting the ash-heaps; / opening and shutting itself like / an / injured fan." Again, the singular images are visually interesting and anticipate the conclusion—the seascape is both beautiful and treacherous.

The scene quickens. There is a succession of changing actions:

> The barnacles which encrust the side
> of the wave, cannot hide
>   there for the submerged shafts of the
>
> sun,
> split like spun
>   glass, move themselves with spotlight swiftness
>   into the crevices—

The barnacles play tricks on the eyes. The sense of the water's stillness has been dissipated. Nothing is inert; the poet's eyes, the water, the light—all are fluid. The color changes; there is a "turquoise sea / of bodies." The coast is rocky.

> The water drives a wedge
> of iron through the iron edge
> of the cliff; whereupon the stars,
>
> pink
> rice-grains, ink-
> bespattered jelly-fish, crabs like green
> lilies, and submarine
> toadstools, slide each on the other.

The effect is kaleidoscopic, but the precision of the images gives one the experience of standing alongside the sentient poet.[5] Then the action of the eyes is arrested by the wrecked ship:

> All
> external
> marks of abuse are present on this
> defiant edifice—
> all the physical features of
>
> ac-
> cident—lack
> of cornice, dynamite grooves, burns, and
> hatchet strokes, these things stand
> out on it; the chasm-side is
>
> dead.
> Repeated
> evidence has proved that it can live
> on what can not revive
> its youth. The sea grows old in it.

The ocean, the source of life, is also a place of conflict, danger, and destruction. The sense of dying life within the sea garden hovers over the poem in much the same way that a theme hovers over a Picasso painting without being articulated. The poem's final

statement, "The sea grows old in it [the damaged and deteriorating vessel]," is similar to the "barnacles which encrust the side / of the wave" in reversing the usual habit of "saying and thinking," but different in the fact that the old sea is no illusion. The complexity of the statement stimulates a meditation on time and change in "the world's body" that the dissolving images clearly define.

The typography delineates the music of the poem. On a minor scale, the hard rhymes are dominant: "wade . . . jade," "keeps . . . heaps," "side . . . hide," "pink . . . ink-," "ac- . . . lack"; but the sibilants in "keeps" and "heaps" introduce the words that also mimic the sound of the sea: "swiftness" and "crevices," "the" and "sea," "this" and "edifice." The old-fashioned word "edifice" attracts attention to itself and contrasts with "spotlight swiftness" at the same time that the language echoes the slapping and shishing of the waves. Alternations in stress patterns of syllables for pairs of rhyming words, "an" and "fan," "green" and "submarine," "all" and "external" or "dead" and "repeated" lighten the music; and the unrhymed last line of each stanza points up the subtle discordant tones. The final eye rhyme is a musical pun: "it can live / on what cannot revive. . . ." The form is synonymous with the content.

The modulations of sound and images, the expressive use of space in the line and stanzaic arrangements—all work together in the contemplation of a scene to which the fish alert the observer. In the poem, Moore's vision is both imagistic and extra-imagist. By describing movement in space she was able to escape the Imagists' tendency toward stasis; this tendency was frustrating, for example, to Williams because it limited the choice and development of subjects. The

major reason she was not a "pure" Imagist, however, is apparent in the "vivid exposition consonant with the best use of metaphor," as Moore said of Eliot's verse. Fascinated as she was with the visual object and the phenomenal world, she always respected the natural shapes, colors, textures, and autonomous physical values of what she saw. In this she was like the modern painters she admired, was aligned with Williams, and was not a visionary or mystic; but her penchant for exposition was strong and seldom denied in the poems, as the commentary beginning with "All" in "The Fish" indicates.

"An Egyptian Pulled Glass Bottle in the Shape of a Fish" (1924) pointedly illustrates the way in which Moore combines a static image with remarks suggested by an object. The poem sounds, at first, as if an art lecturer is talking about the usefulness, the relation of function to form, and the beauty of the bottle. Appreciative of the patient, anonymous glass blower, the lecturer also describes the object in language exact enough that one can perceive it:

> . . . art, as in a wave held up for us to see
> in its essential perpendicularity;
>
> not brittle but
> intense—the spectrum, that
>   spectacular and nimble animal the fish,
>   whose scales turn aside the sun's sword by
>   their polish.

Responding to the words for the strength, the delicacy, and the emission of light waves, as well as to the quick turn of the lines in the verse, one can imagine for a moment that the static bottle is a fish in water.

One also glimpses in the lecturer's prose a poet whose vision comes from an interest in the thing itself.

A familiar example of the many poems in which Moore integrates expository and visual action is "A Grave" (1921). The voice of the poem is that of a self-conscious moralist thinking about a man who has blocked the line of sight for others looking at the sea from the shore. The man's inconsiderate intrusion on the scene provokes a reprimand masked as a lesson on the limits of an anthropocentric view of nature in the presence of the ruthless, grasping, impersonal beauty of the ocean: "it is human nature to stand in the middle of a thing, / but you cannot stand in the middle of this[.]" The action of the poem is both in the mind of the persona and the rustling, advancing waves of the sea. Fir trees stand reserved, saying nothing, exemplary by comparison with the seething moralist, the man who does not budge, and the repressive ocean. If the man's look is rapacious, so is the force of the water. The moralist, consequently, seeks comfort in the fact that "the sea has nothing to give but a well excavated grave"—grim humor but not the whole truth; there is another vision:

> men lower nets, unconscious of the fact that they are
> desecrating a grave,
> and row quickly away—the blades of the oars
> moving together like the feet of water-spiders as if
> there were no such thing as death.

The life of the sea, the networks of foam, the birds swimming through the air, the activity of tortoises about the feet of the cliffs, the pulsation of lighthouses, the floating bell-buoys—all external to the self —are fully visible. The water looks "as if it were not that ocean in which dropped things are bound to

sink— / in which if they turn and twist, it is neither
with volition nor consciousness." Willful man, willful
and conscious moralist, even those who win life from
the sea—all human beings are at its mercy. The unconscious ocean has caught the imagination of the
persona who comes to momentary rest in an impersonal state beyond the petty annoyances, the protest,
the ungenerous view with which the moralist began.
The poem's long lines, in free verse, move the voice
beyond the self and its limitations. The "you" of the
poem becomes everyone and disappears, while a dangerous sea stretches the mind, quickens the attention,
and corrects the views that repress an awareness of all
that is larger than the mortal will or consciousness.
What is striking about the poem, however, is the
simultaneous movement and countermovement within it. Words for the changing sea are drawn from concepts of the unconscious mind, but the action of the
sea effects changes in the conscious mind; at the same
time, the poem goes in contrary ways, and the sea
becomes a trope for the mind.

The natural, monolinear progression from image
to image and the remarks integrated with them in
"The Fish" or the contrarieties of "A Grave," expert
as the poems are, may not seem startlingly innovative.
The design of "The Buffalo" (1934) is more radical,
affording an instance of Moore's many experiments
with complex structures. The poet recalled in 1960
that she thought it "would probably outrage a number
of people because it had to me a kind of pleasing jerky
progress." Readers, nonetheless, have not found it
troublesome, since they have been interested in the
character of the animal: an independent spirit willing
to do a day's work in the service of man. The relation
of the poem's "hero," the Indian water buffalo, to the

unusual form has gone almost unnoticed except for Laurence Stapleton's perceptive comment that the poem is a visual mosaic.[6]

Unlike "The Fish," the poem breaks between the title and the first line. The opening subject is color—black, niger, hematite, soot-brown. The initial point made about black is that contradictory meanings have been ascribed to it; but then the poet wonders whether or not the subtle, lustrous dark to dark greyish red of the bison's horns and its soot-brown tail-tuft have any "significance." These rudiments, with the title, may tempt one to think the poem is going to be about the American bison, inaccurately known as the "buffalo" in its native land. The subject of the next stanza is, disconcertingly, an American painting of the ox Ajax by the regionalist John Steuart Curry (who wanted his work to have a significant message to his countrymen in the heartland). The ox is placidly "pulling / grass—no ring / in his nose—two birds standing on the back [.]" Is this ox domesticated in comparison to the bison (which is a wild ox)? The poem does not ask that, but perhaps the theme is to be wildness versus tractibility or, perhaps, tame excitement, on which the poet once said she thrived? Or is the theme to be related to the purposes of art?

In spite of an ellipsis between stanzas, the one following begins "The modern / ox does not look like the Augsburg ox's / portrait." (The reference is to a woodcut from *Historia Animalum* by Konrad von Gesner, a sixteenth-century naturalist.) "Yes," / the poet says, "the great extinct wild Aurochs was a beast / to paint. . . ." Just as she chooses two features to represent the bison, she notes only that the big aurochs had a stripe and a six-foot horn spread. Amid the fractured images, the connections or associations are multiple if

one wishes to follow the salient details beyond the poem. The name "aurochs," or the wild ox of Europe, for example, has sometimes erroneously been applied to the European bison or wisent. Or the Indian buffalo's horns may be over six feet long, spread outward and upward, approaching each other toward the tips, like the horns of the extinct aurochs. Perhaps the theme is the value of art to preserve relationships that would otherwise be lost? The poem's progress is indeed jerky.

Then, presto, there is an excursus into the fact that domestic dairy cattle descended from the wild aurochs: amusingly "decreased / to Siamese-cat- / Brown Swiss size or zebu- [Asiatic ox] / shape . . . ; to red- / skinned Hereford or to piebald Holstein." So, one may suggest, the theme must be the jerky "progress' of human civilization, its costs and its benefits.

"Yet / some would say that the sparse-haired / buffalo has met / human notions best. . . ." Finally, after twenty-two lines of animal history, among other things, the poet is going to paint the subject the title announced! But not before she introduces further contrasts with (1) the elephant, "jewel . . . in the hairs" (decorated for a religious procession) or "jeweller" (valuable for ivory tusks); (2) Vermont twin oxen yoked together "to haul maple-sap" (on Calvin Coolidge's New England farm); and (3) a freakish "Over-Drove Ox" drawn by Thomas Rowlandson (the caricaturist famous for lampooning John Bull during the War of 1812). Following those apparent asides in eleven-and-one-half additional lines, the buffalo emerges from the "little intricate grids of visual symmetry"—to use Hugh Kenner's phrase for Moore's stanzaic patterns—that precede it. The de-

sign involves the reader in a mental exercise much like that one experiences in seeing a face embedded within overlapping and contrary planes emerge from them for Picasso's cubist portraits of Reine Isabeau (1909), Daniel-Henry Kahnweiler, or Ambroise Vollard (1910).

For the last twenty-six-and-one-half lines, the poet's eyes are on the buffalo. Moore's buffalo can be a stubborn ox, a bold, even savage mammal, but will stand patiently all day in mud when there is work to do, "cheerfully assist" the Buddha, charge a tiger, and be led by small boys to stable. This fierce, tranquil, useful, mettlesome creature "need not fear comparison / with bison, with the twins, / indeed with any / of ox ancestry." It can be prized for itself.

The consideration of the symbolism of the color black at the beginning of the poem is, after all, not quite tangential: black can mean "prudence," or it can mean "unpropitious." (The unstated link between the title and the opening line is "the buffalo is black.") There are simultaneous contrary meanings, shades of color, divergent images, and nuances of gesture about which one can speculate. Opposed to the emphasis on black, furthermore, are splotches of white—the "white plush dewlap" of the Brown Swiss cattle, the "white-nosed Vermont ox" in snow, the albino feet of the Indian buffalo, and the "white Christian heathen"—but in between there are the red Hereford and the "piebald Holstein." Both the clash of particulars and the continuities have as their pre-text Gerard Manley Hopkins's "Pied Beauty" (1910) with its praise of God "for dappled things—; / For skies of couple-colour as a brinded cow;" for

> All things counter, original, spare, strange;
>   Whatever is fickle, freckled (who knows how?)
>   With swift, slow; sweet, sour; adazzle,
>   dim;
> He fathers-forth whose beauty is past change:
>   Praise him.

Whereas Hopkins's poem makes explicit the theme that the images express, Moore's poem gathers the observations into a form that expresses the theme. The conflict between one's traditional expectations of a linear form and one's response to Moore's multiple perspectives, images, and subjects is resolved by her appreciation of "things counter, spare," and coupled in "The Buffalo."

The ingenuities of the structure, by which Moore develops without stating the theme from an earlier experimental poet she admired, recalls a comment she quotes approvingly from *Counter-Statement* (1931) (essays by Kenneth Burke, with whom Moore had been associated at the *Dial*). Reviewing Burke's poems, *Book of Moments* (1955), she notes that he had written, in the essays, that "by innovation is not meant something new but an emphasis to which the public is not accustomed." Readers unaccustomed to Moore's change of emphasis in poems like "The Buffalo" continue to overlook the importance of the way in which the structures themselves express the content. But Moore also cites Burke's point that "a work has form insofar as one part leads a reader to anticipate another part and be gratified by the sequence." The lack of connectives, which she once told Williams she "despised," tends to cause readers to be uncertain about what to expect as they come to her new sequences, even when they are variations on themes or forms from the past.

"No Swan So Fine" (1935), for example, is a son-

net, consisting of fourteen lines of two equal stanzas, more sparsely rhymed, more dissonant, and more irregular metrically than the classic models. The structure is an adaptation of the sonnet's traditional forms, and is as pertinent as the language itself in clarifying the poem's thematic continuities. An elaborate description of a "fine" china bird preempts the center of attention, in ironic contrast to a simple description of a living swan. Both birds are poised between the poem's first and last sentences—two different contexts that control the tonal values in the use of the same word, "dead," the point on which the poem's meanings turn. The design, like that of any good sonnet, makes prosaic connectives superfluous.

The title is echoed grammatically and rhythmically by the first words: " 'No water so still as the / dead fountains of Versailles.' " The poet then repeats and develops the image of the title:

> No swan,
>
> with swart blind look askance
> and gondoliering legs, so fine
>   as the chintz china one with fawn-
> brown eyes and toothed gold
> collar on to show whose bird it was.

She goes on to describe attentively and lovingly the Louis XV candelabrum tree in which the swan perches among the sculptured flowers: cockscombs, dahlias, sea-urchins, and everlastings. In contrast with the flowers, the two swans, and (by the poem's strategies) the fountains, "The king is dead."

The "dead" fountains clearly prepare the reader for the common awareness that the king and everyone else who once lived at the court of Versailles are dead. The description of the china swan, obviously a collec-

tor's item in rococo style, suggests the usual irony that a work of art may survive its owner and be appreciated by later generations who think it even more impressive than a live bird. Surely, however, the controlling theme is not the superiority of art over "life's faulty excellence" or the commonplace expression that "Art is long, life is short." The poet must be playing with those concepts, although one thinks she probably has some reservations in regard to those views when she begins with the quotation, " 'No water so still as the / dead fountains. . . .'"

The quotation, from a feature story with the title "Versailles Reborn: A Moonlight Drama" by Percy Philip, in the *New York Times Magazine*, May 10, 1931, is one of many clichés to which Philip is given. Offensive in its sentimentality, the tale is conventionally fanciful: " 'Seven moons since last the fountain played,' grumbled a bronze tortoise. 'Now they never let us have a good splash except on the first Sunday of each month in summer.' " And the "moon gazing down into the gardens could see her reflection, pale and quizzical in the still waters of the Grand Canal. . . . There is no place where she likes better to admire herself, for there is no water so still as in these dead fountains at Versailles." Or "Melancholy is queen now of all their company. It is she whose stillness rests like a grey cloud over the gardens and the water in the fountains." The occasion for the hackneyed romanticism was that the nearly completed work of restoring the palace would "assure the preservation for another 200 years." All Versailles, Philip said, was in an uproar. The facts are, then, that the waters were still, but the fountains were not dead.

One can see, without returning to the source, both the inaccuracy of the word "dead" to describe

fountains in which there is still water and the correc-
tive in the simple, unadorned, unequivocal statement
that the king is dead. Moore thereby pertinently points
up the lack of precision in the use of language and
pokes fun at clichés.

For Moore, as for any good writer, exhausted language has no impact and gives no pleasure. "Stock
oaths, and the result is ennui, as with stock adjec-
tives," she commented in an essay on Pound's *Cantos*
(1931). She also observed that "added to the imagination is the idiosyncratic force of the words—the terse-
ness in which some reflower and some are new." She
continued: "Of Mr. Pound and words, Dr. Williams
says, 'He has taken them up—if it may be risked—
alertly, swiftly, but with feeling for the delicate living
quality in them, not disinfecting, scraping them, but
careful of the life.' " Years later she wrote, in "Teach,
Stir the Mind, Afford Enjoyment" (1952), "Our debt
to Ezra Pound is prodigious, . . . most of all, for his
insistence on liveness as opposed to deadness. 'Make
it new,' he says. 'Art is a joyous thing.' "

Moore was, as she confirmed to Donald Hall in
1960, really isolated from modern poetry until 1916,
the year in which she read Pound's original study *The
Spirit of Romance* (1910). Like her visit to "291," her
discovery of the book was significant. Pound's plea for
art that "never bores one" but gives joy, revives the
mind, and instructs painlessly was important in the
development of Moore's aesthetic principles. And
while she disclaimed any literary influences, there is
no doubt that the generative activities of Pound, along
with Williams and other modernist poets as well as the
painters, encouraged her to "make it new" whether
she was trying an old poetic form or choosing a single word. She would even write a sonnet on an or-

nate subject that occupies a central place between
" 'dead' " fountains and a dead king. She lucidly demonstrates that she has the right to talk about language.
The swan is fine, just as the candelabrum tree in a
capricious, graceful style is fine; they are described as
if the poem's life depended upon them, and it does.
The poem says simply "listen," "look." "As for com-
prehension of what is set forth," Moore remarked in
"Teach, Stir the Mind," "the poet has a right to expect
the reader, at least in a measure, to be able to complete the poetic statement; and Ezra Pound never
spoils his effects by over-exposition." Neither does
Moore. That is one of the beauties of the forms: they
explain the poems. Structures often serve the same
purpose in modern art.

"Nevertheless" (1944) is another example of a
series of images and related concepts approximating
the painters' experiments with perspective. The subject is the strawberry; the poem is like a still life by the
analytical cubists who reduced objects to their basic
shapes and qualities, split the objects open, and reor-
ganized the images in a two-dimensional plane.

After beginning as if she were in the middle of a.
conversation, "you've seen a strawberry / that's had a
struggle," Moore concentrates on essential elements
of the subject she analyzes in all its complexity. She
chooses the first images for the berry that had survived

> yet
> was, where the fragments met,
> a hedgehog or a star-
>> fish for the multitude
>> of seeds. What better food
>
> than apple-seeds—the fruit
>> within the fruit—locked in

> like counter-curved twin
> hazel nuts?

The hedgehog rolling itself up to make a ball (with a point) is the image for the shape of the strawberry; the spiny-haired animal suggests a magnified view of hairs on both the berry and the back sides of the plant's leaves. Many starfish have a brushlike effect, but in other species there is a velvet over the surface; the commonest colors of the stars are shades of yellow, orange, pink, or red: all salient details for the connoisseur of strawberries. The starfish, with its water vascular system, easily relates to the fact that the berry is 90 percent water by weight. As a student of botany, Moore knew that the strawberry is not a berry but a fruit and is much more than a single fruit; it is a greatly enlarged stem end or receptacle in which the many true fruits (popularly called seeds) are embedded: hence "apple-seeds—the fruit within the fruit." The poet then splits the strawberry open and looks at the inside, which is like "counter-curved twin / hazel nuts."

To the analytical poet, the strawberry is good food and also an object of thought correlative with the natural attributes, the hardy, rugged strength, the fortitude, of the species. She compares the rubber-plant leaves and stalks to the *kok-saghyz*, an Asiatic dandelion cultivated for its fleshy roots that have a high rubber content and are rather difficult to eradicate: frost doesn't harm the roots—"they still grow / in frozen ground." She recalls an epiphanic moment of having once seen where

> there was a prickly-pear-

leaf clinging to barbed wire,

> a root shot down to grow
> in earth two feet below

The strawberry's runners (or stolens), coming out of the axils of the leaves, touch the ground and take root. The poem's images also continue to multiply: the roots are compared to carrots that form "mandrakes," or a "ram's-horn" sometimes; the runners are compared to grapevine tendrils as they knot and coil to attach the plant to a support. Therefore, the poet talks of victory, weakness, menace, and the power to overcome strength itself.

It is as if the strawberry (which is widely distributed) evokes the world's garden and the cultivation of the fruit evokes a moral universe. "What is there / like fortitude! What sap / went through that little thread / to make the cherry red!" With the red cherry, the strawberry is whole, and the poem is complete. There is so much life in the still life that the poet may well be permitted an exclamation or two. Nevertheless, in spite of the struggle to survive, in spite of the tedious complexities, there are coherent relationships. Moore's perception of identity in seemingly disparate things and her explanations of one by another are reminiscent of Emerson's poetic theory as well as the techniques of the analytical cubists. The poem itself is representative of the triumph of art over fragmented vision. Moore's art is not a puzzle, but characteristically a composition in which fragments form singular new wholes.

III

An interest in design and pattern was an aid in Moore's mastery of the problems that arise from a vision of the complexities of knowledge and perception, of being too much conscious and conscious of too much, as F. R. Leavis observed of T. S. Eliot's poem *The Wasteland* (1922). Moore's work in "several" voices, *Marriage* (1923), like *The Wasteland,* is without narrative continuity and takes its form from the collage in which diverse fragments are assembled without a center of gravity. The longest of her experimental compositions, it is in free verse.

Its simplest antecedent is a quatrain she published in 1915 as a "found" poem, "Counseil to a Bacheler":

> If thou bee younge, then marie not yett;
> If thou bee olde, then no wyfe gett;
> For younge mens' wyves will not be taught,
> And olde mens' wyves bee good for naught.

She indicated that the *verse trouvé* was an "Elizabethan Trencher motto—Bodleian Library [with title and modification of second line]." Never reprinted, it is the first instance of Moore's habit of preserving lines or expressions that she liked. After the fun she had in giving her own title to the quatrain, touching it up, and publishing it under her signature, she began to use quotations sparingly but inventively in many of her poems.

By 1923, the "art" of quotation, which she never gave up, reached large proportions, probably with the encouragement of the example of the literary 'fragments' Eliot shored against the ruins in *The Wasteland.* Moore's "Novices" (1923), a criticism of deficiencies

in the "conscious artistry" of "scared egos," ends with thirteen lines of which ten are passages adapted from other writers to praise "the spontaneous unforced passion of the Hebrew language" superior to the work of tyros with an antipathy toward "the antique." The effects of the "reverberations and tempestuous energy," of "action [that] perpetuates action and angle . . . at variance with angle / till submerged by the general action" in Old Testament literature are transmitted by Moore's design itself. One feels that a poetry has been both unleashed and controlled in cadences moving with immediate power. Unlike some of Moore's collages, "Novice" does not particularly involve readers in the relation between a source and her use of a passage from it; the reader's pleasure in the construction is not appreciably changed by a knowledge of the porcupines from which Moore pulled the quills.

In *Marriage*, on the other hand, the play between the subject and the texts the poet brings to bear on it is often part of the point. Attention to the contiguities and to "the general actions" within the structure will make clear, I hope, that the work does not run off the page and that the "notes" do not take over, as Eliot felt had happened in commentary on *The Wasteland*. Both works represent literary efforts that the small "found" poem "Counseil to a Bacheler" seems hardly to have foreshadowed. They belong to the modern consciousness.

Marriage is an assemblage of which Moore said, "I was just making a note of some things I'd come on that took my fancy—either the phrasing or the sound," "words that I didn't want to lose, . . . and I put them together as plausibly as I could."[7] It would have been no exaggeration for her to have said "hilariously" or

"wittily" instead of "plausibly." She tried to be helpful without being immodest or giving herself away. She questioned whether or not *Marriage* was a poem and insisted that it was not a theory of marriage at all, "doesn't even approach it." Given a large number of disparate and conflicting elements in a collage, the form is a precarious contrivance. The elements tend to carry on guerilla warfare with one another, and the arrangement incurs the risk of seeming impenetrably chaotic or of being arbitrary rather than unified. Whether Moore intended it or not—and I suspect she did—the collage becomes appropriately witty for the subject of marriage, its tensions, disharmonies, and irreconcilables. (Picasso, as one of the originators of the collage, or synthetic cubism [1912–1914], understood the humorous possibilities of the form.) The attitude of the poet and the tones of the many voices in *Marriage* as text plus the incongruities of the texts beyond the text should allay some of the criticism of readers who have not enjoyed the esprit with which Moore views a paradise lost.

The prologue is rather prosaic, in the manner of a half-serious comic talking out of both sides of the mouth about "This institution, / perhaps one should say enterprise," in which one has believed but about which "we still are in doubt." The dry voice could be male or female, married or unmarried. The persona flattens out an old joke about a public announcement of a private intention by referring to marriage as "public promises / of one's intention to / fulfill a private obligation," because one shouldn't be naughty vis à vis sacred matters. There is nevertheless the admission that "criminal ingenuity" is required to avoid the lure of "this fire-gilt steel" golden tradition, "committing many spoils"—with innuendos of sin and loot.

And, by the end of the twenty-line prologue, everyone is incriminated in the editorial "we," whose doubts the speaker voices after a broadside against "Psychology which explains everything" but really "explains nothing."

The principal actors in the comic routine are Adam and Eve, both of whom are beautiful. Part 1 is initially devoted to Eve, seen apparently from the point of view of the male who is startled by her handsome looks. She is incredibly talented—"able to write simultaneously / in three languages" and talk at the same time—but riddled with contradictions, wanting "commotion" and demanding "quiet." She is "the central flaw / in that first crystal-fine experiment, / this amalgamation. . . ." The words of one of the great Puritan ministers, Richard Baxter, in praise of " 'that strange paradise / unlike flesh, stones, / gold or stately buildings, / the choicest part of my life' " are excised from the nearly forgotten classic of Protestant devotional literature, *The Saint's Everlasting Rest* (1650). The ironies of the encomium continue in remarks that may refer either to the good minister or to self-gratulatory men, slyly "constrained in speaking of the serpent— / shed snakeskin in the history of politeness / not to be returned to again— / that invaluable accident, exonerating Adam." One is suddenly also not sure whether the ambiguous ironies are from the point of view of a polite man, a woman, or the persona of the prologue. Moore has seen to it, however, that Eve shares the center of attention for forty lines of chatter. Adam will get sixty-nine lines. Equality, thy name is Adam?

No, the female will have her say. The center of consciousness clearly shifts to Eve, who soliloquizes: "it's distressing—the O thou / to whom from whom, /

without whom nothing—Adam[.]" Adam is compared
to the poetry of the twentieth-century philosopher,
George Santayana, " 'something feline, / something
colubrine[.]' " Eve cannot forget the serpent. Ex-
egeses of the Fall customarily overlook the woman's
view that the seductive snake was a transfigured male
Satan, of whom Eve speaks as "a crouching mythologi-
cal monster." Seen as part grotesque, part arabesque
in a "Persian miniature of emerald mines, / raw silk,"
or in a "paddock full of leopards and giraffes— / long
lemon-yellow bodies / sown with trapezoids of blue,"
man is also talented. "Alive with words, / vibrating
like a cymbal / touched before it has been struck," he
knows how to prophesy and has natural force. There
is more: praise for the masculine style from William
Hazlitt; a sarcastic reminder that man forgets that
woman has "a quality of mind" that is stereotypically
said to be "instinctive" and is obviously not to be
trusted; and a return to the worldly wisdom of the
"saintly" Richard Baxter on marriage as a mixed
blessing, " 'hell, heaven / everything convenient / to
promote one's joy.' " The woman runs on: " 'he experiences a solemn joy / in seeing that he has become
an idol.' " (The allusion is to Anatole France's book
for children, *Filles et Garçons* [1900]—any girl knows
"man's joy" is that he is a baby boy.) Oh, he is
"plagued," impassioned, unnerved by the sweet nocturnal song of the nightingale, "dazzled by the apple,"
and "stumbles over marriage." More formidable than
the Wife of Bath, her great grandmother and prototype, Eve has no scruples. She even clips the nineteenth-century rationalistic anarchist William Godwin,
who pronounced the institution " 'a very trivial object
indeed' " that, as she says gleefully, "destroyed" the
philosophical attitude in which he stood as a man "un-

fathered by a woman." Will she never stop talking?
Garrulity, thy name is woman, mother of man. But if
form is synonymous with content, Eve gives Adam
more time and attention than he gave her.

It is, however, Moore who is responsible for the
wit implicit in the arrangement. The woman's expression reveals other possible, conceivable attitudes,
such as her confident assumption of the right to speak,
pleasure in ridiculing man, and grudging admiration
for him. There are women who would not give him the
time of day, or night, and there are women who would
not protest so energetically. The poet is known for the
axiom in "Silence" (1924): "The deepest feeling always shows itself in silence; / not in silence, but restraint." In *Marriage,* restraint is not synonymous with
Adam's constraint.

Part 2 of the poem begins with a brief discourse
of thirty-two lines by an unidentifiable persona, probably the comic of the prologue, on the god of marriage: "Unhelpful Hymen! / a kind of overgrown
cupid / reduced to insignificance" by both advertising
and Adam's experiment (the garden of Eden, the eating of the "potent" apple, the ritual of marriage?
Again, the phrase covers a multitude of sins). Whatever the ambiguities of the "experiment," there are
"ways out but no way in—" (to the garden). The persona grants that Hymen gives "good" Victorian advice, found in Anthony Trollope's comic novel,
Barchester Towers (1857): the best age to be blinded by
love is "from forty-five to seventy. . . ." With that
reservation, the permissive Hymen can commend love
as "a fine art," "an experiment, / a duty," or "merely
recreation." One cannot expect love without friction
or calamity; it is even a fight to be affectionate, as the
open-minded persona knows. He or she therefore

matches the genial god with a citation from the thir-
teenth-century priest, Robert of Sorbon, for whom the
great center of learning and French philosophy was
named: " 'no truth can be fully known / until it has
been tried / by the tooth of disputation.' "

Juxtaposed with the ineffectual Hymen are thirty-
two lines introduced by the marriage emblems: a
"blue panther with black eyes," and a black one "with
blue eyes. . . . 'Married people often look that way[.]' "
These fierce, solitary, flesh-eating creatures are
merely said to be graceful; one must give them the
path. Zigzagging back and forth, the persona inter-
poses an image on the cruelty of "a black obsidian
Diana," a variation of the black panther, her virginal
hand spiked to prove her affection "to the bone," an
image followed much later by comment on the equivalent power that men sometimes "make" one feel.
Abrupt shifts insinuate themes of mixed emotions,
lack of emotion, the lost self or the self lost, freedom
and servitude, a little laughter and generous humor,
frankness and deception. There are brief notations on
the ironic story of the banquet—tête á tête—of king
Ahasuerus (conquered by Esther, a loving wife who
saved her people from death); "orchids like snakes'
tongues"; and the "imperious humility" of French ladies ready to receive gentlemen at tea: the variety
suggests that only a synthetic collage could contain
such a pastiche. The perspective is clearly not linear;
the center does not hold. Williams spoke of *Marriage*
as an "anthology of transits," Moore as an "anthology
of statements." It is almost—but not really—a disjunc-
tive harangue. The persona drops out of sight or
leaves the stage.

As might be expected, "He" and "She" crowd
one another in center stage for Part 3. In thirty-seven

lines of operatic dialogue, they bare their teeth dis-
putatiously with help from a satire on "The Rape of
the Lock," a book on the Syrian Christ, the president
of Bryn Mawr College speaking at Mt. Holyoke (the
first college for women in the United States), George
Adam Smith's *Expositor's Bible*, Ezra Pound, Charles
Reade, and Edgar Allan Poe. Ranting at cross purposes, the two are united only by the charges they
bring against each other. Women are not music to the
ear, but poison; men are monopolists unfit to be the
guardians of another's happiness; women are "mum-
mies" to be handled carefully, and a wife is a coffin
refusing to be buried, an adoring child to a distinguished parent; marriage is a play there isn't enough
time to sit and watch. Almost out of breath, the central
characters finally sound as if they are listening to one
another: She says "You know so many artists who are
fools," and he replies, "You know so many fools / who
are not artists." (The repartee is adapted without
credit from Poe's "Purloined Letter.") Both are plagi-
arists, but the man has the first and the last words. The
persona, in the meantime, recovers sufficiently to pro-
nounce twenty-five lines in judgment on the self-love
of these savages. Beyond redemption, they disaffect all
those who are not visionaries.

The epilogue of thirty-four lines opens with a
passage from commentary on La Fontaine's fable,
"Love and Folly": "Everything to do with love is mystery; / it is more than a day's work / to investigate this
science." (Hence the broadside in the prologue: "Psychology which explains everything / explains nothing,
/ and we are still in doubt.") Then, in a whirl of words,
in one long-winded sentence, the undaunted persona
characterizes love. It is, of course, rare: the "striking
grasp of opposites," a "cycloid inclusiveness," the

"triumph of simplicity," a "charitive" tempestuous
wind threatening the lives of the prisoners of the faith
or its disciples, a "frightening disinterestedness,"
something one feels a long time like true sorrow, "the
essence of the matter: / 'Liberty and union / now and
forever[.]' " The persona's commentary following the
shibboleth for heterogeneous states, the familiar in-
scription for the statue of the "archaic Daniel Webster," statesman, politician, compromiser, in Central
Park, is the essence of wit. The great debater stands
with "the Book on the writing table; / the hand in the
breast pocket." What Book—the Bible, the laws, stat-
utes of limitations, rights and obligations, collective
wisdom and nonsense? And the equivocal gesture of
"the hand in the breast pocket"—over the heart where
it should be? The dramatic pose makes one want to
hoot. He could outwit the devil.

Moore lets herself go, freely but adroitly and
amenably, in *Marriage*. Although she veers toward dia-
tribe, she never loses control of her *plaisanterie*. She
well knew she had dared misreading in relation to the
fact that she never married. Having ridiculed an experience she later said was "the proper thing for everybody but *me*," she volunteered the quixotic
comment that "you don't marry for practical reasons
but for *im*practical reasons." Or, amused that she was
"diagnosed as 'a case of arrested emotional development,' " she could also ridicule herself: "Prudence,"
she wrote, "is a rich, ugly old maid courted by In-
capacity." These attitudes underlie the bantering
tones and good humor, the high and low comedy of
Marriage. "So," she said, "people daren't derive a
whole philosophy of life from that." And, with credit
to the collage, one last pun in the spirit of this poem
that is not a poem: it has no center of gravity.

IV

Another of Moore's literary antics is a tour de force, "To Victor Hugo of My Crow Pluto" (1961), and the companion piece in prose, "My Crow Pluto—A Fantasy" (1961). Apparently bothered by the response of readers to both *Marriage* and "My Crow," she explains in "A Burning Desire to Be Explicit" (1966) that both were written for amusement. Speaking of the fact that she was beset by charges of obscurity, she comments that "an even somewhat experienced person" feels gratitude for "clues to meaning." She thereafter disingenuously remarks, "I can scarcely be called *avant-garde*, and might say that 'My Crow Pluto' is narrative, not an attempt at abstract writing. It says that crows entertain me . . ."; and then, in almost the same breath, she makes one of her repeated references to "my lines" *Marriage* as "but a little anthology of terms and phrases that had entertained me." The synthetic form of the collage, relatively daring at the time of its publication, differs from the poem and fantasy about "My Crow," however, in that the later experimental pieces belong to a classic genre. They are parodies of the most notorious of Poe's poems, "The Raven" (1845), and "The Philosophy of Composition" (1846), which is the disputed account of the calculatedly conscious way the author went about writing "*a* poem that should suit at once the popular and critical taste."

Satirizing the tricks of both thought and manner in Poe's work, Moore chooses a pedestrian crow instead of the more romantic, intelligent raven. But both birds belong to the same family, the Corvidae, and they are similar in appearance. Poe, needing a bird with imitative skills, decided that the symbolic bird of

dark prophecy was preferable to the gaudy parrot.
Moore's Pluto, ironically superior to both raven and
parrot, is "the true / Plato" and speaks "pseudo /
Esperanto" or "crow-Esperanto," "madeinusa." Her
use of the artificial international "bird" language in
the verse is the twentieth-century poet's way of joking
about Poe's stated aim—"kept steadily in view"—of
"rendering the work *universally* appreciable," as the
nineteenth century expected it to be.

In one of several efforts to suggest that she was
not writing "doggerel" but parody, Moore said she
went over the Esperanto with Floyd Zulli, of the Department of Romance Languages at New York University, who verified all but a single phrase, "botto e
totto," which she told him casually she had seen
"somewhere."[8] (She provides, handily, the English
"vow and motto" as an equivalent in the text of the
verse and in the "impromptu" dictionary following
the poem.) Esperanto especially suits her wordplay,
because it is liberal in the use of a sound Poe liked for
effect. Explaining that he chose the "long *o* as the most
sonorous vowel, in combination with *r* as the most
producible consonant," he arrived at the commonly
quoted refrain, "Nevermore." Moore merely notes "I
wanted an 'o' all the way through."[9] She is thereby
faithful to the Greek origins of parody, "a song sung
alongside another," but Moore is not sonorous; the
o's multiply like nonsense syllables in a comic chant,
leaving one saying, "Ridiculous. No Moore."

The "Fantasy" is as important as the poem in the
parodic, fictive maze, and is the first of Moore's efforts
to provide clues to the spoof rather than an analysis of
how "My Crow" was written. "Since runover lines in
verse seldom read well," the narrator begins, "it suddenly occurred to me to continue a two-syllable line,

two-line stanza about a crow . . . but I am changing to prose as less restrictive than verse." Poe preferred to write poetry, but found the pay less restricted for prose. And while the persona for "The Raven" is a student "weak and weary" pondering "once upon a midnight dreary" over "many a quaint and curious volume of forgotten lore," Moore's persona listens to "Dr. Zulli's 6:30 Sunrise Semester" on "Landmarks in the Evolution of the Novel" over Channel 2. (Poe specialized in the novel, the new or original.)

Adopted by Pluto, whose rookery was in Fort Greene Park, Moore's student narrator finds him to be, like Poe's raven, an intuitive, knowing bird ("savio / ucello" in Moore's poem). She had, she testifies, always wanted a crow; she had received a mechanical one for Christmas but needed feathers to replace those that blew off her hat. Pluto also liked many of the same foods she liked and was "a dream come true." In Poe's poem, the nameless bird is from "Night's Plutonian shore"; he intrudes on the student's lonely mourning for the lost Lenore and on his "dreams no mortal ever dared dream before." Emblematic of never-ending remembrance, as Poe says in "The Philosophy of Composition," the ungainly raven limits himself to the repetitive "Nevermore," and the experience turns from ludicrous fancy, to ominous mystery, to nightmare. Moore's narrator could not induce her crow to say "Nevermore." If she inquired "What was the refrain in Poe's 'Raven,' Pluto? he invariably would croak 'Evermore.' " He was, however, clever enough to supply a word if the student missed one when she was taking down Dr. Zulli's TV lecture.

Like Poe's raven, which "perched upon a bust of Pallas just above my chamber door— / Perched and sat and nothing more," Pluto "favored a bust as a

perch—a bronze by Gaston Lachaise," cast and given
to the narrator by Lincoln Kirstein. (Lachaise did a
bust of Moore which is now in the Metropolitan Museum of Art; Kirstein was among the editors who published her poetry; both men were friends of hers.) The
bust was, appropriately, "near the typewriter which
interested" the bird. He was also "fanatically interested in detail" such as the lettering on the stationery
from women's magazines; he attracted attention at the
drugstore and Key Foods, but she had to keep an eye
on him; and he could even fly to the bookcase to fetch
her *Webster's Dictionary for the Vest Pocket:* all of which are
oblique figurative references to Poe himself. He contributed frequently to women's magazines, has been
probably inaccurately described as a drug addict, did
not eat well when he was out of work, and so forth. It
is even likely that the shenanigans about the pocket
dictionary, which she says contains a section on "National Bankruptcy Law," allude to the financial failure
of the one magazine Poe owned.

Addressing her "dear crow," however, Moore's
poetic persona "has to let" him go "a bel bosco" ("to
lovely woods"). She tells, in the "Fantasy," of taking
him to the Connecticut woods where she liberated
him. She said to Pluto, " 'Spread your wings. Fly,'
although 'emancipated' is more accurate, since he was
already free. 'Fly?' Losing him was not simple but the
spirit of adventure finally got the best of him." Poe's
demonic raven, "never flitting, still is sitting, / still is
sitting, / On the pallid bust of Pallas. / . . . And the
lamplight o'er him streaming throws his shadow on
the floor; / And my soul from out that shadow that lies
floating on the floor / Shall be lifted—nevermore!"

Moore's "Crow" is free because he is "tuttuto /
vagabondo," a complete gypsy, also suggesting Poe's

unsettled, peripatetic life. And although she rarely used an epigraph for her poems, she chooses for "Crow" the Poesque figure from Victor Hugo: "Even when the bird is walking we know that it has wings." Poe occasionally resorted to the epigraph for his verse, but typically selected inscriptions from other writers for the tales. The association of Poe and Hugo, to whom Moore's poem is addressed, perhaps occurs because the American writer's French connections—Baudelaire and Mallarmé—are considered by historians of literature as central to the beginnings of modern poetry. Poe was, of course, first championed by Baudelaire, who felt indebted especially to him but also to Hugo for their evocation of the ambience of mystery and for knowledge of the technical resources of verse that rescued French poetry from sterile conventions. Hugo, like Poe, was also a great popular writer. And the sonorous long *o* conveniently aids Moore in the rhyme scheme, as do the names of Plato and Pluto and the description of the crow as "pigeon-toe." Pluto–Plato Crow is, however, a "serafino / uvaceo" (a grape-black seraph); Poe, often called "The Raven," became to Mallarmé "the angel" who gave "a sense more pure to the words" of the tribe ("Le Tombeau d'Edgar Poe"). Crow, then, is apparently an emblem for Poe himself.

Like Poe, again, Moore's bird shares with her persona the credo, "lucro / è peso morto"—"profit is a dead weight." In 1963, she published a brief essay with that statement as a title; the tone is serious. The ironies of the point in "Crow" depend upon the biographical cliché that Poe's "Raven" brought the impoverished author fame and ten dollars. (He said "the bird beat the bug ['The Gold Bug'] all hollow.")

Enjoying a sensational success that no American

poem had previously been accorded, "The Raven" is unsuccessful poetically. Of interest for its narrative and dramatic lines, it is also metrically skillful, but neither the light rhythms nor the rhymes are compatible with the action and atmosphere of the poem; the form is not synonymous with the content. Critics, pointing to the hypnotic versification as banal or to the conflict between it and the grotesqueries of the poem, see the work as one of the evidences of Poe's increasing physical and mental deterioration. Despite the serious strains in "The Raven," the modes are so mixed that its popular reception is taken as an index of the questionable taste of a period in which Poe was unable to keep his bearings as a genuinely original man of letters. (When Moore talked about her versification for "My Crow," she said, "I didn't quite succeed.")

Having herself been compared to Poe for "passages of pure poetry" and "technical virtuosity," Moore acknowledged that she was influenced by his prose; Laurence Stapleton noted that the early draft for at least one of the poems, "A Grave," also shows an indebtedness to Poe's fine verse, "The City in the Sea" (1831, 1845). In her imaginative tricks, Moore is the ideal parodist because of her appreciation of Poe as a writer, because of the "feather touch" of the ridicule, and because of the ironic levities of the social as well as the literary criticism. She too aimed for originality, if not novelty. She too had her difficulties in satisfying both popular and critical tastes.

V

Marianne Moore's virtuosity and her fearless assumption that she could find ways "to objectify what it is indispensable to one's happiness to express" continued throughout her career. The liberating activities of the modern artists and her literary fellows were reinforced by the example of earlier American poets—Poe, Whitman, Dickinson—in their willingness to work against established traditions. Asked in 1953 whether or not there were qualities that distinguished a poem as "American," Moore responded that she did not see how one can speak of "a typical American poem," because of the extreme variety in American verse. "A tendency to defy convention does seem to me typically American; but when American verse disregards rules and defies precedent and yet is poetry," she said, "it is so because depth of experience, imagination and 'ear' make it so; because it is stamped by firmness of personality."[10] The defense of freedom from proscriptive "rules" against which she pits "personality" is a reiteration of both the basics of modernism and the belief of her great nineteenth-century predecessors in their own genius and individuality. Like them, she is often labeled idiocyncratic, eccentric, quirky, both by those who find individuality irritating or threatening and by those who delight in it. "I was a little different from the others," she said when she recalled her gratitude to Alfred Kreymborg, who published three of her early poems, including the long version of the famous "Poetry" (1919). "He thought I might pass for a novelty, I guess."[11] She could have said that she insisted on her freedom to be herself.

Freedom did not mean for the eclectic Moore that anything goes. Hers is a freedom from "overconscious

correctness" and from rigidities that stymie spontaneous joy. Discussing Edmund Spenser's poetry, for example, she approves of his "coining words to suit the
rhyme," the "gusto in even the least felicitous of his
defiances," and "the impulsive intimacy" of words
that bring "the whole thing to life." Valuing "the natural wording of uninhibited urgency at its best," she
also recognized the need of a counterpoise to anar-
chical license. She asserted simultaneously that "gusto
thrives on freedom, and freedom in art, as in life, is the
result of a discipline imposed on ourselves. Moreover,
any writer overwhelmingly honest about pleasing himself is almost sure to please others."[12] The confident
belief in her own autonomy is nowhere more evident
than in the fact that she defied precedent by opening
verse to new rhythms, which she disciplined herself to
write despite the objections of readers with old-fashioned ears.

In retrospect, the most radical characteristic of
what Moore called her "observations, experiments in
rhythm, or exercises in composition" was her increasing reliance on syllabic rather than accentual-syllabic
or accentual verse forms. Syllables and words are
stressed as they would be in natural speech or free
verse, but the control, unlike that of cadenced verse,
is in the number of syllables that occur within the line.
Although Moore said in 1969 that she hated the syllabic method, and although she was not the originator of
the form for poetry in English, she was the first major
American practitioner of the method later adopted by
other poets such as W. H. Auden and Donald Hall.
Syllabic verse provided her with both a freedom and
a discipline that she desired. Liberation from what has
been called the lust for stress, or what she spoke of as
the "subservient singsong," enabled the discovery of

understated rhythms and the reanimation of language from the source common to any writer—prose. Rhythm, she once explained, was her prime objective. "If I succeeded in embodying a rhythm that preoccupied me, I was satisfied." The increased flexibility nonetheless approached the sound of prose, a quality disliked by readers who want a poetry rich in sensuous music. The differences between poetry and prose are often slight in American verse of the twentieth century, which has cultivated the colloquial and even the vernacular in an effort to enliven the genre. Moore, however, is not primarily a conversational poet, despite frequent evidences of demotic speech combined with literary language in the collages. What she wrote was also not prose, but verse with the awkwardness or the ease of the rhetoric of prose. Having said in 1919 that "My work jerks and rears," she exaggerated slightly, but she persisted in her efforts to find effective rhythms for her voice, and by mid-career if not earlier she wrote syllabic verse of heightened power and singular nuances. After 1929, for instance, she ceased to write free verse.

The units of the syllabic form are governed by the pull of sentences and paragraphs. As early as 1919 she explained to Ezra Pound, who inquired about her "metric," that the verse she had written had been "an arrangement of stanzas, each stanza being an exact duplicate of every other stanza." The form of the original, or first stanza, she pointed out, was "a matter of expediency, hit upon as being approximately suitable to the subject."[13] In 1960, she told Donald Hall that she never "planned" a stanza, although she might "influence an arrangement or thin it, then try to have successive stanzas identical with the first. Spontaneous initial originality—say impetus—" seemed "difficult to

reproduce later." She then quoted Stravinsky, who had said about pitch, "If I transpose it for some reason, I am in danger of losing the freshness of first contact and will have difficulty in recapturing it later." She also said in 1969 when she once again discussed the methods by which she worked, that "after the thing is done," she supposed she did "count the syllables" to know how nearly she had followed "a set example in the second stanza from the first," but that she "never possibly could think of it until *after*" she had written the poem. Then she saw how it "mathematically comes out." Asked if she could hear the number of syllables in a line without counting them, she immediately replied, "Oh, yes, I don't think about the mathematics."[14]

When she deliberately broke up a pattern that she set, she said it was to make it sound more natural. She amplified the idea:

And it ought to be continuous. For instance, that little thing (they tell me, at college, it was the first thing I wrote): "I May, I Might, I Must."

> If you tell me why the fen
> appears impassible, I then
> will tell you why I think that I
> can get across it if I try.

There, everything comes in straight order, just as if I had not thought it before, and were talking to you. Unrestrained and natural. Well, that's an extreme example, too. I don't do that well. I'd *like* to.

Self-critical, she admitted that some of her work sounded "thought up and worked over. . . . But I like to have it all natural and consecutive, no matter how it counts on the page."[15]

She always thought of the way the poem looked

and liked "to see symmetry on the page," but the visual design ceased to be as important as the spoken rhythms. She damagingly admitted, however, that she "never realized until we got tape recorders and records that the spoken line is different from the one on the page sometimes." Beginning with the first disc in 1944, she recorded during her lifetime thirty of the poems and seven of the fables she translated from La Fontaine. (Among them are only four of the poems published between 1915 and 1925; two of the group are "The Fish" and "To a Chameleon.") She found in trying to read aloud that some of the lines wouldn't read. To make the verse "read right," she thereafter made minor changes in phrasing for *The Complete Poems*. She wanted to correct the tendency of the visual pattern to mislead people into thinking that the line is the vocal unit in her verse. Except for emphasis "as if you were stopping, and couldn't go on any further," she said, she did not ordinarily want the reader to pause at the line breaks. "I would have the poems read straight, with commas—or punctuation—showing where to pause."[16] As she shifted attention from the "grids of visual symmetry" influenced by the use of the typewriter, and as the grids of sound became foremost in her work, she was more appreciated by the public that values poetry. She became, in fact, a public poet and a public personality.

She did not, however, have a flair for "dramatic reading." In the recordings, she is decidedly without artifice, cunning, or pretense. The voice is not high-colored or commanding, rasping or sweet. There are subtleties of tension, quick rhythms, crisp or quiet tones, and slight changes to suggest the matter-of-fact or the humorous, a gentleness or severity. Whether she is relaxed or rushed, she is not given to grand

climaxes or great swells of emotion. She is sometimes
conversational and sometimes close to light music.
While there is no luxury of sound, there is the sense
that she enjoyed the sound of words and that she took
care in conveying the meaning as well as the measures
of the verse.

Among the poems Moore chose to record is
"What Are Years?" (1940), in which the syllabic verse
has the formality, order, and perfection of ritual. The
poem reads well either silently or orally, and it is indebted for its rhythmic and strophic structure to the
scriptures used in responsive readings at religious ser-
vices. Essentially a wisdom psalm, it is a meditation on
the themes of fallibility and strength, resolute doubt
and mighty singing, mortality and eternity. The first
questions move back and forth as if they were a choric
chant: "What is our innocence, / what is our guilt?"
The answers have a haunting finality: "All are / naked,
none is safe." That very finality demands further questioning:

> And whence
> is courage: the unanswered question,
> the resolute doubt,—
> dumbly calling, deafly listening—that
> in misfortune, even death
> encourages others
> and in its defeat, stirs
>
> the soul to be strong?

The reply resounds with priestly assurance as the
figures turn irreversibly toward the conflict at the center of man's being:

> He
> sees deep and is glad, who

> accedes to mortality
> and in his imprisonment rises
> upon himself as
> the sea in a chasm, struggling to be
> free and unable to be,
> in its surrendering
> finds its continuing.

The composure of the voice rising and falling inspires a succinct recapitulation of the theme: "So he who strongly feels, / behaves." With confirmation of the acceptance of the wisdom, the idea is then continued, repeated, and enlarged in a new figure, followed by a choric summary:

> The very bird,
> grown taller as he sings, steels
> his form straight up. Though he is captive,
> his mighty singing
> says, satisfaction is a lowly
> thing, how pure a thing is joy.
> This is mortality,
> this is eternity.

The voices of the antiphon are inviolable. The measured poem has one line that breaks the syllabic pattern of 6, 6, 7, 9, 5, 9, 7, 6, 6; the line, "the sea in a chasm, struggling to be," is ten syllables. Within the confines of the movement, there is only one extra word, "be," which carries beyond the limitations of one's self. (The center word of the center line is "himself.") The word "be" is echoed by "free and unable to be," but the restriction, "the surrendering," is the source of the strength for "continuing," the last word of the strophe and the stanza. "Continuing" is prepared for by "stirs," the last word of the first stanza, and anticipates "eternity," the last word of the chant.

Carried by the disciplined rhythms, one can hardly misread the poem aloud. The lines of force and the symmetrical pattern capture the voices and strengthen the laxest, weakest, and most troubled of readers who straighten up with a will to redeem the time.

"The Mind Is an Enchanting Thing" (1943) is another of the poems Moore recorded. The subjects— the qualities and behavior of the mind in the act of thinking about itself—are proved by the images, the metaphors, and the commentary that change so rapidly that one is hardly arrested by the action. Yet, attracted by the spontaneous changes and the spirited rhythmic movement within the poem, one is prepared to agree with the right-minded, surprising conclusion of the argument.

Although it is not ritualistically formal, the work shares with "What Are Years?" the exactness of the syllabic count in each stanza and a single exception to the design. The prevailing pattern of 6, 5, 4, 6, 7, and 9 is broken in stanza four, whose final line consists of ten syllables. There Moore makes an Emersonian point about the mind: "it's conscientious inconsistency." If she is alluding to Emerson's familiar observation that a "foolish consistency is the hobgoblin of little minds, adored by little statesmen and philosophers and divines," she goes him one better in the mischievous inconsistency of one little extra syllable that underscores the prosaic line. In a Moore poem, as in any good poem, everything counts effectively, but the writer can also ignore the count to enact a subject rhythmically, whether the language is prosaic or figurative.

The poem not only describes the mind's enchanting ways but also verbally enacts its contradictory power to disenchant, analyze, speculate, and question:

"It tears off the veil; tears / the temptation, the / mist the heart wears, / from its eyes—if the heart / has a face[.]" When the mind is thinking, the rhythms can become wittily abrupt even within syllabic controls. The punctuation, of course, does its work as it should.

Moore's poetic principles allow for the reader's participation in the activities of the mind. Her humor is partly underwritten and partly hidden, for instance, in the analogy between the kiwi—a flightless bird—and the mind "feeling its way as though blind" and walking "along with its eyes on the ground." The kiwi is known for having lots of feathers (as a "rain-shawl" —protective in a downpour) and an apeteryx-awl (as a beak—sharp, boring). The kiwi also has the largest nose of any bird, and its sense of smell is so acute that it can detect worms underneath the ground—facts Moore implies as if she were telling an "in" joke ("the poet has a right to expect the reader, at least in a measure, to be able to complete the poetic statement"). The mind, she says in the next stanza, "has memory's ear / that can hear without / having to hear." She is no longer teasing; she relies on the poem that is articulated to evoke the continuities that are unspoken. That is one of the reasons she is a difficult but fascinating poet.

And, in case one has missed the humor as well as the "conscientious inconsistency" of which the mind is capable: "Unconfusion submits / its confusion to proof; it's / not a Herod's oath that cannot change." With visions of the head of John the Baptist brought in upon a platter to a woman who asked Herod for it after he had promised her anything she wanted and would not renege, one cannot insist that the poet's approbation of the power of the mind to change is

simply a woman's poem. "Conscientious inconsistency" is preferable to a severed head.

Long before, in "The Labors of Hercules" (1921), a criticism of stereotypes in thinking, Moore had written: "It is one thing to change one's mind, / another to eradicate it—," which she deleted from the final version. Becoming more tempered and skilled in verse forms as well as more certain of her own acts of mind, the poet who renounced the lust for stress was followed by one who stopped hitting readers over the head. If her verse does not usually soar or sing, it has that sense of sleight-of-hand synonymous with a freedom resulting from the discipline she imposed on herself to become a "modern" poet.

A self-deprecating humor and a modesty masked the extent of her daring in the development of the impressive forms that do not deny but go beyond the traditions of verse. As John Ashberry, reviewing *The Complete Poems* in 1967, observed, "there is a point at which her importance gets lost in the welter of minutiae that people her poems, and in the unassuming but also rather unglamorous wisdom that flashes out between descriptions of bizarre fauna and rare artifacts." Despite "the obvious grandeur of her chief competitors," including William Carlos Williams and Wallace Stevens, Ashberry said, "I am tempted simply to call her our greatest modern poet."[17]

3

Art Is Always Actually Personal

I

To be a poet meant for Marianne Moore that she had to master her trade, but also that she had to be herself. The integrity of what she made depended on her integrity as a person. She was always cognizant of the disparity between the perfection of forms and the human limitations, her own and others' imperfections, with which one lived. That consciousness is the source of her self-examination and criticism in relation to what she valued and admired. The poems, therefore, record the hazards of her experience in mastering qualities of which she disapproved in herself without sacrificing her own quick singularity and independence.

In "Literature the Noblest of the Arts" (1925), she quotes George Saintsbury on Trollope: "If you have any sense of the particular art you can't help feeling the skill with which the artist wheels you along till he feels inclined to turn you out of his barrow and then deposits you at his if not your destination." With characteristic humor, she writes years later in "A Carriage from Sweden" (1944), "carts are my trade." The model is a handmade cart, "a vein of resined straightness," "that inner happiness made art."

Although Moore has been associated with objectivist poetry because of her respect for things in their own right, she is also a subjective, an introspective, and a personal poet. She rarely apologized for her predilections, which reveal the woman who made the poems. In "Subject, Predicate, Object" (1958), she declares: "It is for himself the writer writes, charmed or exasperated to participate; eluded, arrested, enticed by felicities." She concludes the poem "In the

70

Public Garden," which she read to a crowd of five
thousand at the Boston Arts Festival in 1958, by saying
one is

> glad that the Muses have a home and swans—
> that legends can be factual;
>> happy that Art, admired in general,
>> is always actually personal.

We assume she is speaking in her own voice, not
simply because phrases such as "My first," "I recall,"
"let me," "And I?" occur in the poem, but because the
word "personal" sums up the point of view, and because Moore habitually, if not consistently, used that
point of view in her verse. My guess is that when she
began to write she was naive in regard to questions
that critics debate as they try to distinguish between a
fictive voice in the first person and the autobiograph-
ical "I." While the poet's personal papers still have
not been published and there is no "life," there is
nothing in print that compares with Emily Dickinson's
caveat in an early letter (1862) to T. W. Higginson:
"When I state myself, as the Representative of the
Verse—it does not mean—me—but a supposed person."[1] Yet at least by the time Moore wrote "Melanchthon" (1919), in which there are two predominant
voices, she was attentive to the distinctions between
the stated "me" and imagined projections that mirror
or oppose the self as she developed the skill of wheeling readers along to her destination. She was also
careful about such distinctions when she discussed
other writers. She observed, for instance, in a lecture
on Wallace Stevens as "A Bold Virtuoso" (1952), that
he "embeds his secrets, inventing disguises which assure him freedom to speak out." For all the play in
Moore's verse, however, she does not wear as many

disguises as Stevens or play as many games with "supposed persons" as Dickinson. Moore was inclined to play herself. Discussions of her work have taken that tendency for granted, and it probably explains the necessity she felt to make comments suggesting experiments with personae in *Marriage* (1923) or "My Crow" (1961). She wrote many poems like "The Fish" (1918), in which she is the unremarked observer whose aim is to achieve "the likeness of the thing visualized," but the strategy in most of the work is that of "In the Public Garden," which encourages the reader to identify the observer and participant as Moore herself.

Although the poetry and the mind of the poet are not the same, there are similarities between attitudes in the verse, the interviews she gave, and the prose she wrote; there are also changes in attitude that make us aware of Moore's resilience as well as the angularities and the jagged edges of her truths. An example is her pronouncement on poetry: "I, too, dislike it." Having fired the blast at the beginning of "Poetry" (1919), she let the sound reverberate through the years; and although she drastically revised her apologia more than once (1921, 1924, 1967), she never suppressed that opening salvo. She told Donald Hall (in an interview for *McCall's* magazine, December, 1965) that she rather resisted the idea of writing poetry. "I disliked poetry, anything partly true and improbably lengthened out to *sound* true. As a child, I had no use for it. We had to recite things in school, learn them by heart. . . . And I had to learn something called 'The Little Red Hen.' " She remembered that the "hen's cackle was imitated: " 'Cut-cut-cut-cudaw-cut.' That—well—had no verisimilitude for me. I thought, Anything but awkward fictitiousness." She was no child when she

admitted the reservation in "Poetry"; and after years of practicing the art, she was hardly gesturing when she said that she was glad the Muses had a home. Criticism of "no verisimilitude" or "awkward ficti- tiousness" and appreciation that "legends can be fac- tual" are less contradictory than "I, too, dislike it" and "happy that Art" is "admired in general." But Moore's change of mind is anticipated in the original version of "Poetry" (1919) by the conclusion: "if you demand . . . / the raw material of poetry in / all its rawness and / that which is . . . / genuine, you are interested in poetry"; the view is trimmed and restated in the final version (1967): "Reading it, however, with a perfect contempt for it, one discovers in / it after all, a place for the genuine."

Moore seems to have believed that she had a di- vining rod for locating the genuine, and she probably did. "The poet commits himself to that one integrity: antipathy to falsity," she said in "A Bold Virtuoso." She praised T. S. Eliot's "contempt for sham," "terse- ness synonymous with a hatred of sham," and "disgust with affectation." E. E. Cummings's *One Times One* was "a thing of furious nuclear integrities." Or describing Llewelyn Colum, she refers amusingly to his dislike of "a naturalist with an umbrella," shams, and "pick- thank" science. Sincerity was another variation of the genuine, and in Moore's view, originality depended on it, even when it took the form of "lethal honesty," which was "something apart from the stodgy world of mere routine." Naturalness also was inseparable from the genuine. "The natural wording of uninhibited ur- gency," "natural reticence," "helpless sincerity," "helpless naturalness," and "indescribable natural- ness" were her terms of approbation for Henry James, who was opposed to "the artificial" and the "touch of

affectation." Notes from D. H. Lawrence had "the effect of naturalness" and belonged for Moore with Mabel Dodge Luhan's comment: " 'Inessentials' seemed deadly to him who knew how to savor a piece of crusty bread on the side of a hill." One of Moore's charms as a person was the confidence with which she was genuinely, honestly, naturally herself. For her that course was both a moral and an aesthetic principle throughout the fifty-five years that she published verse.

II

As a young supplicant, Moore could be bluntly direct and haughty. In "Feed Me, Also, River God" (1916)— apparently suggested by Ezra Pound's figure, "Art . . . is not unlike a river"[2]—she says "I am not . . . indefatigable, but if you are a god you will / not discriminate against me. Yet—if you may fulfil / none but prayers addressed / as gifts in return for gifts— disregard the request." Raising bluntness to arrogance in "To Be Liked By You Would Be a Calamity" (1916), she retorts to a person who has attacked her:

> You tell me frankly that you would like
> to feel
> My flesh beneath your feet,
> . . . I can but put my weapon up, and
> Bow you out.

> Gesticulation—it is half the language.
> Let unsheathed gesticulation be the steel
> Your courtesy must meet,
> Since in your hearing words are
> mute, which to my senses
> Are a shout.

Talking in "Roses Only" (1917) to a woman who does not seem "to realize that beauty is a liability rather than / an asset," the young poet justifies her honest rebuke by reminding "the rose" of a "predatory hand" and commending the protective thorns as "the best part of you." The tones in "To an Intra-Mural Rat" (1915) are acerbic and flippant rather than funny: "You make me think of many men / Once met to be forgot again / Or merely resurrected / In a parenthesis of wit. . . ." None of these frank little verses appear in *The Complete Poems,* but none are juvenile, either. Moore was in her late twenties and willing at the time to have them printed.

Moreover, she included in *The Complete Poems* several other pieces from the same period that show the imperiousness of her character. "To Statecraft Embalmed" (1915) begins abusively: "There is nothing to be said for you. Guard / your secret. Conceal it under your hard / plumage, necromancer." The "bird" who is the subject seems almost too pathetic to be trounced as pitilessly as any political enemy was ever trounced:

> . . . transmigrating from the
> sarcophagus, you wind
> snow
> silence round us and with moribund talk,
> half limping and half-ladyfied, you stalk
> about. Ibis, we find
> no
> virtue in you—alive and yet so dumb.
> Discreet behavior is not now the sum
> of statesmanlike good sense.
> Though
> it were the incarnation of dead grace?

"To a Prize Bird" (1915), on the other hand, is addressed to George Bernard Shaw, whom Moore admires: "You suit me well. . . . / Pride sits you well, so strut, colossal bird. / No barnyard makes you look absurd; / your brazen claws are staunch against defeat." Granted, it was the Shavian intellectual clowning as well as the polemics that she enjoyed, but brazen claws are sharper than "unsheathed gesticulation" or thorns, and she appreciated all of them.

Speaking of the "almost combative sincerity" of Eliot, she observed that "by doing his fighting in prose he is perhaps the more free to do his feeling in verse." Moore was tactful in prose, pointing to what she liked and contributing to the cause of literature itself. She fights in verse. Criticizing a critic in "To a Steam Roller" (1915), she does not hesitate to try her heavy "wit" against the heavy weight: "The illustration / is nothing to you without the application. / You lack half wit. You crush all the particles down / into close conformity, and then walk back and forth on them." She says sarcastically: "Were not 'impersonal judgment in aesthetic / matters, a metaphysical impossibility,' you / might fairly achieve / it." Even her final remark, which attempts to lighten the satire, may be amusing but is waspish: "As for butterflies, I can hardly conceive / of one's attending upon you, but to question / the congruence of the complement is vain, if it exists." This is the poet who years later (1960) quotes George Grosz (once a Dada satirist himself): " 'In art there is no place for gossip and but small place for the satirist.' "³ As the young moralist, however, she liked the stimulating effect of satire. Ridiculing "the little assumptions of the scared ego" and the attitudes of beginning writers who "offended poetically," she charged that they were "blind to the right word," and

"deaf to satire / which like the 'smell of cypress strengthens the nerves of the brain[.]' "

During the early years of writing, Moore began to discipline her hauteur and to write poems that are more engaging. In "Critics and Connoisseurs" (1916), she maintains her critical sense or moral severity, but she is more open, speculative, and tempered. The subject is poetry in relation to unconscious and conscious fastidiousness, determination and ambition, conveyed in an easy confluence of images and commentary. The opening remark, "There is a great amount of poetry in unconscious / fastidiousness," carries Moore beyond the strictures of the rational at the same time that it permits her to take advantage of a habit of mind she valued. She sanctions "a / mere childish attempt to make an imperfectly ballasted animal stand up" or "to make a pup / eat his meat from a plate" rather than the "hardihood" of a swan she remembers reconnoitering for food in the river at Oxford but resisting what she "gave it to eat"—her trope for the critic and "ambition without / understanding in a variety of forms." The swan's "conscious fastidiousness" is also compared with "a fastidious ant" she happened to see "carrying a stick north, south, / east, west," and then abandoning it "as useless and overtaxing its / jaws with a particle of whitewash—pill-like but / heavy" only to start over with the same procedure.

> What is
> there in being able
> to say that one has dominated the stream
> in an attitude of self-defense;
> in proving that one has had the experience
> of carrying a stick?

"The poet's hardihood," Sir Herbert Read wrote about "Critics and Connoisseurs," "must not be proof against the impact of random sights and sounds, flotsam and jetsam, bright objects not usually accepted as poetic pablum." But he recognized that Moore demanded much of herself and was consequently ambitious to write verse that would not be insipid or soft. "Ambition without understanding," he observed, "is too fastidious because it is too rigid, too blind to variety and novelty. To have ambition with understanding, to have an open or innocent sensibility," he believed, "is to allow significant images to rise from the depths of the unconscious." This meant, for Read, that the poet "must flow with the stream of consciousness; that is to say, abandon" the "conscious ego."[4] Moore, however, was less interested in the unconscious depths than in being both conscious and freely carried beyond the conscious self. This was the sense in which she wanted to be natural, helplessly natural.

"Critics and Connoisseurs" is important for what it tells us about Marianne Moore as a poet and a person. In it, she discovered an approach to writing that she was to develop as her own and to follow frequently as she matured. She is sharp in the distinctions she illustrates, yet the discriminations are finely drawn and so inextricably linked that, as Read noted, it is difficult to quote anything less than a complete poem. It is also difficult to comprehend the work without attending to the discriminations and subtleties by which they are linked within the individual poems. She compared her work to research. "I want," she said, "to look at the thing from all sides: the person who has seen the animal, how the animal behaves, and so on." She thought of herself as an observer, her poems as observations. They were ways of knowing the world and, since she

was often the person looking, ways of knowing herself, albeit she was not always able to adhere to the principle of looking at a thing from all sides as she tried out her responses and observations.

Having discovered a method in "Critics and Connoisseurs," Moore can be seen to zigzag when she is exasperated or enticed. "Those Various Scalpels" (1917), for instance, is one of her harshest poems. A scathing description of another woman, the poem begins with the title, which is followed by lines that explain it without explaining it: "those / various sounds consistently indistinct, like intermingled echoes / struck from thin glasses successively at random[.]" These are words that cannot, annoyingly, be discerned, but as Emily Dickinson would say, "she dealt" them "like Blades— / How glittering they shone—". Even the woman's hair, "the tails of two / fighting-cocks head to head in stone," reminds Moore of "sculptured scimitars" that repeat the curve of the woman's ears "in reverse order." The eyes, predictably, are "flowers of ice and snow / sown by the tearing winds on the cordage of disabled ships"—victims all? A hand is raised in "an ambiguous signature." And the cheeks are "rosettes / of blood on the stone floors of French chateaux, / with regard to which the guides are so affirmative—[.]" A hard woman with too much makeup—falsely reminiscent of real blood spilled years before? The other hand is "a bundle of lances all alike " but "partly hid" by extravagant jewelry, Persian, Florentine, or gaudy, colorful costume pieces. Then finally the costume: "a magnificent square / cathedral tower of uniform / and at the same time diverse appearance—a / species of vertical vineyard rustling in the storm / of conventional opinion." The description is flamboyant and vicious; it has the

gusto of an observer both taken and repelled by the subject.

Writing about the poem to Eliot in 1950, Moore said, "it seems to me to grow tired at the end"; the end is indeed equivocal. "Are they weapons or scalpels?" the poet asks; the difference might be worth considering, although the answer is a feint:

> Whetted to brilliance
>
> by the hard majesty of that sophistication which is
> superior to opportunity,
> these things are rich instruments with which to
> experiment.
> But why dissect destiny with instruments
> more highly specialized than components of
> destiny itself?

The conclusion, it can be argued, is apt for the poet herself and is for the most part as incisive as the instruments she uses to dissect the victim. The reader, however, is not certain whether the final question is directed toward the cruelties of the subject or turned by the dissecting poet on herself. One might say, as a woman who bore real scars observed, "When a knife cuts you once, you're wary of the knife," but Moore was not inclined to be wary about what she disliked. She wanted to be fearless, and she could be savage as well as gracious. The poem's conclusion is weak because Moore has not resolved the conflicts within herself. It is, of course, unattractive to be a moralist without magnanimity.

Knowing how to use both weapons and scalpels, which were hardly ever dull, Moore still retained a sense of innocence. She spoke of the innocent earth, she was always nostalgic for the life of purity and sim-

plicity, and she had a pristine quality evident in her habits of mind. By 1919, she had written, "In the Days of Prismatic Color":

> not in the days of Adam and Eve, but when Adam
>   was alone; when there was no smoke and color
> was fine, not with the refinement
>   of early civilization art, but because
> of its originality; with nothing to modify it but the
>
> mist that went up, obliqueness was a variation
>   of the perpendicular, plain to see and
> to account for: it is no
>   longer that. . . .

If the poem hardly seems to be written by the same person who wrote "Those Various Scalpels," at least one point in the exposition will confirm that it is: "Principally throat, sophistication is as it al- / ways has been—at the antipodes from the init- / ial great truths." The glimpse of humor in the remark about sophistication is preferable to "Scalpels," not necessarily as poetry but as a personal attitude, for one who hankers after plain truths. Humor was one effective means of resolving conflicts between savagery and innocence. Humor kept the poet valiant, honest, and gracious.

The young comedienne, then, began to write about people in tones that reveal her to be less self-righteous and less narrow in her sympathies than some of the earliest poems indicate. One of the freest and liveliest of pieces, "To the Peacock of France" (1917) is in praise of the great dramatist Molière. She rollicks through the poem for which the first line sets the tone: "In 'taking charge of your possessions when you saw them' you have become a golden jay." For

that she is tolerant. The sense of spectacle, the transformations of borrowed sources, the charm and seri-
ousness of his comedy, the strength of his hatred for
hypocrisy and affectation, the biography—uncertain
beginnings, sombre moods, energy and persistence,
worldly glitter, and the success as well as the outrage
he experienced—the insight, the pleasure Molière
affords: all are expressed with levity and narrative distance in the poem.

> Scaramouche said you charmed his charm away,
>   but not his color? Yes, his color when you liked.
> Of chiseled setting and black-opalescent dye,
>   you were the jewelry of sense;
>   of sense, not license; you but trod the
>   pace
>   of liberty in market-place
>   and court, Molière,
>   the huggermugger repertory of
>   your first adventure, is your
>   own affair.
> "Anchorites do not dwell in theatres," and peacocks
>   do not flourish in a cell.
> Why make distinctions? The results were well
>   when you were on the boards; nor were your
>   triumphs bought
> at horrifying sacrifice of stringency.
>   You hated sham; you ranted up
>   and down through the conventions of
>   excess;
>   nor did the King love you the less
>   nor did the world,
>   in whose chief interest and for whose
>   spontaneous delight, your broad
>   tail was unfurled.

Comedienne that she is, Moore is hardly artless or
unsophisticated. Men as birds, prize birds, vain birds,

successful birds with integrity caught her fancy. The poem to Molière is more memorable than the one to Shaw, and she herself is on her way to "success" without a "horrifying" sacrifice of stringency.

With a talent for mixing people and animals, she might have been a cartoonist. In a poem first titled "My Apish Cousins" (1917) and later changed to "The Monkeys" (1935), on the artistic, literary, or social "scene" as a zoo, the caricatures are quickly sketched. The monkeys "winked too much and were afraid of snakes"; the zebras were "supreme in / their abnormality"; the elephants, with "fog-colored skin," were there; "the small cats"; and the parakeet, "trivial and humdrum on examination," destroyed "bark and portions of the food it could not eat." The humor is broad, and more mischievous than savage: "I recall their magnificence, now not more magnificent / than it is dim." The circumlocutionary cut is followed by the whimsical "truth": "It is difficult to recall the ornament, / speech, and precise manner of what one might / call the minor acquaintances twenty / years back." If one reads the poem straight, Moore would have been ten years old when she went to that party; it was probably one of the Bohemian gatherings she attended on her first trip to New York only a year before, or a tea given by someone like Professor Cheetah in Eliot's "Mr. Apollinax" (1916). But she remembers verbatim the astringent remark of one "cat"—"that Gilgamesh [legendary king, part-god, part-man, warrior and builder, who knew all things] among / the hairy carnivora." And he is a cat after her resolute heart: "They have imposed on us with their pale / half-fledged protestations, trembling about / in inarticulate frenzy, saying, / it is not for us to understand art. . . ."

Who are they? Other people at the party, art critics, academics, arrogant snobs? It hardly matters, since the air is familiar. One wonders also if the admirable cat is patron, aristocrat, or commoner. He has clearly been patronized. "They," he says, find "it all so difficult," and examine "the thing / as if it were inconceivably arcanic, as symmet- / rically frigid as if it has been carved out of chyrsophrase / or marble—" They are not talking of Michelangelo, and they don't know what they are talking about. Gilgamesh has looked at the "thing": "strict with tension, malignant / in its power over us and deeper / than the sea when it proffers flattery in exchange for hemp, / rye, flax, horses, platinum, timber, and fur." The thing must have been at Gallery 291. The independent cat will not be flattered. He knows the depth, the worth, and the seductive power of art; he perceives clearly the exaggerated compliments art pays to one's intelligence, the satisfactions of one's ego and emotional needs, and what it takes of real goods, perhaps irrationally, senselessly, so that one will barter everything one has of any value for it. If this is a romantic view of art, it was the young poet's view. It is, however, as if we had opened her sketchbook and found a cartoon and a chiaroscuro drawing on the same page.

While every poem was a new beginning for Moore, her apprenticeship was coming to a close. She realized "the imperiousness natural to all art" and the confidence one needs to write with authority, as she pointed out in the essay on Saintsbury. She knew, too, that literature was a strict taskmaster, even though she had discovered more than one means of making carts and wheeling readers along to her destination. She had kept her integrity, but she had another important lesson to learn if she was to be as helplessly sincere as

the writers she wished to emulate. She must admit the malignant in herself; she must be more openly self-critical.

The offhand title "Snakes, Mongooses, Snake-Charmers, and the Like" (1922) suggests a relaxed, natural poise that we may regard as typical of Moore in her maturity. She is thinking of a friend "who would give a price" for "those hideous bird's claws, for that exotic asp and the mongoose— / products of the country in which everything is hard work, the country of the grass-getter, / the torch-bearer, the dog-servant, the messenger-bearer, the holy-man." The poem's primary topic, however, is the asp; but the poet looks at the person who would like to have the poisonous asp as well as at the asp and herself looking at both of them. She is both sympathetic toward the friend and narratively detached from him:

> Engrossed in this distinguished worm nearly as wild
>   and as fierce as the day it was caught,
> he gazes as if incapable of looking at anything with a
>   view to analysis.
> "The slight snake rippling quickly through the grass,
> the leisurely tortoise with its pied back,
> the chameleon passing from twig to stone, from stone
>   to straw,"
> lit his imagination at one time; his admiration now con-
>   verges upon this.

Then we see that she also is engrossed in the worm. She is attracted to the sensuous beauty, the movement, the formal perfection of the sacred asp:

> Thick, not heavy, it stands up from its travelling-basket,
> the essentially Greek, the plastic animal all of a piece
>   from nose to tail;
> one is compelled to look at it as at the shadow of the

                                                              alps
    imprisoning in their folds like flies in amber, the
                               rhythms of the skating-rink.
    This animal to which from the earliest times, impor-
                                  tance has attached,
    fine as its worshipers have said—for what was it inven-
                                                   ted?

She extricates herself by her questions, one answering
the other: "To show that when intelligence in its pure
form / has embarked on a train of thought which is
unproductive, it will come back? / We do not know;
the only positive thing about it is its shape; but why
protest?" So she turns abruptly and unequivocally on
herself in honest criticism, which is as emancipating as
humor: "The passion for setting people right is in
itself an afflictive disease. / Distaste which takes no
credit to itself is best." As Vernon Watkins observes
in his "Ode" to T. S. Eliot, "the self-corrected alone
is honest." Moore would ask herself thirty years later
whether scruples are always attractive.[5]

III

Moore's keen attention to animals is one of the best
known of her occupations. Speaking to the question of
her "the inordinate interest" in them, she is almost
too quick as she asserts: "They are subjects for art and
exemplars of it, are they not? minding their own business." They "do not pry or prey—or prolong the conversations; do not make us self-conscious; look their
best when caring the least." It is as if she is giving
someone a deserved comeuppance. She goes on to
qualify her remarks by second thoughts; she recalls
that in a documentary she "saw a leopard insult a

crocodile (basking on a river bank—head visible on the bank)—bat the animal on the nose and continue on its way without so much as a look back. Perhaps I really don't know." Now, mischievous poet that she is, what did she mean by that? Perhaps Moore's reasons for liking animals were that they were not human; they lived in an amoral universe; and they were natural. It was not that she preferred them to people. She customarily liked them both. ("Everything I have written," she once said, "is a result of reading or an interest in people.") It was, I think, safer to talk about animals than to talk about individuals or herself. People, she knew, are inclined to look back; they have a bad conscience or feel guilty if they bat someone else on the nose. They also talk back when insulted. Finally, for all Moore's composure and delight in animals, they are vulnerable creatures, as the example of the crocodile affirms. Like her humor, like her recognition that she was attracted to the malign and susceptible to self-righteousness, a coordinate interest in animals freed Moore to participate imaginatively in an imperfect world in which she could be arrested or enticed by felicities or by not knowing.

"Peter" (1924) is a "strong and slippery" cat, who likes to sleep and has bad dreams.

> Sleep is the result of his delusion that one must
> do as well as one can for oneself. . . .
> Demonstrate on him how the lady placed a forked stick
> on the innocuous neck-sides of the dangerous southern
> snake.
> One need not try to stir him up; his prune-shaped head
> and alligator-eyes are not party to the joke. . . .
> when he has been got the better of in a dream—
> as in a fight with nature or with cats, we all know it.
> Profound sleep is not with him a fixed illusion.

Springing about with froglike accuracy, with jerky cries
when taken in hand, he is himself again;
to sit caged by the rungs of a domestic chair
would be unprofitable—human. What is the good of
hypocrisy?

If Peter's judgment is sometimes fallible, he has his
nerve. He is susceptible to calming influences, but he
is not given to the pretense that he is something other
than what he is.

He can talk but insolently says nothing. What of it?
When one is frank, one's very presence is a compliment.
It is clear that he can see the virtue of naturalness,
that he does not regard the published fact as a surrender.
As for the disposition invariably to affront,
an animal with claws should have an opportunity to use
them.

This is Marianne Moore talking, and she is not talking
about moral imperatives. She is enjoying the independence and the insolence of a natural cat.

To leap, to lengthen out, divide the air, to purloin, to
pursue.
To tell the hen: fly over the fence, go in the wrong way
in your perturbation—this is life;
to do less would be nothing but dishonesty.

Having exchanged the figure of people as cats for
the subject of cat *qua* cat, the poet found her imagination arrested by birds as they are. The swiftest flyer of
all sea birds, the pirate of the air, is described joyously
in "The Frigate Pelican" (1934). She associates the
frigate-bird that cruises rapidly or glides in the air,
gains speed by diving into the wind, and hangs mo-
tionless in the breeze, with both literature and music.

The first association is with Dr. Johnson's "spiritual autobiography," *The History of Rasselas*. The bird "realizes Rasselas's friend's project / of wings uniting levity with strength." (The friend, an artist who attempted to construct wings that should leave vultures and eagles behind, failed as he dropped into the lake of the "happy valley" from which he and Rasselas had hoped to escape to see the misery of the world.) "This / hell-diver, frigate-bird, hurricane- / bird; . . . the storm omen when / he flies close to the waves, should be seen / fishing," but the poet prefers to describe what the bird "appears to prefer"—stealing "from industrious crude-winged species / the fish they have caught." He is "seldom successless," a "marvel of grace, no matter how fast his / victim may fly or how often may / turn." (At the time Moore finished the poem she wrote: "Everything I do is clumsy but may get more felicitous if I keep on working." "Clumsy" is not the word for it; her mother thought it "excellent."[6])

The care with which the poet stresses the piratical behavior of the bird that she simultaneously admires is consistent with the objective of looking at "the animal" from all sides. The care is hardly different from that she takes in an essay published the same year (1934) on a writer for whom she had high regard: "Idealism which was willing to make sacrifices for self-preservation was always an element in the conjuring wand of Henry James." But what of the observer who thinks her poetry clumsy by comparison with the grace of the hell-diver? She would write (in 1943) about Wallace Stevens "that the imagination and the imaginer are different from images and imager, from the nature-loving Narcissus who sees only himself in every pool." She sees not herself but herself as she would

like to be in the images of the pelican. The poem is
quickened because the poet lets herself go not with
abandon but with imagination's energy.

> The others with similar ease,
>   slowly rising once more,
>   move out to the top
>   of the circle and stop
>
> and blow back, allowing the wind to reverse their
>   direction—
>   unlike the more stalwart swan that can ferry the
>   woodcutter's two children home. Make hay;
>   keep
>   the shop; I have one sheep; were a less
>   limber animal's mottoes. This one
>   finds sticks for the swan's-down dress
>   of his child to rest upon and would
>   not know Gretel from Hänsel.
>   As impassioned Handel—

The comparisons could hardly be more pointed or
more light-hearted, even cavalier. The successful frigate is not like reliable, work-a-day creatures even when
they are characters in fairy tales; but like Handel,
"meant for a lawyer and a masculine German domestic / career" who "clandestinely studied the harpsi-
chord / and never was known to have fallen in love,"
the bird "hides / in the height and in the majestic
display of his art." A subject of art, and an exemplar
of it, he glides or quivers, "full of feints," and is "an
eagle / of vigilance."

Then the poet's ecstasy is broken: *"Festina lente.*
["Hasten slowly" or "Go slow in order to arrive more
quickly at a work well made."] Be gay / civilly? How
so?" Then: " 'If I do well I am blessed / whether any
bless me or not, and if I do / ill I am cursed.' " The

bird's vigilance reminds the observer of her own need to be vigilant; the poem is not a spiritual autobiography, but it turns to self-examination and definition. "Art," Moore says in an essay on W. H. Auden (quoting R. G. Collingwood), "is not magic, but a mirror in which others may become conscious of what their own feelings really are. It mirrors defeats and it mirrors escape."

"The Frigate Pelican" concludes:

> We watch the moon rise
> on the Susquehana. In his way,
> this most romantic bird flies
> to a more mundane place, the mangrove
> swamp to sleep. He wastes the moon.
> But he, and others, soon
>
> rise from the bough and though flying, are able to
> foil the tired
> moment of danger that lays on heart and lungs
> the
> weight of the python that crushes to powder.

Uniting levity with strength, Moore and her bird literally transcend threats to their survival, even though one is a pirate and one is a poet.

Moore's earth may be innocent, but life for creatures who inhabit it is often dangerous, and preservation of the species as well as self-preservation is a subject about which her vulnerable animals helped her to write without sanctimoniousness or falsity. "Bird-Witted" (1936) is a discordant song of innocence and experience in face of danger, and it is as fiercely partisan as any poem she ever wrote. The homely humor and simple ironies depend on the common knowledge that birds have small brains but strong emotions and that the mockingbird not only excels as a singer but is

endearing for devotion and bravery, attacking even
man himself in defense of the young. Beyond the
humor is the savagery the devotion unleashes, savagery that is part of what the poet knows.

The scene is a pussy willow tree beneath which
three wide-eyed, open-mouthed young mockingbirds
as large as their mother wait for her to bring something that "will partially feed one of them." Feeble,
solemn fledglings, they squeak intermittently like
"broken carriage-springs"; and "when/from the beak/
of one, the still living / beetle has dropped / out, she
picks it up and puts / it in again." Even the line breaks
ally the poet with the mother. Although her big babies
squeak, they have pussy willow–surfaced coats which
they have learned to dress, and they will learn to fly,
perforce to sing, as the harassed mother once sang.

> What delightful note
> with rapid unexpected flute-
> sounds leaping from the throat
> of the astute
> grown bird, comes back to one from
> the remote
> unenergetic sun-
> lit air before
> the brood was here? How harsh
> the bird's voice has become.

The humor has vanished. The word "harsh" in the
matter-of-fact exclamation clangs against the wistful
memory of music and spring light.

The scene becomes another "tired moment of
danger." A cat creeps "toward the trim / trio on the
tree-stem." Ignoramuses that they are, the young
birds make room for him. A foot "finds the twig on

which it / planned to perch." The mother—the parent
—as taut as the awkward lines, comes

> darting down, nerved by what chills
> the blood, and by hope rewarded—
> of toil—since nothing fills
> squeaking unfed
> mouths, wages deadly combat,
> and half kills
> with bayonet beak and
> cruel wings, the
> intellectual cautious-
> ly creeping cat.

Generally regarded as an expression of a feminine consciousness, "Bird-Witted" also depicts the
old conflict between the power of emotion and the
seemingly superior force of intellect. Because one is
on the side of mother courage against a ruthless cat,
one is tempted to succumb to the triumph of emotion.
Moore's discipline of both her feelings and poetic intelligence in the perfection of the narrative does not
lessen one's sympathy for the mockingbird but per-
suades us, no matter how partisan we are, that human
beings are apt to be like mockingbirds and cats. If one
is partisan, as Moore is, there is need to acknowledge
the "bayonet beak and / cruel wings." She is still the
poet of "various scalpels," and one would not have
her otherwise, but her personal triumph, to which the
apprenticeship and the mature work contributed, was
the integration of heart and mind, the simultaneously
sympathetic account and tempered narrative. Survival
of crises makes some creatures harsher and others
more creeping; it made Moore, at her best, wiser in
her concern with equity. She says, as she had not said
before, that even the most virtuous are cruel in com-

bat. "What is our innocence, / what is our guilt?" she asks in "What Are Years?" (1939). "All / are naked, none is safe."

The will to survive and the practice of the arts of survival were never academic questions for Moore. She expressed surprise when Donald Hall reminded her in 1965 that she had said the quality of being without fear helped her when she edited *The Dial* magazine in the twenties. "I did?" she replied, and recalled that someone had once said to her, "You must be a very timid person, you're so brave." Then she added, "True or not, I can tremble and shrink." Perceived as an armored animal, the humble animal, or a wild animal in need of a carefully made cage, she never denied the proclivities.

Reckoning with what it meant to be tough minded, enlarging her sympathies with endangered species, and becoming more cognizant of the fundamental vulnerability in the most resolute of wills, she also mocked herself. In "His Shield" (1944), which she mentioned along with "What Are Years?" and "The Buffalo" as poems she liked, she exposes herself to ridicule that she earlier had turned on others. She puts herself to an acid test, and she does not flinch. Ambidextrously reviewing a group of animals that are "battle-dressed," the poet parodies her own style as she talks about armature. She hilariously makes up a couple of names for the first animal on parade—"pinswin or spine-swine"; and because he has all his edges out, she says parenthetically that he is "edge-hog miscalled hedgehog[.]" Inebriated with sounds, she reels off the words: "echidna and echinoderm" (the spiny toothless burrowing mammal with an extensile tongue and the prickly little marine animals such as starfish, sea urchins, and related forms) "in distressed- / pin-

cushion thorn-fur coats," followed by "the spiny pig or porcupine"; and, as grand finale, "the rhino with horned snout" (which it rarely has to use because it is large enough to dissuade all predators but man).

A distressed poet has only words to fight with: "Pig-fur won't do[.]" The bristles are coarse and at best make only a stiff brush. So, "I'll wrap / myself in salamander-skin like Presbyter John." Although the poet uses the name from ancient apocryphal tradition, she also takes advantage of medieval lore in which Prester John was the legendary Christian monarch of a vast, wealthy empire she describes as "unconquerable country of unpompous gusto," where "greed / and flattery were unknown"—a land without vice or strife or envy, a land of peace and justice, a literary fiction. In such a kingdom, armor would hardly have been necessary, but there were other realms, and the enigmatic John was a crusader. (The reader has to supply the narrative continuity, and may make the wrong connection.) As the story goes, John left the ideal world, and as the poem goes, he is salamandrine: "A lizard in the midst of flames, a firebrand / that is life, asbestos-eyed asbestos-eared, with tatooed nap / and permanent pig on / the instep; he can withstand / fire and won't drown." One could envy him his "inextinguishable" power: "His shield / was his humility." John knew that he was mortal—"he revealed / a formula safer than / an armorer's: the power of relinquishing / what one would keep; that is freedom." Humility, Moore would say in a lecture in 1948, is an "indispensable teacher."

Having made the leap from the mythical to the actual, from literary fiction to spiritual truth, the poet might be expected to show evidence that she had learned to wear the shield. It is, however, as if the poet

is too lacking in sharpness of edge or point to understand the lesson of the humble John. She advises:
"Become dinosaur- / skulled, quilled or salamander-
wooled, more ironshod / and javelin-dressed than a
hedgehog battalion of steel, but be / dull. Don't be
envied"—the fate of the clever and superior?—"or
armed with a measuring-rod." Is she advising against
being calculating or echoing Ezra Pound's delineation
of his poetic aims: "I am not trying to use an inch-rule
but a balance"? Like all qualities, spiritual humility is
immeasurable. Yet the changes of tone in Moore's
didactics also leave one questioning the relation of
being dull or not being envied to unpompous gusto or
genuine goodness. What began as a parodying of her
own style in the parade of armored animals almost
ends with the relinquishing of any claim to wisdom
other than tongue-in-cheek advice as an affirmation of
an indispensable lesson. There is, nevertheless, the
added balance of the directive, "Don't be armed
. . . with a measuring rod." She becomingly, modestly,
finally does not detract from the example of the wise
Presbyter. She is, in fact, wearing his shield.

   She never quite finished with the subject of animals and defense. At the peak of her maturity, she
brought out one of the most memorable of her poems,
"Apparition of Splendor" (1952), which could be jus-
tified by Emerson's view that "your goodness must
have an edge to it—else it is none." The apparition,
nevertheless, does not depend on that incisive point,
nor is the splendor separate from it. In the poem,
Moore recalls a walk in the woods where—to put the
matter in everyday language—she could hardly believe that a real porcupine had shown up before her
very eyes. She thinks of a comparable surprise. Although Dürer's imaginative graphic of a rhinoceros

partakes "of the miraculous / since never known literally," it "might have startled us equally / if black-and-white spined elaborately," that is, if it had been a porcupine.

An experienced observer of wild life and a raconteur, Moore captures the sense of immediate excitement precipitated by the appearance of the compactly arched little animal. (She stood as still as she had when she looked down on a spiny fern, or peered at a long, plumed, barbed egret in hope that the bird would open its mouth or turn slightly so that she could see it better.) "Like another porcupine, or fern, / the mouth in an arching egret / was too black to discern / till exposed as a silhouette[.]" The solitary porcupine is by nature slow-moving, shows little fear of other animals, is not antisocial, and will not fly away. It also will not attack unless it is attacked. The "double-embattled thistle of jet— / disadvantageous supposedly—has never shot a quill." Fortunately armored, the porcupine is unpopular prey since it can drive a powerful, muscular tail against an enemy, and the quills, easily detached from the skin, remain with the barbed end in whatever they touch; but the spiny creature never throws those spears at will, so an interested observer has nothing to fear. The poem might have been titled, "How To Look at a Porcupine or Anything Else" with the capacity for enchantment, imaginative appreciation, informed intelligence, sensitivity, clear eyes, and without touching:

> Was it
> some joyous fantasy,
>   plain eider-eared exhibit
>   of spines rooted in sooty moss,
>
> or "train supported by porcupines—

> a fairy's eleven yards long"? . . .

And the reply? "Anything more than the truth," as
Frost wrote, "would have seemed too weak. . . . / The
fact is the sweetest dream. . . .":

> as when the lightning shines
>   on the thistlefine spears, among
>   prongs in lanes above lanes of a shorter prong,
>
> "with the forest for nurse," also dark
>   at the base—where needle-debris
> springs and shows no footmark;
>   the setting for a symmetry
>   you must not touch unless you are a fairy.

One is in the forest of pine trees and ferned paths, a
spiny investiture where all is quietly, beautifully consonant: an exact mystery.

But the spell is broken. There is a larger world,
and there is another lesson for that world: "Maine
should be pleased that its animal / is not a waverer,
and rather / than fight, lets the primed quill fall." The
observer is attracted by the porcupine's fearless
symmetry, a subject of art, but is herself a moral being,
unable to forget her own and other human beings'
unconscionable ways. In her universe of correspon-
dences and conflicts, there is also the voice that is both
personal and public saying to the "Shallow oppressor,
intruder, / insister, you"—and the "you" is anyone,
including the poet, with characteristics the names
specify—"you have found a resister." As the pejora-
tives are spun off in the moment of recovery, there is
the suggestion of a tirade restrained by the fortuitous
delight of having seen the porcupine. The poem does
not surrender the moral or the comic voice absolutely,

then, but lets the quills fall where they may; for Moore, the porcupine is also an exemplar of art.

IV

The poems of Moore's later years have the spontaneity and immediacy of "Apparition of Splendor" in revealing an active mind still open to experience. "Then the Ermine:" (1952) is so close to the experience about which the poet is writing that the language in which the poet thinks about it almost resists apprehension. As natural as the poem's movement is, it veers toward the impenetrable, yet the situation is a familiar one—a contest of wills; the poem is an account of both the poet's internal debate and behavior in the contest.

The conflict was provoked by the fact that "I saw a bat by daylight; / hard to credit / but I knew that I was right." Bats are almost completely nocturnal, and although they may be active in the twilight of evening or early morning, only two species occasionally hunt by daylight. The bat, then, is not a "believe-it-or-not," even if the insistence on being right implies confrontation with someone who would doubt what Moore calls "an unconformity."

The attention focuses first on the Ermine, symbol of chastity because of its white fur, and the motto associated with it, "rather dead than spotted[.]" The heraldic animal and the motto of a competitive young knight who had performed honorable actions (but who became angry because he thought he had received a "wrong" when the judgment went against him in Sidney's *Arcadia*) point up the jousting in the poem. The irony in the reliance on easy slogans, of which the knight's is the first, will become apparent

when the second, *Mutare sperno vel timere* ("I spurn to change or to be timid") is put to the test. In so important a matter as her "word," the poet is reluctant to change; but when she says that the bat "wavering like a jack-in- / the-green" (a figure in May Day capers) charmed her, she finds herself bristling. Shall she insist that she is right—there is, granted, "reason to think not"—or graciously restrain the inclination to argue the fact? After all, the discrepancy between the declaration of principle and the anecdote of the bat "wavering about me / insecurely" is rather absurd. The situation is clearly just a conflict of wills.

The argument was, or would have been, foolhardy. "Instead of hammer-handed bravado / strategy could have chosen / momentum with a motto:/ *Mutare sperno / vel timere*—*"* which was the slogan of an unyielding, arrogant, self-interested, politically powerful and shrewd Duke of Beaufort and Cardinal of Winchester (who was also tender-hearted and suffered monstrous guilt on his deathbed). Moore's "I don't change, am not craven; / although on what ground could I / say that I am hard to frighten?" is an anticlimax of the most humorous kind. But, she says, "Nothing's certain." (One hears "You must be a very timid person, you're so brave.") Consequently, she will capitulate.

"Fail," she says to herself, but is saved by her humor: "and Lavater's physiography / has another admirer of skill in obscurity— / now a novelty." (John Kasper Lavater included physiognomy, the art of judging human character by facial features, in an elaborate system for describing natural phenomena; the work is a matter of curiosity to people who delve in forgotten lore. The theory failed to survive empirical scrutiny.) The poet is making fun of herself again.

She then develops one of the most fanciful, or outrageously witty, or private of her conceits: "So let the *palisandre* settee express it, / 'ebony violet,'/ Master Corbo in full dress, / and shepherdess, / an exhilarating hoarse crow-note / or dignity with intimacy." A change of topic? Furniture of the mind? Something stationary on which to sit to regain one's poise? Of "People's Surroundings" (1922), she had written that "They answer one's questions," but ironically concluded, "In these noncommittal, personal–impersonal expressions of appearance, / the eye knows what to skip; / the physiognomy of conduct must not reveal the skeleton. . . ." A rosewood settee, the wood of a dark red or purplish color streaked and variegated with black, is no heraldic charge, but it has its charms as a contrast to the unspotted white fur of the ermine. The poet—is she both La Fontaine's Master Corbo, "dropping the prize [cheese] as his huge beak sang false," and an Arcadian shepherdess like the one described by Sidney as she knits and sings, her voice comforting her hands to work, and her hands keeping time to her voice's music? Moore has indeed changed her strategy, if not her character or her leaning toward obscurities.

By having averted a violent outburst of feeling, however, she counts on new insight, strength, energy, even delicacy like that concentrated in the natural image of a hardy little perennial that grows in temperate zones but does not shrink in its simple perfection and intensity of color: "Foiled explosiveness is yet / a kind of prophet, / a perfecter, and so a concealer— / with the power of implosion; / like violets by Dürer; / even darker." Ebony violet conceals the violent colors, but is darker.

Many readers prefer the younger Moore who did

not mind being right and did not conceal her righteous wrath or its skeleton in allusive dress. There are
later poems, however, that delight without baffling;
"The Sycamore" (1955) is one. To draw a sycamore
as an albino giraffe against a gun-metal sky, Moore's
figure for her tree, would be an ineffective distortion,
and yet the figure is extraordinarily graphic for the
height, the pleasing line, and the color of the sycamore. "Didn't Aristotle say," she asked Donald Hall,
"that it is the mark of a poet to see resemblances
between apparently incongruous things?" The mind's
eye knows what to skip; no one need strain to see that
a tall tree can be compared to the tallest of living
quadrupeds also known for its long slender neck that
moves gracefully. "Without / leaves to modify, /
chamois-white as / said, although partly pied near the
base, / it towered where a chain of / stepping-stones
lay in a stream nearby; / glamour to stir the envy / of
anything in motley—" or, for that matter, an "all-
white butterfly."

Despite the forebodingly dark sky and the chain
of stepping stones, the poet's mind—clarified by a
brisk walk—is exuberantly carefree. Because she is
Marianne Moore, however, she momentarily checks
herself: "A commonplace: / there's more than just one
kind of grace." Heightened consciousness is, of
course, always short-lived: "We don't like flowers that
do / not wilt; they must die, and nine / she-camel-hairs
aid memory." (She helpfully provides a note explaining that she-camel-hairs are the drawing brush of the
Iranian miniaturist Imami, about whom she had read
in *The New York Times.*) A "she-camel" herself, given as
she is to appreciation of all kinds of animals and
plants, yet almost serenely accepting life's transience,
Moore would naturally think the embalmed look of

artificial flowers distasteful. But how brusque and matter-of-fact is Moore's way of saying that death is the
mother of beauty, how direct and understated and
minimal the reason for art. The restrained moments in
turn, then, give way to a frolicsome mood that brings
us up short once again as she finishes off the poem.
Hers is no vapid memory.

> Worthy of Imami,
> the Persian—clinging to a stiffer stalk
>   was a little dry
> thing from the grass,
> in the shape of a Maltese cross,
>   retiringly formal
>   as if to say: "And there was I
>   like a field-mouse at Versailles."

She-camel, or familiar Scarlet Lightning (the blossom
shaped like a Maltese cross) seared by heat and cold,
or fieldmouse—she is still an innocent abroad exaggerating what it is like to see the sights of the "old"
world. "Prizing Henry James," she said, "I take his
worries for the most part with detachment; those of
William James to myself when he says, 'man's chief
difference from the brutes lies in the exuberant excess
of his subjective propensities. Prune his extravagance,
sober him, and you undo him.' "

Another of the exuberant poems, "The Arctic Ox
(Or Goat)" (1958) is for all its comic air basically rational. Moore said she liked the poem as well as anything
she had written, and there is no cause to doubt her
sincerity. She may have liked the poem because she
liked the animal—a fur bearer you do not have to kill
to wear its fleece: "your coat is warm; your conscience,
better." She always was a conservationist, and she was
old-fashioned enough to want a good conscience.

There are also other reasons for her commendation of the goat. "It smells of water. . . . / Its great distinction / is not egocentric scent / but that it is intelligent." Basking in the blizzard, "these ponderosos could dominate / the rare-hairs market in Kashan and yet / you could not have a choicer pet." The goats have winning ways:

> They join you as you work;
> love jumping in and out of holes,
>   play in water with the children,
> learn fast, know their names,
> will open gates and invent games.

She could have been a composer of jump-rope rituals on the children's counting-out formula.

She was seventy-one years old when she counted this one out. As old man, W. B. Yeats said of his Chinamen ("who know nothing of tragedy") that when "accomplished fingers begin to play" the musical instrument that one of them carries, the "ancient glittering eyes are gay."[7] Without betraying sorrow or pain, Moore was not a tragic poet. She fought but she did not raise a heroic cry in the midst of despair; hers was not the voice of traumatic experience and existential anguish. She wanted, on the contrary, to be sensible. She even casts the single eye of reason on marriage. She says of her goats:

> While not incapable
> of courtship, they may find its
>   servitude and flutter, too much
> like Procrustes' bed;
> so some decide to stay unwed.

And if they are compared with other animals: "Camels are snobbish / and sheep, unintelligent; / water buf-

faloes, neurasthenic— / even murderous. / Reindeer seem over-serious. . . ." But the ascetic oxen (or goats) survive on "Mountain Valley water, / dandelions, carrots, oats— / encouraged as well by bed / made fresh three times a day— / to roll and revel in the hay." So one last twirl of the rope:

> If you fear that you are
> reading an advertisement,
>   you are. If we can't be cordial
> to these creatures' fleece,
> I think that we deserve to freeze.

It is not, and does not pretend to be, a great poem.

Other works published during the final decade of Moore's life are revisions or new versions of attitudes to which she had always been given, personal attitudes expressed in the manner of one overheard thinking to herself. In "Tell Me, Tell Me" (1960) she is as irrational as she ever became, and she is furious. The poem is an exercise in "How to Curb Your Tongue." She is exasperated by an egocentric "tailor-and-cutter jury" with a "propensity to bisect, / mis-state, misunderstand / and obliterate continuity." She wants to blast away at flatness set on "some cindery pinnacle" and the viper's snarled "traffic knot." "Tell me," she cries, without opening her mouth, "where might there be a refuge . . . ?"

In contrast to "grievance touched off on / any ground"—that of the viper or the poet or both?— there is an apparition of splendor. "It appeared: gem, burnished rarity / and peak of delicacy— / . . . the absorbing / geometry of a fantasy: / a James, Miss Potter, Chinese / 'passion for the particular,' of a / tired man who yet, at dusk, / cut a masterpiece of cerise—[.]" She explains in the poem that she is "re-

ferring / to Henry James and Beatrix Potter's Tailor."
(She will not explain everything. In the story of *The
Tailor of Glouster*, the poor old man, "worn to ravel-
ling," could not sew together the pieces that he had
cut to make the mayor's wedding coat for want of a
single skein of cherry-colored twisted silk; but the
mice he had rescued from the cat in the kitchen take
over the work while he sleeps and rescue him from
weariness and poverty. And, under the influence of
the good mice, even the bad cat is "repentant.")
Moore's Jamesian tailor " 'breathed inconsistency and
drank / contradiction,' dazzled / not by the sun but by
'shadowy / possibility.' " He inspires her to vow to flee
"to metaphysical newmown hay, / honeysuckle, or
woods fragrance."

In "A Burning Desire to Be Explicit" (1966),
Moore tells about a woman who wanted to know

> *"What* is metaphysical newmown hay?"
> . . : "Oh, something like a sudden whiff of
> fragrance in contrast with the doggedly
> continuous opposition to spontaneous conver-
> sation that had gone before."
> "Then why don't you *say* so?" the impressive
> lady rejoined.

Back at the party in "Tell Me, Tell Me," the poet
considers other strategies. She might ask, or in her
way imply, that the dogged opponent "T. S. V. P." She
does not hope for a responsive silence. She might be
rude and say *"Taisez-vous?"* She is tempted. " 'Please'
does not make sense / to a refugee from verbal feroci-
ty." Exasperated as she is, however, she knows that to
say, "Will you shut up?" would be ineffective as a
means of escape from the social predicament. After
"Then the Ermine:" one is hardly surprised by the

poet's admission of perplexity and willingness to conclude: "Even so, 'deference'; / yes, deference may be my defense." The woman who once fought to survive has become the woman who has to protect herself. She is still "superior" and outwardly poised, having resisted her own righteous anger.

Then, as if she had been asked, she writes "A *précis?*" for us. The children's story "of how the cat's mice when set free / by the tailor of Glouster, finished / the Lord Mayor's cerise coat" saved both the tailor and the vulnerable poet—a poet who is, she says specifically, "a reader," and who is happily "rescued . . . / from being driven mad by a scold." She calls the poem "this told-backward biography." And autobiography? Not quite, because—at her own expense—she had an occasion to talk about another use of literature, not as an escape from "reality" but from "madness." The poem is one of the funniest defenses of literature, and one of the most mundane, imaginable. "For God's sake," she might have said, "let me hold my tongue and write." Or read.

The conflict between being ingratiating and being plucky is not one of great moment, but civilized people—and perhaps women especially—have for centuries had to resolve it. For Moore, who did not suffer fools gladly, and who despised hypocrisies but wanted to be tolerant and sociable, one's character and ardor, naturalness itself, depended on the way one coped with just such a conflict. Another poem, "W. S. Landor" (1964) expresses energetically—with "uncircuitous simplicity"—and without need for any "explanation" the poet's pleasure in vehement and uncompromising character:

There

is someone I can bear—
    "a master of indignation . . .
meant for a soldier
    converted to letters," who could

throw
a man through the window,
    yet, "tender toward plants," say, "Good God,
the violets!" (below).
    "Accomplished in every
style
and tint"—considering meanwhile
    infinity and eternity,
he could only say, "I'll
    talk about them when I understand them."

She had been reading the introductory note by Havelock Ellis to Landor's *Imaginary Conversations,* which are characterized by as wide a range of reading and eclectic interests as Moore's own dialogues with herself. The violets are one of the grace notes, but the voice is that of the poet who extolled a prize bird in 1915.

"An Expedient—Leonardo da Vinci's—and a Query" (1964) is, summarily, a tribute to another of Moore's heroes, an artist who inaugurated a radical new style, a fascinating and baffling personality whose achievements are said to have "fixed the imagination of modern man." Although Moore is relaxed, contemplative, but alert in the poem, the sudden and unpredictable transitions from one to another of Leonardo's and her innumerable interests are appropriate to the contradictions and anomalies of his—and her—nature.

It was patience
    protecting the soul as clothing the body
from cold, so that "great wrongs

were powerless to vex"—
and problems that seemed to perplex
him bore fruit, memory
making past present—
like "the grasp of the gourd,
sure and firm."

She never wanted to be vexed by wrongs she herself
suffered; she wanted to do well: " 'None too dull to /
be able to do one thing well. . . .'" (" 'If I do well I am
blessed / whether any bless me or not, and if I do /
ill I am cursed,' " is one of her leitmotifs.) Then comes
the abrupt comic observation that an orator who
knows only one word is not worthy of praise. But
Leonardo's height kept "polecat or snake" away from
the verdure of his vine:

With a passion,
he drew flowers, acorns, rocks—intensively,
like Giotto, made Nature
the test, imitation—
Rome's taint—did not taint what he'd done.
He saw as treachery
the all-in-one-mold.
Peerless, venerated
by all, he succumbed

to dejection.

Moore would have been sharply critical of any
inference that she thought her poetry equal in significance to the work of Leonardo. She did not fix the
modern imagination; she chose her animals and her
people as subjects from which she could learn to do
one thing well, write her own original verse. Yet she
had much in common with the Renaissance attitudes
of Leonardo. She subscribed to the view of art as an

intellectual and empirical activity—"research" was her
word for it; she also knew, as he did, that science and
imagination interact in strange ways. He, for instance,
made a life-long study of the motion of water, but like
Aristotle's poet he compared the motion to the curls
in human hair, and the "Deluge" drawings show the
transposition into fantasy and art of years of study of
nature from an objective point of view. Readers of
Moore's sketch of Leonardo have tended to focus on
the word "dejection" as a sign of her own state. The
questions she asks indicate a different mood and reveal other concerns:

> Could not
> the Leda with face matchless minutely—
>   have lightened the blow?
>   "Sad" . . . Could not Leonardo
>   have said, "I agree; proof refutes me.
> If all is mobility,
>   mathematics won't do":
> instead of, "Tell me if anything
>   at all has been done?"

Having placed his faith in mathematics, which was
more important to him than painting was, he realized
that if everything were in continuous movement it
could not be controlled by mathematics. The realiza-
tion, as the poet says simply, was a blow. A spirited
woman—remarkable in her resources, her grasp of
expedients for endurance and inner happiness—
Moore certainly knew dejection, discouragement,
disappointments, defeats; even though she liked to be
right, she knew the salutary effect of admitting that she
had been wrong. The poet's questions reveal, it seems
to me, her sympathy for an inconsolable human being,
downcast both by the experience of failure and the

awareness that he was wrong but unable to take consolation from what he had done supremely well. It is further pertinent that she is troubled—as who is not? —by Leonardo's lack of self-knowledge as well as his need for reassurance in a crisis of misjudgment, neither of which can be factored out from the restlessness of the creative mind, the fallibility of genius, and the innocence of his worth. I doubt that Moore overrated her work, and I am sure that she had reservations about its peerlessness; but critically astute as she was, how could she have said she liked "The Arctic Ox (or Goat)" as well as anything she had written, except for its lack of solemnity or her modesty? It sometimes took surprisingly little to bring her inner happiness. That, I think, was one of the secrets of her innocent, lively imagination.

The poet's mind, open in the act of observing itself and the world, had once been for her "an enchanting thing"—"an enchanted thing," but in a poignant, personal poem of her old age, "The Mind, Intractable Thing" (1965) she cries out, as she rarely did, "Why can't it help me?" At the moment she utters the cry, she interjects a cynically humorous, realistic comment that the mind "even with its own ax to grind, sometimes / helps others." The complaint does not, of course, mitigate the pain; and as if she thinks better of that mind than her carping complaint indicates, she quickly changes her mind. "O imagnifico," she pleads directly in the eloquent language with which one speaks only to gods or persons worthy of adulation. But the eloquence falls away in a split second; as she continues the supplication, the vocative is more equivocal, perhaps teasing: "Wizard in words—"; then, finally, the voice is steadied and yet heart-breaking: "poet—was it—as Alfred Panzini defined you?"

Panzini, who compiled a dictionary of contemporary
Italian language (1905), had defined "imagnifico" as
"creator of images"; it is that power of the mind, the
poetic power, which always had Moore at its mercy:

> Weren't you refracting just now
> on my eye's half-closed triptych
>   the image, enhanced, of a glen—
> "the foxgrape festoon as sere leaves fell"
> on the sand-pale dark byroad, one leaf adrift
>   from the thin-twigged persimmon; again,
>
>   a bird—Arizona
> caught-up-with, uncatchable cuckoo
> after two hours' pursuit, zigzagging
> road-runner, stenciled in black
> stripes all over, the tail
>   windmilling up to defy me?

The images are fine; her memory is sharp; but she
cannot go on to develop them.

Honest, as always, she has long since learned a
humility that did not trouble the self-assured young
woman writing "Feed Me, Also, River God." Measuring herself against the fleeting images—intensified or
defiant, coming and going beyond her will—she pays
homage to the superiority of the mind, the creator of
images: "You understand terror, know how to deal /
with pent-up emotion, a ballad, witchcraft. / I don't.
O Zeus and O Destiny!"

In the act of writing out her sorrow, the emotion
is released unashamedly with that helpless naturalness
and, to use a phrase from Denis Donoghue, with "that
fatality of cadence"[8] a lifetime of discipline rewards.

> Unafraid of what's done,
> undeterred by apparent defeat,

> you, imagnifico, unafraid
> of disparagers, death, dejection,
> have out-wiled the Mermaid of Zennor,
>   made wordcraft irresistible:
> reef, wreck, lost lad and "sea-foundered bell"—
> as near a thing as we have to a king—
>   craft with which I don't know how to deal.

When talking about "real poetry" in 1967, Moore gave "The Ballad of the Mermaid of Zennor," by Vernon Watkins, as an example. "It has such grand resonance," she said. "I know it by heart."[9] When she could not lay her troubles by, when inevitable, burdensome human frailties made her feel afraid, deterred, and apparently defeated, art itself, poetry, was both a consolation and glorious reminder of her own insufficiencies. For the poet whose change in diction from one word to the next is a subtle event, the stylistic changes of the last three lines of "The Mind"—the plaintive music, the ordinary symbol of earthly power from which we are distanced, and the prosaic but personal protest that the poet's resources are inadequate —verbally dramatize the falling away of life. Yet, just as the phrasing of "imagnifico," "wizard in words," "poet" is a version of the holy trinity reordered (father, holy ghost, son), the three strains of an aging voice reverberate, no matter how unruly the mind, with a superior force Moore cannot refuse to heed but against which she valiantly, defiantly, intractably sets her well-wrought poem.

These poems, which embody and reveal conflicts within Marianne Moore herself, vis à vis the kind of person she was or wanted to be, may not seem of great moment if we compare them to literature of which the subjects are painful sexual conflicts, emotional violence, hysteria, genuine madness, or human betrayals,

brutalities, and corruptions in the struggles for power as well as resistance to it. The value of the personal poems, however, is precisely that Moore depicts the ordinary little attitudes human beings encounter in living with themselves and others, attitudes that determine how we carry ourselves as social animals in our vulnerable relations with other persons whom we are attracted to or repelled by. The poems may also seem of minimal significance in a century of overwhelming spiritual, economic, and political crises, but Moore was not indifferent to those crises. Just as she did not ignore herself, she did not ignore issues much larger than herself. She writes about them with the same integrity and attention to pertinent forms that characterize the expressions of her own mortal voice and her efforts to *be* in the world. All of her work, in fact, is the work of a poet in the world.

4

The Spiritual Forces

" All severe and renunciatory minds," Richard Chase wrote of Emily Dickinson, "have a center of meaning and a source of energy to which, after wandering far and wide, they return again and again."[1] For Marianne Moore that center was Christian faith, which is implicit in the language of her verse and the precepts integral to its perspectives. It is neither possible nor desirable to separate Moore's spiritual convictions from her poetic achievement. Art, she writes in "When I Buy Pictures" (1921), "must acknowledge the spiritual forces which have made it."

When she says, "The world of the soul? As difficult as it is to define the soul, is 'creativeness' perhaps as near a definition as we can get?" she may be in accord with the romantic rhetoric of praise for the artistic vision; but she attributes the point to a member of the Presbytery to which she belonged,[2] and she is testifying to what she called "the radiance of the soul." She believed that the human being is in essence the creature of God and therefore good; she also believed that people are the children of fallen Adam and therefore sinful. There is little evidence that, like Dickinson, she quarrelled with God or stamped a tiny foot against him. Moore, on the contrary, quarrels with herself and her moral shortcomings: "That belief in God is not easy, is seemingly one of God's justices; . . . imposed piety . . . and religious complacency are serious enemies of religion."[3]

She resolves the conflicts between a naturalistic view of phenomena and—to use her phrase—"the mythographers of worship" with customary poise: "Mystical belief which is not unthinking belief, seems

116

to find that science does not discredit the supernatural but reinforce it. That is to say, we see that reverence for science and reverence for the soul can interact."

In discussing whether or not "culture can exist without a positive religion," she makes a historical argument: even though culture "partakes of varied elements" and, by extension, modes of behavior, "culture so far, has not existed without religion and I doubt that it could." Moreover, "if everything literary were deleted, in which there is some thought of deity," she continues, " 'literature' itself would be a puny residue; one could almost say that each striking literary work is some phase of the desire to resist or to affirm 'religion.' " She does not, like Yeats, proclaim that the arts have taken "upon their shoulders the burdens that have fallen from the shoulders of the priests"; she desires, rather, to affirm a love for God that elevates the human soul above all temporal life.

The ground of being for Moore is the mystery of the created world, and God is the first principle of her thought. While she seeks to bring the awareness of that mystery to consciousness out of the silence, God is not named—except when the use of the word is attributed to someone else—in the poetry she chose to preserve. Religious feeling at its most profound is for her unspoken, private, and personal. There are, however, poems that are religious in their imagery, symbolism, and allusive language. Two early ones, "Sun" and "A Talisman" are expressions of her supreme belief in the sovereign power of the God she does not name. Of the pair, "Sun" is the more personal, more enigmatic, and more beautiful.

The poem's publishing history indicates its importance to her. Written in 1910,[4] it was first printed in 1916 with the title "Fear Is Hope." Omitted from

both her *Selected Poems* (1935) and *Collected Poems* (1951), it reappeared with the title "Sun" in the *Mentor Book of Religious Verse* (1957) and was placed at the end of Moore's last individual volume, *Tell Me, Tell Me* (1966). "Hope and Fear accost him" was the epigraph for the final version of the poem.

Opening with the medieval couplet, " 'No man may him hyde/From Deth holow-eyed," the poet asserts in a clipped tone that "this inconvenient truth does not suffice." It is a Blakean "cry of the flesh and cry of the soul," answered in an act of meditation which begins, "You are not male or female, but a plan / deep-set within the heart of man." The ambiguous "you" is repeated three times before "Sun," the appositive, is hailed. The illuminating experience is, in the language of the classic confession of Christian orthodoxy, based on the belief that the life of Jesus was human life as God had intended human life to be, and, more crucial, that it was part of the plan by which God wanted to restore his grace to man and to break the power of death. The imagery of triumph is muted in the enigmatic lines that follow:

> Splendid with splendor hid you come, from your
>   Arab abode,
> a fiery topaz smothered in the hand of a great prince
>   who rode
>   before you, Sun—whom you outran,
>   piercing his caravan.

Moore, writing on T. S. Eliot in 1936, says "as God's light is for man, the sun is life for the natural world." The controlling image of the sun is archetypal, rich in associations with gods and acts of reverence. The facts that the sun is a self-luminous object shining by radiation derived from energy sources

within itself and that it is a source of warmth, light, and
energy for the planet earth which shines by reflected
light only, as well as the illusion that the sun is the
largest and brightest of stars, make it an inevitable,
common figure in iconographies. In Moore's religious
cosmos, the sun is a dynamic symbol that partakes
more irreducibly of the realities of Christian faith than
of the phenomenal world. Her sun is God's light, light
on light.

In the first stanza of the poem, however, the sun
is "Splendid with splendor hid," which implies a dark
night of the soul and hazard. "You come from your
Arab abode"? From the East, both the general direction of sunrise and the place on the mythographers'
maps for the beginnings of the Judeo-Christian religion? The native region of the historical Jesus of
Nazareth and a people who believed in one deity? The
initial version of the poem describes the sun as "An
incandescence smothered in the hand of an astrologer / who rode / Before. . . ." Are the intricacies of
the relation between the Babylonian priests, their
ideas—particularly their astrology and belief in "One
God," Itu, from whom all other gods spring—and the
Christian godhead pertinent? And why the changes
from "incandescence" to "fiery topaz" as well as from
"an astrologer" to "a great prince"?

The meanings ascribed to precious stones in astrological lapidaries were handed on from the ancient
world to the medieval and Renaissance Christians.
The oriental topaz had healing virtues, making its
wearer beloved and safe, increasing prudence and wisdom, and curing madness. According to the *Lapidary
of Alfonso X,* of Spain, the "vertue" of the stone "is such
that if one were to put it in a place full of scorpions or
snakes or any other poisonous reptiles, it would chase

them away."[5] The topaz became, in medieval Christian tradition, dependent upon its knight for its virtues. Although one does not know with certainty which of the structures of esoteric meanings are at work in the two versions, the poet's substitution of "a fiery topaz" for "an incandescence" is imaginatively effective. The substitution of "a great prince" for "an astrologer" seems to indicate that the poet underwent a change from an interest in the evolution of religious belief to a desire for sharper focus on the Christian mystery. It is clear that the celestial sun, "displaced" but transfigured into a precious jewel "smothered" in the hand of a great prince, no longer an astrologer, who rode before the sun, violates natural law and belongs to the domain of the supernatural. Within the logic of the poem, however, the passage is a development of the foreboding, which is one of the themes of the epigraph, "Hope and Fear accost him," as well as a narrative return to the confession of Christian belief in the coming of the historical Jesus, the substantiation of God's plan. Reflecting the golden light of the hidden sun, the "fiery topaz"—smothered but not extinguished—ironically could not save the great prince. "When you talk about Jesus Christ," as Martin Luther stressed, "it is well to start with the fact of his wounds." The primal sun in the hands of the incarnated Christ—the prince, not of darkness, but of peace and righteousness—was dependent on that prince and his willingness to sacrifice himself to effect God's plan; the sun, then, miraculously "outran" the prince (the knight?), piercing his caravan. The poet's use of present tense in "Splendid with splendor hid you come" confirms the continuing grace of God to those who believe in his omnipotence and the paradox of the crucifixion—the death that saves life:

> O Sun, you shall stay
> with us; holiday,
>   consuming wrath, be wound in a device
> of Moorish gorgeousness, round glasses spun
> to flame as hemispheres of one
> great hour-glass dwindling to a stem. Consume
>   hostility;
> employ your weapon in this meeting-place of
>   surging enmity!
> Insurgent feet shall not outrun
> multiplied flames, O Sun.

The pierced Christ is mysteriously girded with "the Spirit's sword," the sword of God's "own deathless word"—in the figures from the hymn, "Send Thou, O Lord, to Every Place, Swift Messengers" (1887) by Mrs. Merrill R. Gates.[6] The poem stanzaically and artfully holds Christ's death and deathless power in counterbalance.

The brilliance with which the imagery breaks out to affirm the everlasting beauty of God's light in the world should not distract the reader from an awareness that the lyric cry is a prayer both urgent and resolute. "The device of Moorish gorgeousness" is a cosmic hourglass, to borrow a phrase from May Swenson's "Cardinal Ideograms." As Swenson says of the hour-glass, "Note the enigmatic shape, / absence of any valve of origin, / how end overlaps beginning." It is a diagram of Marianne Moore's universe: two globes, the phenomenal and the spiritual in equilibrium. And yet, the two dwindle "to a stem"—the mortal life between the two spheres. Furthermore, the hourglass, as a measure of time, is both in time and out of time, whereas the poet's voice is mortal only.

The music of the rhymes in the opening stanza of "Sun" is interrupted by the sound of the inescapable

fact of one's death in time, the inconvenient truth that
does not "suffice," but the prayer for the "holiday, /
consuming wrath" to "be wound in a device"—a continuing arabesque—completes the suspended music.
The poem's initial title, "Fear Is Hope," and the revised equation in which "Hope and Fear" accost the
human being, are consistent with Christian teaching—
that faith inspires true repentance, which is spurred by
"fear of God" and primarily distinguishes the devout
from the wicked but simultaneously inspires confidence, love, and joy in the radiance of eternal light.
"Insurgent feet shall not outrun / multiplied flames,
O Sun." That is hope.

The magnificence of "Sun" is hardly comparable
to the simplicity of "A Talisman" (1910), but that
modest poem also uses the symbolism of ancient religion to depict the hope of immortality. The poem
brings together the figure of the shepherd, a stum-
bling shepherd, who found a seagull "of lapis lazuli, /
a scarab of the sea, / with wings spread—" and the
subject of "the dead." The poem, criticized for its
commonplace sentiment, does not draw out the
remembered account of the angelic message, given to
those shepherds keeping watch over their flock by
night, that "a savior" had been born to them and all
people [Luke 2:8–20]. The poet, criticized also for the
inaccuracy of the description of the seagull, takes the
liberty of giving the bird the color of the azure sea and
fusing a private emblem with the image of the scarab
that possessed magic potency and symbolized "the
after-life" for the pre-Christian Egyptians. The use of
the hieratic symbol from the old dispensation follows
the custom of transforming and reinvigorating archetypal images available to them by the early Christians,
for whom the sacred beetle became a symbol of resur-

rection. The seagull, scarab of the sea, therefore parts "its beak to greet men long dead." It is for the shepherd a promise of a new dispensation. For the poet, "A Talisman" is complimentary to the great poem, "Sun," and the two together promise the development of authoritative new verse so indebted to her religious heritage it is tempting to say that without its influence on her imagination she could not have realized the singularity of the poetic forms.

Perhaps the weakest of all the early verse, "Appellate Jurisdiction" (1915) should be forgotten except for the fact that it speaks explicitly of sin and is the only extant verse in which Moore refers directly to God. Although the poet declares that "fragments" of sin are part of her, she insists on doubting that "new brooms" will sweep her heart clean, and questions whether or not God shall redeem her. While she acknowledges God's power to review the judgment she makes of herself, she does not sound as if she believes herself especially wicked. "Appellate Jurisdiction" reveals, nevertheless, that to be a religious poet was not always easy for Moore. She can be credited with having dared expose herself at her worst, and with never reworking or reprinting the ordinary little poem.

"Melanchthon," for which the first title was "Black Earth" (1918), is another matter. Revised slightly and reprinted a dozen times, including a translation into Italian, it did not, however, appear in Moore's final *Complete Poems.* Her one comment on it was in a letter of January 9, 1919, to Ezra Pound: "Black Earth . . . was written about an elephant that I have, named Melancthon [sic]." It is an extraordinary poem, daring in its lines of force and contours; yet it does not have the power it purports to embody. Unlike "Sun," the "beautiful element of unreason in it"—to

use the poem's concluding words—is too apparent, consciously formulated, schematically drawn, deliberately controlled, and therefore rational. The elephant is seen from two perspectives: the first- and third-person points of view. There are three parts: the transition from the first to the second part occurs in stanza seven, from second to third in stanza fourteen, and the third part concludes with three stanzas. The elephant is the persona for the first part; its voice merges with that of the poet in Part 2; and the poet speaks Part 3. (There are three, two, and one questions in each of Parts 1, 2, and 3.) The poem's subjects are the body and soul, black earth and spiritual poise, substance and essence, for which the elephant is symbol: "Black / but beautiful. . . ."

The elephant who speaks for himself, "the more-than-animal"—in Charles Tomlinson's phrase[7]—is a natural creature, pleasing himself, enjoying the sun, accepting circumstances, wishing for a rebirth, even submerging himself in the great river where he becomes greyed and patined by the sediment rather than cleansed by the water. The elephant feels enriched "by unpreventable experience," sounds placid or philosophical, and is almost complacent. Yet he is a questionner. The first of his questions is rather casual, as he admits that "the blemishes stand up and shout when the object / in view was a / renaissance; shall I say / the contrary?" It is as if the honest elephant could easily deny his good intentions; he is not really going to change except insofar as he becomes more decidedly himself. He inhabits a hard black skin, "fibered over like the shell of / the coconut," "black glass through which no light / can filter," like one of Picasso's mirrors containing nothing but blackness and death, it might seem. The elephant's skin, "cut /

into checkers by rut / upon rut" of experience, clearly shows signs of aging—there is no way to stop that. And it is not certain that anyone can learn from the elephant's experience: "it is a manual for the peanut-tongued and the / hairy-toed," that is to say, monkeys who are clever at imitating tricks. Even so, the elephant's awareness that his black back, having carried burdens and kings, is full of the history of power stimulates two slightly more intense but not really agonizing questions: "Of power? What / is powerful and what is not?" These second thoughts bring Part I to an end.

If the elephant, "the more-than-animal," is natural humanity in all its bulk and strength, he has, nevertheless, a soul, which is more powerful than the mammoth body. "My soul," he says, "shall never / be cut into / by a wooden spear." The oblique reference is to "Saint Narcissus," but the elephant is spiritually less self-centered: "through- / out childhood to the present time, the unity of / life and death has been expressed by the circumference / described" by his trunk—he knows he is physically destructible, he perceives "feats of strength to be inexplicable after / all," and he is on his guard. He understands, moreover, that pride is the center of external poise, and from that insight springs his final question: "but spiritual poise, it has its center where?" By his own testimony, he is a creature of faith: "My ears are sensitized to more than the sound of / the wind. I see / and I hear[.]" (He is more trusting than Christ's disciples, who having forgotten to take bread on their journey, are tempted to eat the leaven of the Pharisees and Herod. Mindful of the miraculous feeding of nine thousand people in the wilderness, Christ asks the disciples: "Having eyes, see ye not? and having ears, hear ye not? and do ye not

remember?" [Mark 8:18]) The elephant is also different from either the "tree-trunk without / roots," "the
wandlike body . . . which was made / to see and not
to see; to hear and not to hear" but is "accustomed to
shout / its own thought to itself like a shell"—or the
coral plant that ordinarily cannot live at great depths,
but absorbs "the equable sapphire light" and converts
it into "nebulous green." They are ambiguously spiritual brothers, for whom "The I of each is to / the I of
each / a kind of fretful speech, / which sets a limit on
itself[.]" They are incapable of the difficult conquest
over themselves and by inference are barred from
God. (Perhaps there is an implied allusion to Blake's
epigrammatic lines, "Till I Will be overthrown, /
Every eye must weep alone.") It is also not clear
whether the elephant himself feels that his own speech
has become fretful, or whether the poignant, critical
observation is spoken by the elephant's voice or the
poet's. As in Picasso's painting "The Mirror" (1932),
with its double images of the woman seen from different perspectives, the point of view of the poem
changes: The poet deftly does an about-face and the
elephant is seen in a dimension external to the "I." In
other words, Melanchthon is freed from his introspective revelations when the poet asks the question that
concludes Part 2: "the elephant is / black earth
preceded by a tendril?"

The figure of the "tendril," the threadlike part of
a climbing plant that serves to support the plant, may
seem an absurd image for the elephant's trunk, but
this is only one of the many elements of "unreason"
in the poem. Moore returns to the analogy years later
in "Smooth Gnarled Crape Myrtle" (1935): "An aspect may deceive; as the / elephant's columbine-tubed
trunk / held waveringly out— / an at will heavy thing

—is / delicate. / Art is unfortunate." The circumference described by Melanchthon's trunk, the delicate tendril, has always expressed for the elephant the unity of life and death, the wholeness of being. But art, like speech, has its limits, and the poet is at a loss for an image to describe the soul. The fact that she asks, nevertheless, if the elephant is black earth "preceded by" a tendril also implies the debate familiar to Christians about whether "essence precedes existence" or "existence precedes essence"; and the question reinforces the mystery of the relation between the body and soul.

The elephant's opacity, his blackness, is explicitly compared to the wandlike body and the coral plant that "vacillate like / a translucence of the atmosphere." The elephant is at least steadier, is "that on which darts cannot strike decisively the first / time, a substance / needful as an instance / of the indestructibility of matter; . . . / the name means thick." (The Greek term for the now obsolete classification in which the elephant was grouped—pachyderm—means "thick skin.") There is an imponderable quality, an inexplicable strength and solidity in that ponderous, corporeal mass that continues to survive in the natural world. The poet, therefore, asks the final, assertive, but barely rhetorical question: "Will / depth be depth, thick skin be thick, to one who can see no / beautiful element of unreason in it?"

It is characteristic of Marianne Moore to have named her first elephant after Philipp Melanchthon, the sixteenth-century "teacher of Germany" and influential Protestant theologian, whose family name, Schwarzerd, which literally meant "black earth," became hellenized in keeping with humanistic custom when he distinguished himself in classical studies. By

naming an elephant for the theologian, Moore indicates her affection for both and dignifies her animal.
She knew that the association between man and elephants goes far back in mythology, that in Hindu legend male and female elephants spring from a "cosmic
egg," and that to the Buddhists "white" elephants are
revered as creatures related to the gods. She will come
back to the wisdom of the huge old beasts in an allegorical poem, "Charity Overcoming Envy" (1963),
and in a vision of peace, "Elephants" (1943), for which
"Melanchthon" had prepared her years before.

A poem closer to "Melanchthon" in date of composition takes up and develops the subject of spiritual
poise emblematically rather than explicitly in the geo-
graphic-mythographic context of a religious poet in a
secular age. Moore assembles a "strange fraternity" of
creatures from nature, history, folklore, and allegory
for the two maps—terrestrial and celestial—she draws
in the complex work, "Sea Unicorns and Land Unicorns" (1924). The sea unicorn, or Arctic narwhale
(*Monodon monceros*), unusual in that the male possesses
a long, twisted, pointed ivory tusk projected like a
horn, was associated in folklore with the fabled unicorn (in Greek, *monceros;* in Latin, *unicornis*), which
remains an enigmatic symbol whose interpretations
still keep some of its mystery. These two creatures,
one real and one imaginary, are counterparts just as
lions in the sea and on the land are counterparts—"a
strange fraternity"; and they along with sea snakes
(the sea serpent of which there are many legendary
accounts), bears, penguin kings, and historical per-
sonages inhabit the western world mapped by the
poet. The poem unfolds like a story of recovery—and
comes to rest in contemplation—of the "miraculous
elusiveness" of the allegorical unicorn.

The subject of the first thirty-eight lines, including the title, is the terrestrial map with the narwhale and unicorn, lion and sea-lion as the devices for the four corners of the map. On it, the poet brings together representatives of the human imagination in a period when old conceptions of the world combined with the excitement of the exploration of a new world. The initial reference is to the sixteenth-century Christian poet, Edmund Spenser, with whom Moore shares the conviction that Nature, the phenomena in space and time, is not the ultimate reality. From Spenser's "epic marvelous," *The Faerie Queene,* Moore borrows a phrase describing "mighty monoceroses with immeasured tayles." The amusing image from Spenser and the mention of a seemingly insignificant date, 1539, establish her perspective—the cartography is medieval and modern. The poet is like the "early modern" mapmakers of the sixteenth century who enlarged the old-world concepts in which mythical elements occupied such an important place and for which corrections had to be made to take into account changing views without losing the awareness of the unknown that countered the self-centered geography of the past. Unicorns and their respective lions are the "very animals" described by those cartographers.

Quoting from one of them as typical, Moore credits the source as an English translation of the work of Olaus Magnus in historiography, but equally pertinent to the poem is the priest-humanist's *Carta Marina* (1539), the first detailed map of Scandinavia and the north with any pretensions to accuracy. Other references, either in the notes or the text, are to less admirable but more adventurous men of history: Thomas Cavendish, freebooter and third circumnavigator of the globe; and Sir John Hawkins, first English slave

trader, naval administrator, and "Christian" philanthropist. They not only bring back from their travels treasures such as "the horn of the sea unicorn" (a protection against poisoned drink) to Queen Elizabeth, "who thought it worth a hundred thousand pounds[.]" These daring fellows also return with "immeasured" accounts ("tayles") mingling fact with fiction about the marvels of the new world and the abundance of exotic animals: sea unicorns "swimming where they like, / finding the place where sea-lions live in herds, / strewn on the beach like stones with lesser stones— / and bears are white;" or " 'land unicorns and lions; / since where the one is, / its archenemy cannot be missing.' " The geography is at least "true."

The poet is entertained by the deductive reasoning based on incorrect assumptions and by the combining of fancied antipathies in traditional notions to which credulous people are given. She is less entertained by the moral contradictions in human beings or by the natural conflicts between them in various spheres of life. The poet, then, reverses the matter in the statement on a civilized community:

> Thus personalities by nature much opposed,
> can be combined in such a way
> that when they do agree, their unanimity is great,
> "in politics, in trade, law, sport, religion,
> china-collecting, tennis, and church-going."

The list of human activities is from the American Henry James's observations of the English character. Moore also reminds the reader of the art of "embroidering" in brilliant colors " 'polished garlands' " and fourfold combinations of "strange animals" and disparate images of "agreeing difference." As a twentieth-century heir to a long tradition from which much

has been gained, much preserved, and much lost, she can talk serenely about the new English coast "and its land lion oddly tolerant of those pacific counterparts to it, / the water lions of the west." But that talk is only after a bow to "Britannia's sea unicorn with its rebellious child," the American in the new land. "Ostentatiously indigenous," it should be noted.

She completes the salient outlines of the "western world" with the figures of the "strange fraternity," "these sea lions and land lions, / land unicorns and sea unicorns:" The colon, marking the completion, serves as the sign for a transition passage of four lines in which the image of regal power, the heraldic lion "civilly rampant, / tame and concessive like the long-tailed bear of Ecuador" is juxtaposed with the image of another kind of lion "standing up against this screen of woven air / which is the forest:"—images for the social and natural realms. Following the second colon, a single line states the subject to be developed in Part 2, the thirty-nine lines that conclude the poem: "The unicorn also, on its hind legs in reciprocity."

If the poet's earthly map indicates the irregularities and crossed lines of post-medieval history, the second of her maps charts the territory of the unicorn. The unicorn, common to many cultures, is not an exclusively Christian symbol, but one rich in associations transfigured by the art of Christianity. Moore recovers the religious imagination of the medieval world and reinterprets the legends in a fable for a post-Christian era. The unique animal "etched like an equine monster on an old celestial map" has warily disappeared for centuries and reappeared "yet never to be caught." Haughtiest of beasts and a "puzzle to hunters," the unicorn rebels proudly against dogs "which are dismayed by the chain lightning / playing

at them from its horn" but which also derive "agree-able terror" from its not being consumed by the fire that enflames it. Capable when endangered of throwing itself with "head foremost from a cliff, / it walks away unharmed[.]" The "feat," the poet says, is one she has not seen except in pictures. There is, however, a record on "the printed page" and "by word of mouth" that while the unicorn is " 'impossible to take alive,' " it can be "tamed only by a lady inoffensive like itself— / as curiously wild and gentle"—the Virgin Mary. The "unicorn 'with pavon high,' " the haughtiest of beasts, willingly becomes submissive to a power that is equal to its own but paradoxically superior, and "approaches eagerly; / until engrossed by what appears of this strange enemy, / upon the map, 'upon her lap,' / its 'mild wild head doth lie.' " Beyond "agreeing difference" and "reciprocity," the quietly dramatic surrender of the prideful self brings transcendent peace.

Sharing a common view that historical developments had cut much of civilization off from "the sense of the whole of life,"[8] Moore wished to write poetry in which she would contribute to the recognition of that wholeness. The belief that the natural world is not the totality of existence, as real as it was for her, was evident in "Melanchthon," which symbolized the union of the physical and spiritual. "Sea Unicorns and Land Unicorns" is more intricate and more beautiful in tracking the supremacy of the religious over the secular realm. To write a twentieth-century poem in which she joined the earthly and heavenly maps was to risk their being relegated to a museum of the mind. Readers have been ironically apt to think of the first map as a "museum piece" at the same time that they have responded to the second as a traditional religious alle-

gory of the unicorn. For many of them, the pre-Christian unicorn is a symbol of Christ. For Moore, I think, the "multiplied flames" of the "Sun" symbolize the resurrected Christ, whose "curiously wild and gentle" mother embodies the gift of divine and irresistible grace by which she too is qualified for the vocation of blessing the wildest, haughtiest, most elusive of beings. The unicorn is Moore's embodiment of the mystery of spiritual poise.

Complementing "Sea Unicorns and Land Unicorns" as well as "Melanchthon" and "Sun" are "The Pangolin" (1936), "The Paper Nautilus" (1940), and "Rosemary" (1954).

II

"In this place of surging enmity," Moore finds another impressive animal, "The Pangolin." The focal theme of the poem is grace. "To explain grace," she writes, "requires / a curious hand." The poet is nothing if not curious. She not only wants to know; she wants to write about everything she knows. And how curious to write about grace in a poem for which the initial subject is that artichoke with a tail, that "roller" ("pangolin" means roller) thought by "simpletons" to be "a living fable / whom the stones had nourished." The pangolin is, in fact, an ant-eater. Belonging to the natural order, he has—as one can expect in Moore's animals—"certain postures of a man."

> Sun and moon and day and night and man and
> > beast
> > > each with a splendor
> > > > which man in all his vileness cannot
> > > > set aside; each with an excellence!

The pangolin is "armored"; he has sting-proof scales overlapping scales as well as a "graceful" giant tail "tipped like / an elephant's trunk with special skin," and lives in "a nest / of rocks closed with earth from inside, which he can thus darken." When he is threatened, he also can climb trees or roll himself up in a ball that cannot be unrolled. Clever as he is to protect himself, he nevertheless suffers discomforts. His ear, nose, and eye apertures are susceptible to ant stings. " 'Fearful yet to be feared,' " he retaliates. (What creature would not?) Otherwise, he is not aggressive and "draws / away from danger unpugnaciously, / with no sound but a harmless hiss. . . ." So, he "endures." He has his virtues, even if he hisses; and he has a "fragile grace": a "machine-like form and frictionless creep of a thing / made graceful by adversities, con- / versities." He is, clearly, a work of art, and the poet delights in him as a model of exactness. The natural ease of his movements, however, is only one kind of grace, rather a limited and cautious kind. To explain grace requires more than that.

The poet's serious play with language testifies to the amplitude of the word. "If that which is at all were not forever, / why would those who graced the spires / with animals" and gathered to rest on the cathedral porches "have slaved to confuse" the concept of grace with (1) the ideals of social behavior, (2) consideration in business dealings, (3) "the cure for sins" (the gift of divine favor that grants salvation to man), and (4) aesthetic values? The humor of the verb "confuse" may mask the poet's nostalgia for a spiritual order that, despite its imperfections, gave the world an integrated vision by which human activity was measured

and sustained. Randall Jarrell, for example, said of "The Pangolin" that it was "one of the most moving, honest, and haunting poems that anyone has written in our century."[9] Insofar as the view of fragmented man—papermaker like the wasp, tractor of foodstuffs like the ant, builder of suspension bridges like the spider, mechanicked for fighting like the pangolin; and mammal, "serge-clad, strong shod" (a Yahoo?), post-Darwinian, "the being we call human"—is the only view, the poem is haunting. But because Moore believed in Christian grace, supernatural grace both preparatory and prevenient as an actuality, she is an expositor of hope. Moore's essay "Abraham Lincoln and the Art of the Word" (1960) bears directly on that belief:

The largeness of the life entered into the writing, as with a passion he strove to persuade his hearers of what he believed, his adroit, ingenious mentality framing an art which, if it is not to be designated poetry, we may call a "grasp of eternal grace"—in both senses, literal and figurative. Nor was he unaware of having effected what mattered[.][10]

As an example of Lincoln's largeness, Moore choses to quote from his writing: "I dislike an oath which requires a man to swear he has not done wrong. It rejects the Christian principle of forgiveness on terms of repentance. I think it is enough if the man does no wrong hereafter."

In "The Pangolin," "man, the self, the being we call human" is writing master to the world. The poet's phrase is "this world," in which man does not always "grace" spires or behave with Lincoln's magnanimity. He may be a kind of Polonius who "griffons [scrawls, scribbles] a dark / 'Like does not like like that is obnoxious.'" Or he may not be a prattling old fool at all;

yet he is fallible and "writes error with four / r's."
What an attractive way of saying the banal "At least he
knows the word. We all make mistakes." The poet's
amused tone is so relaxed and tolerant that it is far
more effective than stern moralizing or sharp wit
could be. The woman knows how to tease. She has tact
and grace.

"Among animals," she says of man in "The Pangolin," "*one* has a sense of humor. / Humor saves a few
steps, it saves years." Among the many admirable
qualities of Lincoln, for instance, one of the first she
praised was the humor that often "made argument
unnecessary." Moore's joyful humor begins in this
poem with the choice of the slow, timid, crouching
pangolin as the embodiment of the suppleness and
beauty of movement: he "creeps." When she uses the
word "mechanicked" for him, the sound is discordant
enough to undercut that model of exactness as an
epitome of grace. Slipping in a seemingly irrelevant
remark about the sailboat, she does not say that it is
graceful but that it was the first machine, as if to allow
for the nuances. Having made the point, she moves
quickly to the lighthearted, lenient, affectionate look
at a disheartened fellow, man, capsizing in a boat.
"Bedizened or stark / naked, man, the self, the being
we call human, writing- / master to this world[.]" Even
the breaks between "stark" and "naked," between
"writing" and "master" in the roved-over lines contribute to the verbal play, the rhythmic counterpoint
of the poem. The grace of writing, the grace of the
imagination, the grace of humor—all are there in
"The Pangolin." The Christian vision, she seems to be
saying, is a comic vision.

Because of that vision, Moore rises easily to an
affirmation—one of the strongest and surest in all of

her poetry—of belief in generic man. If he has certain postures of the pangolin, vulnerable man is still man:

> he has everlasting vigor,
>> power to grow,
>>> though there are few creatures who
>>> can make one
>>> breathe faster and make one
>>> erecter.
> Not afraid of anything is he,
>> and then goes cowering forth, tread paced to
>> meet an obstacle
> at every step. . . . The prey of fear, he, always
>> curtailed, extinguished, thwarted by the
>> dusk, work partly done,
> says to the alternating blaze,
>> "Again the sun!
>> anew each day; and new and new and new,
>> that comes into and steadies my soul."

Ridiculous as he is, he has a soul, and it can be steadied.

Like "The Pangolin," "The Paper Nautilus" is a description of a model of exactness from nature. The comic spirit of "The Pangolin" is modulated to wit and "beauty's light momentum" in "The Paper Nautilus," whose themes are hope and love, which—with faith—have formed the basis for Christian catechisms. The word "hope" occurs with less frequency than the word "love" in Moore's poetry, but it is there in "The Steeple-Jack" (1932) and "The Hero" (1932), which come first in both the *Collected* and *Complete Poems,* and in the invocatory poem, "Sun." Hope is also the emotion that stimulates man's apostrophe to the sun and "each new day" with which "The Pangolin" concludes. Although chronologically a few poems came between "The Pangolin" and "The Paper Nautilus,"

Moore always placed the two in sequence when she assembled her verse for publication, as if to suggest that the belief in grace and the capacity to hope and love are consonant.

"The Paper Nautilus" is seen in a social context, established in brief critical comments about authorities whose hopes are determined by "mercenaries"—writers "trapped" by superficial fame and creature comforts. In contrast to them is the watchful nautilus, who gives herself and "her perishable souvenir of hope"—her thin, glass, papery shell—to procreation. The nautilus constructs the shell to cradle her eggs hidden "eight-fold in her eight arms" (like the Hindu mother goddess Shakti?), and the arms in turn coil around the shell to protect themselves from predators. Intently guarding the eggs day and night, scarcely eating until they are hatched, she is "hindered to succeed." When the eggs are freed from the shell, they free it. They leave "its wasp-nest flaws" and the "close / laid Ionic chiton-folds / like the lines of the mane of / a Parthenon horse"—things of beauty and aesthetic interest. Moore, describing the compact and highly organized invertebrate animal with customary care, ends the poem with the observation that the arms of the nautilus "had wound themselves" round the shell "as if they knew love / is the only fortress / strong enough to trust to." Bearing life, they lead us to imagine they know their catechism.

One of the poem's obvious antecedents is "The Chambered Nautilus" (1858) by Oliver Wendell Holmes, who describes the subject much less accurately than Moore and then draws the "heavenly message": "Build thee more stately mansions, O my soul / . . . Till thou at last are free, / Leaving thine outgrown shell by life's resting sea." Moore's nautilus

poem is more literally about maternal love, and for that reason is thought to pay homage to the poet's mother. It is, however, doubtful that Moore would think of herself as an egg, egghead, or discarded shell, no matter how self-disparaging she is. "The Paper Nautilus" nevertheless combines images and ideas about them in the poet's characteristic mode, which has much in common with what she said of the work of Robert Andrew Parker (the artist who did hand-colored drawings for eight of her poems in 1962). She wrote of Parker, in 1958, that "he is one of the most accurate and at the same time most unliteral of paint-ers. He combines the mystical and the actual, working both in an abstract and realistic way." Observing that one or two of Parker's paintings seem to be "a kind of private calligraphy," she says they "approximate a sig-nature or family cipher." Beyond the "literal," the poem is familial not only because the cephalopod ex-emplifies the nurturing instinct but also because the "paper" nautilus is a witty conceit for the making of poems, the "spawning" of art. In that sense, it bears Moore's signature.

Her metaphysical wit surpasses the stereotypical formulas for the creative process, the work as surro-gate for childbearing, and even "the feminine sensibil-ity" of artists. Precise as Moore is in describing her marine creature, what she chooses to overlook about the nautilus points up the wit and humor as well as the originality of the "sea changes" in the poem. She does not exploit the "facts" that only the female has a deli-cate papery shell and that the male of the genus is about five-eighths of an inch in its longest dimensions while the female is about six inches long—one of the greatest size discrepancies in the animal kingdom. She neglects to say that the nautili are a more primitive and

less specialized group of cephalopoda than the squid or octopus. She does not take advantage of the Greek roots of "cephalopoda"—head plus feet—about which she could have punned as she did in another poem on poetry, "To a Snail" (1924) with its "absence of feet" and its occipital horn. She fails to mention that no light-sensitive organs are known in the *nautilus,* which has eyes like open pits without lenses. (Poetry can be bioluminiscent.) She chooses instead to say that the female "is in / a sense a devil- / fish," and compares her to Hercules "bitten / by a crab loyal to the hydra [the many-headed serpent]." Having begun the poem by criticizing the mundane and material values of society, she recognizes the strength required to dedicate one's being to perilous labors of love. And she does not say that the *nautilus* is the oldest surviving cephalopod; her paper momento is a "perishable souvenir of hope."

In keeping with a twentieth-century view of the impermanence of art, Moore's paper nautilus does not stimulate visions of the soul's more stately mansions, but of "wasp-nest flaws" or a fragile glass shell, "a dull / white outside and smooth- / edged inner surface/ glossy as the sea[.]" Moore's are the modest claims of a comic poet with an inner vision of temporal beauty. Because she is a Christian poet who esteems the everlasting beauty of God, however, she would not entirely agree with Yeats in "Two Songs from a Play" (1928) when he writes: "Everything that man esteems / Endures a moment or a day." "The Paper Nautilus" says that everything mortal creatures make is short-lived, but that making it with dedicated love and care is freeing and is a "fortress" in which one may find refuge. That kind of making, in the Christian view, is an indispensable condition for human society.

"Rosemary" is a poem of small notations on a common herb that takes its name from the dew of the sea. Consisting of three sestets, in which the final syllable of rosemary serves as the motif for the light rhyme, the poem has three subjects: "Beauty and Beauty's son and rosemary." Like Yeats's "Two Songs from a Play" (*The Resurrection*), Moore's verse joins classical and Christian legend. Yeats muses upon the tradition of the virgin birth of Dionysus and Christ, who died and rose under the same astrological sign ("at the spring"), but "Love's pleasure drives . . . love away." While Yeats's parallels are between Athena and Mary, Moore's are between Venus and Mary and their sons Cupid and Christ, born "at Christmas each, in company." Holiday pleasures, the poem gently states, may not be remembrances of holy days. The "garland of festivity" braided in token of those beautiful women and the children to whom they gave birth is not "always rosemary— / since the flight to Egypt, blooming differently."

In the correspondence between the virtues of stones and herbs, rosemary was associated with the topaz, Moore's emblem for Christ in "Sun." Rosemary, that pious herb, not only made one chaste but also bestowed friendship and honor in the sight of God and humankind. For Moore, it is the "herb of memory," its "lancelike leaf" recalling Christ's crucifixion, and the flowers recalling the flight of the holy family to save their son from death. These emblems, both actual and mystical for Moore, bear their true colors to which the bee (busy?) is dumb: the pointed leaf, "green but silver underneath" ("underneath," the only word breaking the rhymes of the poem), and the herbal flowers, "white originally—turned blue," Mary's color. All is not quite legend in the poem. The

fragrant plant "springs from stones beside the sea,"
"feeds on dew," and limits its height to that of Christ,
but its leaves have a bitter taste—the poet's word is
"pungency"—again delicately tracing the point of the
time of remembrance. Hence, the marine rose "is in
reality / a kind of Christmas-tree." The unaccented
rhymes, in keeping with rosemary, have been trans-
formed to the clearly accented rhymes of "sea,"
"three," "bee," and "tree," with which the music of
the poem comes to a rest. The transfiguration of the
shrub into "a kind of Christmas-tree" depends, as is
usual in the silences of Moore's work, on the simple
fact. The rosemary pine is any one of three pines common to the southern countryside and is itself a Christmas shrub. The paradigm of natural beauty and
natural love, Christian beauty and Christian love "underneath" this Christmas garland suggests its appro-
priateness as ornament for all of the religious poems.

III

Coming chronologically between "The Paper Nautilus" and "Rosemary," which affirm the mystery of
love, "By Disposition of Angels" (1948) and "Like a
Bulwark" (1948) were first printed in the year following the death of Marianne Moore's mother. They are
superlative poems because of the intensity of emotion
and the language perfected by spiritual discipline and
Christian vision. The prayer the poet wrote for her
mother's funeral testifies to that vision:

We thank Thee for the valiant dead who have made the
distant heavens a home for us, whose truth and beauty are
even now in our hearts. One by one Thou dost gather us out

of Earthly light into heavenly glory, from the distractions of time to the peace of eternity. We thank Thee for the labors and joys of these mortal years. We thank Thee for the deepening sense of the mysteries that lie beyond our dust, and for the eye of faith which Thou hast opened for all who believe in Thy Son, to behold through the darkness a shining future. May we live in thy faith and love, the hope implanted in us of immortality, until for us also the day shall break in glory, through the grace of Jesus Christ our Savior, Amen.

"By Disposition of Angels" is elegiac. It is also one of only two sonnets in the *Complete Poems*—the other is "No Swan So Fine"—and is the most lyrical verse Moore ever wrote. In a solitary meditation on death and loss and darkness, a high cold star shines steadfastly and inviolate. The star's divine fire is a ministering spirit beyond human reason or mortal grief and solitude.

Moore is indebted for the title to the New Testament story of the life of Stephen, the first Christian martyr. After performing "great wonders and signs," Stephen spoke against those who "had received the law by the disposition of angels" yet had resisted the Holy Spirit. When they heard Stephen, "they were cut to the heart, and they gnashed on him with *their* teeth. / But he being full of the Holy Ghost, looked up steadfastly into heaven, and saw the glory of God. . . ." (Acts 53–55). The subject of Moore's poem is not, of course, martyrdom, but wonder at the evidence of the holy spirit, the active presence of God in the world, even in experiences of pain and suffering.

Are angels, the poet asks, "Messengers much like ourselves"? "Steadfastness the darkness makes explicit? / Something heard most clearly when not near it?"

As Laurence Stapleton has said, the questions "waken the reader's mind so that the following lines open the way to things beyond the ordinary range of feeling: 'Above particularities, / these unparticularities praise cannot violate. / One has seen, in such steadiness never deflected, / how by darkness a star is perfected.' "[11]

For Moore, as she wrote in a 1941 essay on Louise Bogan, "those who have seemed to know the most about eternity feel that this side of eternity is a small part of life." Believing in a reality both beyond the visible and within the silent darkness, Moore is not, however, among the poets given to ecstatic visions of the soul. It was mortality about which she knew the most; and while she was not one to beat her breast sorrowfully, loneliness was for her—to quote from Bogan—"the heart within your side."

The religious imagination transfigures that loneliness without denying it. The second stanza of Moore's elegy returns to the questioning: "Star that does not ask me if I see it? / Fir that would not wish me to uproot it? / Speech that does not ask me if I hear it?" Acknowledging the impersonal nature of the universe, she receives the law: "Mysteries expound mysteries." The cosmos does not depend on human disposition— although that which is alive does not wish to die or to be destroyed; but one is blessed only if one receives the law and does not resist the disposition of angels. Because her heart is open, she is comforted: "Steadier than steady, star dazzling me, live and elate, / no need to say, how like some we have known; too like her, / Too like him, and a-quiver forever." The reticence in the pronouns "her" and "him" seems to suggest that this is the most personal of devotions, and for that reason I think the poem is in memory of her mother,

one of the valiant dead, and the maternal grandfather with whose legacy the poet kept faith.

"Like a Bulwark" was first printed with the title, "At Rest in the Blast," later changed to "Bulwarked Against Fate" (1956), and then given its final title from the volume *Like a Bulwark* (1956). The successive changes not only make the poem more compact but also distance it from an emphasis on peace in death following earthly strife in the title "At Rest in the Blast." The final title is a shorter form of the poem's thematic line describing a person of fortitude.

The language of the verse recalls two famous Protestant hymns, "Our God, Our Help in Ages Past" (1719) by Isaac Watts, and "A Mighty Fortress Is Our God" (1529) by Martin Luther. In the Watts hymn, God is "Our shelter from the stormy blast." Luther's hymn begins, "A mighty fortress is our God, / A bulwark never failing."[12] The images from Luther would encourage a reading of the poem as a song of praise to God, but the poet's phrase, "firmed by the thrust of the blast," her use of "like" in relation to the metaphor from Luther, and the development of the narrative come together in a characterization of a human being whose spiritual life is godly.

The validation of the person begins with the first word, "Affirmed." The judgment is strong; the person was "firmed," the character pent by power that paradoxically held the life firm and gave power to it. The barrage of dissonant sounds, "pent," "hard pressed," "tempest-tossed," "thrust," "blast," "compact," effect the sense of a battered person, one who could take both "the blame" (responsibility for errors or sin) and the assaults. The person might at last have been brought down, but no, the strength was "inviolate. / . . . like a bulwark against fate; / lead-saluted, / saluted

by lead? / As though flying Old Glory full mast." (The figure of the flag was borrowed from an annual report of the John Deere tractor company.) Both the martial images and the questions are "yoked together by violence," the violence of the poet's emotions. But the conflict is resolved as the narrative ends with the signal of endurance which one quickly realizes is a signal of triumph. Full military honors—a twenty-one-gun salute, in the words of Donald Hall[13]—for a heroic person? To have flown the flag at half-staff would have been a denial of a faith secured.

The wit in the fusion of the traditional languages of religious, military, and secular life is so vigorous that it is difficult to remember that the original title was "At Rest in the Blast." The metaphor of the fort seems to follow the line "love / is the only fortress / strong enough to trust to" from "The Paper Nautilus." Yet love is not spoken, except by indirection, in the poem. Love of God, however, inheres in the musical allusions. Love for the person—the "you" to whom the poem is addressed—is inherent in the poet's analogy between a protecting God of the old hymns and the person as a bulwark also "never failing." Like the pronouns in the elegy "By Disposition of Angels," the praiseworthy "you" is not identified. Again, I think, the twenty-one-gun salute is to Marianne Moore's mortal fortress, her mother, a woman of wit, courageous spirit, and devotion to God. Neither "Disposition" nor "Bulwark" has an explicit dedication; for that reason, both of them can be appreciated as personal and as impersonal poems in praise of anyone who exemplifies the spiritual qualities revered by the poet.

IV

During the last decades of her life, Moore continued to write seriously and sometimes wittily of her own devotion to God. Among the variations in her work are four poems that reveal affinities between Christian concepts and the arts: a paean to the Renaissance composer Melchior Vulpius (c. 1560–1615), verses for Saint Valentine's day, an allegory derived from an old tapestry, and a meditation on the painting of René Magritte (1898–1967). The logic of the poet's preferences, to use one of her own phrases, continues to be unmistakably religious.

In "Melchior Vulpius" (1958), the contrapuntalist is praised for the sacred music he composed. It is in the words of the music she hears, " 'God be praised for conquering faith, / which feareth neither pain nor death,' " that the name of God is heard for the first time in the poet's canon. It is, the poem states plainly, the mysterious power of the great artist who has been able to master and direct the power—a beatitude beyond one's understanding—by which her own faith is affirmed. Creativeness, she had said, was as near a definition as she could give for the soul. Yet while she celebrates its manifestations, she interjects a lively note on the human voice: "Mouse-skin-bellows'-breath / expanding into rapture saith / 'Hallelujah.' " There, as usual, is Moore's signature, in the midst of an appreciation of chorales, wedding hymns, anthems, and fugues—the most complicated of all the contrapuntal forms described as "slowly building / from miniature thunder, / crescendos antidoting death— / love's signature cementing faith." The elation of the religious poet, the elan of wit and humor, the exaltation of music, without which as she wrote in "Merciful-

ly" (1968), "life is flat," are her counters to bare existence.

"For February 14th" (1959) is a spirited "line"
addressed to Saint Valentine. The commemoration of
the lover's festival which, ironically, has been separated from the two legendary martyrs for whom the
day is named, suggests the drift toward secularization
of customs that the poet gently remarked in "Rosemary." In "For February 14th," she muses lightheart-
edly, as if debating with herself, about an appropriate
present for the saint to whom she dares write the
wittiest, most unsentimental note in the history of
greeting cards. The verse is not only a parody of commercial cards; it is a brilliant take-off on all those valentine poems about gems, flowers, and songbirds in
the popular gift books of the nineteenth century
(which, as T. S. Eliot once said, suffered from "a dis-
sociation of sensibility").

Moore first confesses that she is late in writing but
identifies herself as an " 'interested law / impelled to
plod in the poem's cause.' " She has borrowed the
awkward wording from a poem which had been written to her, but she is more given to subtle self-prod-
ding than to plodding. Although she tantalizingly asks
Saint Valentine what he might have liked to have, she
doesn't make up her mind. There must be too many
tempting items to choose from. After considering a
diamond (she did not like diamonds, as she had written in "Voracities and Verities" [1947], but the ads say
"Diamonds. And suddenly you feel irresistible.") she
obviously rejects the idea. She proposes, in turn, a
prickly thistle, a sensitive plant—" 'alexander's armil-
lary sphere' "—and paradise birds, perhaps something she could afford, and certainly original. At least
she liked them: the thistle leaf, downy underneath, is

"worth a touch"; the sensitive plant, if sharp to the touch, is a lovely little globular cluster (the wildflower books compared it to a celestial sphere); the paradise birds with their rich black iridescent colors are among the most beautiful in the world, and perhaps they have a pedigree going back to the ark itself. There's no guessing what Saint Valentine would prefer. Too late to send a present anyway. Questions are preferable, even if "questioning is the mark / of a pest!" So one last question: "Why think / only of animals in connection / with the ark or the wine Noah drank? / but that the ark did not sink."

As the dramatic monologuist, in her one-woman morality play, turns to self-chiding, the saint's day becomes an occasion for remembering the Biblical passage "But Noah found grace in the eyes of the Lord" and Noah's trust in that grace, which the poet assumes the saint (and the reader) will know. Although the silent saint receives no present except the confessions of a tardy note from the poet, the poem belatedly recalls the sacred gift of unmerited love for wayward human beings. No wonder, then, that the poet can be lighthearted. She almost convinces one to take Saint Valentine's day seriously. If she is found wanting as a poet who failed to celebrate erotic love, she nevertheless appreciates that there is more than one kind of love and repossesses those traditional meanings of the word about which she cared deeply.

A late-fifteenth-century tapestry gave the poet the figures for a dramatic account of "Charity Overcoming Envy" (1963), representative of a struggle Christian ethics cannot evade. When people are good, it is easy to be charitable toward them; when they violate principles of justice, *caritas* is more difficult and becomes entangled with the moral imperative to take

justice seriously. Charity without justice is apt to be sentimental, but justice is hard and risks being uncharitable or at least misunderstood. This is the intricate problem that the allegorical poem enacts. It is a problem as old as society itself, and as the poem says, "insupportably tiring."

Envy—one of the deadly sins—is worn and obsessed with greed, since "he can only take *some*" of the things owned by others. Charity riding one of the poet's faithful elephants is superior in strength and power to Envy on his dog. (The superiority in itself may be a cause of fear.) Envy, armored in chain mail and steel, cowers from Charity, whose sword is unsheathed. Envy has been "arrested": his cheek is scratched, although he is not severely wounded. The poet says that he is "scarcely scratched." Having acted, Charity is silent, whereas the victim, exaggerating the mild injury, cries out in self-pity: "Blood stains my cheek. I am hurt. / . . . I am hurt." Surprised that he has been "maimed" by *caritas*, Envy agonizes that she will be relentless and Destiny pitiless.

The wise old elephant acts both in the service of Charity and in the interest of truth. He convinces Envy that he is not destined to destruction by Charity; perhaps Envy is indestructible, but he can be overcome, he is overcome. With recognition of Charity's restraint and largesse, of which the knowing elephant gives assurance, "the problem is mastered." The title itself, "Charity Overcoming Envy," carries the meaning of Charity as a double will: overpowering as it checks and as it frees Envy from the obsessive insecurities that threaten humankind. *Caritas* is justice with mercy. For Moore, true justice is an instrument of love and can be its most satisfactory expression. It would be fatal for justice and love to be severed. In the community of the

spirit, they should be inextricable. "The Gordian knot need not be cut."

The poet's setting for that ideal is a field of flowers, a mosaic, a work of art. The place that Envy has occupied is not as carefully cultivated—flowers are bunched together, uprooted, trampled, slithered, and weeds are rampant; the ground of his being is predictably chaotic. Readers, stressing that it did not gratify Moore to bring people to heel or to see them cower, have thought the poem inscrutable or cryptic; it is good allegory by a poet who did not object to being called a moralist. She begins the poem with a hardly innocent question: "Have you time for a story / (depicted in tapestry)?" The story, as the poem says, is one of "Deliverance." Consistent with Christian belief, the coherent structure assumes that there are ethical imperatives that cannot be ignored if humankind is to cope with fallen existence.

While "Melchior Vulpius," "For February 14th," and "Charity Overcoming Envy" verify Moore's long if independent allegiance to a religious tradition, the last of her poems is a poignant reminder of the openness with which she first encountered the twentieth century's bold new artistic visions and of her alert appreciation of work that affirmed spiritual forces under other names than those to which she ascribed. "The Magician's Retreat" (1970) shares the lucidity, the modesty, and the quiet composure with which the artist-painter René Magritte contemplated the darkness and the light of the created world. The title, with the sense of the sleight-of-hand man, points to the value of art as illusion and to the need not for an escape from reality but for a retreat in which to meditate on the silent language of the visible: "I have seen it," the poet says of the image she describes in the

poem. For Moore "the power of the visible is the invisible," and for Magritte the signs of the visible always
evoke the mystery of the invisible as well as the visible.

Whereas the poet's faith was orthodox, Magritte
never believed in "the comfort . . . of some metaphysical religion" of the kind "priests propagandize," and
he observed in 1954 that "the idea of creation without
a creator" was almost a commonplace. Both of them
believed, however, that art should break with complacent mental habits, whether naive or sophisticated,
that discredit any authentic feeling of existence. Magritte hesitated a long time, as he said, in adopting "Le
Salon de Dieu" as the title for a 1958 painting of a
nocturnal sky and daylight landscape because of "the
total ban on saying anything at all about God." Moore
never spoke of the fact that she does not name God in
the poems, but the discretion was self-imposed, as it
must have been for Magritte. She could have said with
him: "It is basic enough to cease being a 'question'
and to stand revealed as an affirmation of the mystery
in which we live. We exist within mystery whether we
know it or not." Words of Magritte serve well as a
justification for Moore: The "refusal to consider the
problem of the reality existing outside of consciousness is tragic, . . . the mental universe, at its 'known'
but extendable limits, touches the authentic unknown," and the work of the artist or poet was "to
transform that mental universe and give it a charm
that adds to the value of life." For both of them, what
they made was insignificant by comparison with "the
beauty that sears our souls."[14]

In "The Magician's Retreat," the ambience is that
of more than one painting in Magritte's hauntingly
beautiful series "L'empire des lumières," with a house

always in "a nighttime landscape and a sky such as we see during the day":

> cloudy but bright inside
> like a moonstone,
> while a yellow glow
> from a shutter-crack shone,
> a cat's-eye yellow crack in the shutter,
> and a blue glow from the lamppost
> close to the front door.
>
> It left nothing of which to complain,
> nothing more to obtain,
> consummately plain.
>
> A black tree mass rose at the back
> almost touching the eaves. . . .

The daylight of Magritte's paintings has grown small and almost been brushed aside in Moore's poem, but the inner force of the light in the dark landscape is intensified by the cat's-eye yellow glow, which is the essence of Magritte's serenity. The capacity of the poet to respond with such rightness to the world she beheld and the world others beheld is one of her greatest gifts. It is seemly that the tribute to Magritte was the last poem to be published by Marianne Moore before her death. As a final testament to her own luminous energy it is as if the multiplied flames of her great sun still burn inwardly and that in her old age there is nothing more love can say or take away.

5

In the Public Garden

I

When she was a young woman, Marianne Moore, her mother, and their friends were active in the Woman's Suffrage Party of Pennsylvania. Moore went to meetings, was a member of the Committee to Organize Cumberland County, went to the fair to distribute leaflets or talk to farmers,[1] and wrote party notes "contributed at intervals" to the *Carlisle Evening Sentinel.*[2] She was bored at the meetings, but recalled that "to be writing . . . anything at all for a newspaper" was a pleasure.

These activities, beginning in 1915, presage the development of Moore as a poet who wrote about public issues, or causes, and appreciated "the fascination of using words in a way that would be effective."[3] A primary cause was literature itself, particularly American literature.

After moving to New York in 1918, Moore attended gatherings of writers and artists sensitive to the historic preoccupation Henry James had stated simply when he said that Nathaniel Hawthorne proved "to what a use American matter could be put by an American hand."[4] America's struggle for cultural independence following the Revolutionary War continued almost unabated throughout the nineteenth century, and it engaged the passions of Marianne Moore's generation. Because many of her contemporaries chose to live in England or Europe both before and after World War I, the issue was a pertinent one at that time as it had been for Hawthorne, Margaret Fuller, Ralph Waldo Emerson, and Edgar Allan Poe in the pre–Civil War period, or Walt Whitman, Mark Twain, and James in the middle and late decades of the nineteenth cen-

tury. Moore's essay, in 1934, on "Henry James as a Characteristic American" confirms her insistence that to be an American is not " 'just to glow belligerently with one's country,' " but to be " 'intrinsically and actively ample, . . . reaching westward, southward, anywhere, everywhere,' with a mind 'incapable of the shut door in any direction.' " "England," published in 1920, is Moore's first high-spirited expression of the amplitude that was for her an ideal toward which one aimed at the same time that the poem was a personal declaration of independence.

Open to the charms of England, Italy, Greece, France, and the Orient, the poem is nonetheless by an American hand. England, "with its baby rivers and little towns, each with its abbey or its cathedral, / with voices—one voice perhaps, echoing through the transept," is not "the mother country" or even "our old home" but, rather, small after the experience of "big" America; the language is no longer "our mother tongue" but still lovely as it echoes in quiet places, in ancient shrines and towns, to which the poet makes her pilgrimages and responds nostalgically. Or "the East with its snails, its emotional / shorthand and jade cockroaches, its rock crystal and its imperturbability, / all of museum quality" is not in a turmoil of change, is not inscrutable, but a civilization to which her response is aesthetic. The suspended syntax, punctuated by colons, that the poet chooses for the long lines in praise of admirable traditions anticipates a change of pace, of style, and of subject. The keen appreciation of a connoisseur of cultures is matched by the humorous exaggeration, the brio of one who enjoys saying the worst that can be said about America: "the wild man's land; grassless, linksless, language-less," a country "where there are no proof-readers, no

silkworms, no digressions," and "letters are written /
not in Spanish, not in Greek, not in Latin, not in shorthand, / but in plain American which dogs and cats can
read!" All that is missing is an "OK?" There are, instead, pert queries about continents of misapprehen-
sion or the dangers of the resemblance between
poisonous toadstools and mushrooms. (There are, by
inference, those who do not know the difference between a destroying angel and a jeweled puffball. Marianne Moore had, she said, "a burning desire to be
explicit," but wanted enough implication to satisfy
herself.)

"England" begins to circle to a conclusion by as-
serting tentatively, although loyally, that no conclusion may be drawn about certain American traits such
as "mettlesomeness which may be mistaken for appetite" and "heat which may appear to be haste." But
one big question:

> The sublimated wisdom of China, Egyptian discern-
>   ment,
> the cataclysmic torrent of emotion
> compressed in the verbs of the Hebrew language,
> the books of the man who is able to say,
> "I envy nobody but him, and him only,
> who catches more fish than
> I do"—the flower and fruit of all that noted
>   superiority—
> if not stumbled upon in America,
> must one imagine it is not there?

Then, "It has never been confined to one locality."
Although she does not raise her American voice—the
tone is light and teasing—the last words are unequivocal, without envy, and without apology. Open-minded
appreciation of other peoples, as well as respect for

the opinions and achievements of humankind argue persuasively, if cannily, for open-minded cognizance of the values of one's own indigenous experience. The poem is a grand tour de force. It anticipates, however, Moore's achievements as an original American writer ranked with Emily Dickinson, a valued predecessor, but distinguished from her by the fact that the twentieth-century poet was accorded recognition within her lifetime, long before she read "In the Public Garden" at the Boston Arts Festival of 1958.

Among Marianne Moore's compatriots who early recognized her work were T. S. Eliot in London, where he was publishing *Poems* in 1920, and Ezra Pound, whose "Hugh Selwyn Mauberly" was "a farewell to London" as he left for Paris in 1920, as well as William Carlos Williams blasting away from Rutherford, New Jersey, for "new vigors of artistic perception, invention, and expression in the United States." Williams would say, for instance, in 1921 that "Only by slow growth, consciously fostered to the point of enthusiasm, will American work of the quality of Marianne Moore's best poetry come to the fore of intelligent attention and the ignorance which has made America an artistic desert be somewhat dissipated."[5]

For America to become more civilized, Moore believed, would require "The Labors of Hercules" (1922). Moreover, if "the wild man's land" were to be cultivated, someone would have to popularize the mule, a hybrid creature, but one "expressing the principle of accommodation reduced to a minimum[.]" (She wrote, thirty-four years later, a psalm of beatitude for "the unaccommodating man" who, when affronted by "private lies and public shame," will not comply.) Although one might be stubborn as a mule, one would need to be, again, persuasive to accomplish

changes in the American mentality—"it is one thing to change one's mind / another to eradicate it," she quipped. For all her humor, "The Labors of Hercules" is a tirade, one long suspended sentence in which the tones become urgent. " 'Charming tadpole notes' / belong to the past when one had time to play them," "one detects creative power by its capacity to conquer detachment," yet the greatest labor is to teach what "one keeps on knowing / 'that the Negro is not brutal, / that the Jew is not greedy, / that the Oriental is not immoral, / that the German is not a Hun.' " Period. The poet, arguing from the old democratic regard for the individual and the equality of persons, attacks "the high priest of caste," whose "snobbishness is a stupidity, / the best side out, of age-old toadyism, / kissing the feet of the man above, / kicking the face of the man below," in language stronger than Walt Whitman ever used. Moore even shouts "we are sick of the earth, / sick of the pig-sty, wild geese and wild men[.]"

The impassioned poem is pertinent to a decade characterized by political corruption, lawlessness, and bigotry. The disintegration of Woodrow Wilson's presidency, the "return to normalcy," and the disillusionment with the vision of "a world safe for democracy" after the "war against the Huns" fed the distrust of the alien and foreign. "Pure" America was in danger of becoming as hybrid as the mule, so Congress, in 1921, adopted policies of rigid restriction on immigration. Hatred of nonconformism and liberalism took new and ominous forms, including the sinister revival of the Ku Klux Klan. Blacks, Jews, Chinese, Catholics, and recent immigrants were alike victims of the Klan as its membership spread throughout the country. Marianne Moore's was one unaccommodat-

ing protest against a resurgence of native know-
nothingism.

Use of the old phrase—"stubborn as a mule"—to
figure the stress of emotion in "The Labors of Hercules" points to Moore's serious play with another
kind of cliché in the question, "You believe man
sprung from monkeys?" reverberating through her
poem "The Monkey Puzzle," published in January,
1925. The poem is her response to the debates of the
early 1920s in the United States over the challenge of
the Darwinian theory of evolution and the origin of
the human species to Christian belief in the inerrancy
of the Bible and a literal interpretation of the account
of the creation of man in Genesis. Because Darwin's
important work, published in 1859, provided evidence
for natural selection of fortuitous variations of animals
and plants rather than evidence of purposive design
for life on earth, intellectuals and scientists with theo-
logical predilections, as well as writers and clergy in
the Victorian age, suffered a crisis of faith that neces-
sitated an inevitable revision of history and conceptions of existence. The issues have been argued by
die-hard Americans again and again during the twentieth century. In 1925, it seemed not merely that reason would not prevail but that fundamental Christians
were a grave threat to freedom of inquiry and free
institutions. The conservative views of the fundamen-
talists won legal sanction when the governor of
Tennessee signed, on March 13, 1925, an antievolu-
tion law, prohibiting the teaching in public schools
and universities of any theories that denied "the divine creation of man as taught in the Bible" and making it unlawful "to teach instead that man has
descended from a lower order of animals." The infa-
mous Scopes monkey trial, in which the court found

John Scopes, a biology teacher, guilty of violating the law, was held from July 10 to 21, 1925, at Dayton, Tennessee, where Moore's poem, "The Monkey Puzzle," would not have been understood.

As a student of biology and a devout Presbyterian, the poet understood the conflict between science and religion. The poem is a complicated crossword puzzle in which she reconciles what she knows with what she believes. The title refers both to the monkey in the evolutionary hypothesis and to the monkey puzzle tree, a tall Chilean pine. The conifer's design is intricate, with intertwined branches and needle-pointed leaves that cover its stiff branches in a tangled network that thwarts the monkeys and other animals attempting to climb the tree. (The scientific name for it, *Araucaria imbricata,* is cited in the poet's note to line 8, which begins "this pine-tree—"). It is for Marianne Moore a tree of life. It is, she says, "a true curio in this bypath of curio-collecting." The poet chooses three "curios"—a lemur, a Chinese art object, and the pine —for the ingenious reasoning from the particulars to the general conclusion that the poem exemplifies.

Nothing if not curious, Moore begins talking casually about one of the three specimens the collector of data will study: the ring-tailed lemur (for which the scientific name is *Lemur catta*) common to zoological gardens. Because the poet-scientist assumes that the reader knows that the arboreal lemur belongs to a lower order and the monkey to a higher order of primates, she speaks of the lemur as "A kind of monkey or pine-lemur / not of interest to the monkey[.]" No reason, then, for man, who belongs to the highest order of primates, to worry; he is more curious than the monkey. For the student of evolution, a lemur is as interesting as a monkey. The lemurs, she neglects

to mention, were forced to sanctuaries in Madagascar and adjacent islands by the related but superior monkeys, so why does the poet, who surely knows the facts, say that the ring-tail is "in a kind of Flaubert's Carthage"? The allusion is to the novel, *Salammbô*, whose characters represent a diversity of races and civilizations, set in ancient Carthage; despite Flaubert's research and efforts at verisimilitude, the book "was what one might call fancy-dress rather than true history."[6] (Although Colette said of it that "one can smell the lions," the "scene painting" probably resembles prehistoric Carthage as little as a zoo resembles the native habitat of animals.) But what an outrageous, educated, hilarious way to talk about a zoo! No wonder the lemur at which the poet wants to look more closely will not come out of the bamboo thicket. Never mind.

One gets at least a glimpse of *Lemur catta,* " 'this Paduan cat with lizard,' " this "tiger"—" 'An interwoven somewhat[.]' " The poet cites no sources for the phrases, but they suggest she has been reading about the subject of her study. The lemur's black tail ringed with white is like the almost black stripes of the tiger, largest of the cat family—"An interwoven somewhat." That's easy. But why Paduan? The lemur's fur, to use another cliché, is like silk, Padua soy, which by folk etymology (influenced by Padua) is derived from *pou de soy,* a variation of the French *pou de soi.* Historians of fabrics are not certain what kind of silk Padua soy was, but indications from paintings are that it was a rich heavy material "with a tabby ground and self-coloured patterns, also in a tabby weave."[7] No wonder Marianne Moore said she wrote poetry to please herself. Readers would have appreciated a note about the tabby material, although they may know about tabby

cats, and Padua soy is in dictionaries, which define it
by the French term in common use among American
women of the twenties. Oh, yes, the lemur eats lizards.
The poem itself really is "an interwoven somewhat"
that tempts impatient critics and readers to say "so
what?" Explanations of fine points as well as fanciful
puns are apt to be tedious, but the poem within the
poem is the care taken by natural historians, writers,
linguists, and even specialists in silks to recover a
sense of the past in view of much that is beyond their
resources or can only be glimpsed.

    The second curio, furthermore, tells the collector
of data more about itself than anything else. In contrast to the lemur, Foo dog is on display. Assertive, it
will not be overlooked or denied attention as an art
object. A kind of small playful lion, the popular Buddhist Foo is, the poet says, more than the pedestrian
"dog." Self-satisfied and witty—note the tail, by the
way—it has survived. If the recalcitrant lemur, however, is a long way from the Madagascar caves, complacent Foo has also been transported from one
country to another. The poet's mind moves too and is
looking ahead to a far superior curio, a pine-tree, a
pine-tiger, more ferocious than a lion, no China dog.
A magnificent conifer, a genuine work of art, evergreen as jade, stark, quilled, awesome—"but no one
takes it" from its natural environment, the gloomy
rain forest where "society's not knowing is colossal."
Standing for ages like the rock of Gibraltar in primeval
splendor, the impressive tree knows " 'it is better to be
lonely than unhappy.' "[8] Monkey puzzle that it is, it is
of great value. The poet does not say whether its value
is economic or scientific; she does not note its rare
value to the evolutionary biologists because it is one
variety of surviving conifers that together provide a

nearly unbroken record of the past. She observes, instead, that "One is at a loss, however, to know why it should be here" [in Chile][9] or "to account for its origin at all." Scientist or poet, inquisitive or ignorant, one realizes the limits of human knowledge when one ventures into the sacred wood.

The poem, like the tree, is perhaps too complicated, although again like the tree, the poem has " 'a certain proportion in the skeleton.' " The proportion is evident in (1) the lighthearted attitude toward the hindrances to human efforts at apprehending relationships between the past and the present, (2) appreciative acceptance of the discoveries attributable to that endeavor, and (3) acknowledgment of the magnitude of human unknowing. Modulations in the poet's voice —amused, casual, witty, serious, contemplative—express her pleasure and devoted interest in the mystery of the created world. The conclusion of "The Monkey Puzzle" is reminiscent of Whitman's "puzzle of puzzle of puzzles, / And that we call being. . . . (Round and round we go, all of us, . . .)" in "Song of Myself." Marianne Moore's reconciliation of the conflict between scientific fact and Christian faith is ultimately simple and poignant: "but we prove, we do not explain our birth."

II

"An Octopus" (1924) is one of the great American landscape poems, and it may seem quixotic or far-fetched to consider the work in relation to subjects of public controversy. "Only something like alchemy," John Ashberry has said, "could account" for it. "We start with an octopus, evoked with the customary

precision ('dots of cyclamen-red and maroon on its clearly defined pseudopodia'), but the creature seems to be a glacier or else the two are superimposed, for now we are in the landscape of sierras and fir trees, while the author continues tracking imperturbably among excerpts. . . . switching landscapes, language and levels with breathtaking abruptness, rising from botanical note-taking to pinpoint emblems of supernatural clarity that could be out of Shelley:

> the white volcano with no weather side;
> the lightning flashing at its base,
> rain falling in the valleys, and snow falling on the
>   peak—[10]

Indebted to the Romantic ode for the form of the poem, Moore begins with a description of the landscape, is spurred by the sight of it to move to insight, and in the end returns to a view of the landscape with renewed understanding of it. "An Octopus" is not, however, by a Romantic poet looking into nature to find her own image and finding it everywhere. The poem has been read as a voyage of discovery; it has also been suggested that the transcendent images of stillness and whiteness—"this fossil flower without a shiver," after all the richness of color and violent action—stand for eternity; or the mountainous fossil is the symbol of the art of nature and of the human capacity for art.[11]

"An Octopus" is, first of all, a figure for the spectacular lofty volcano and ice-carved canyons of Mount Rainier—which the poet identifies by the Indian name, Tacoma—in the state of Washington. A "map of Mount Rainier, showing the octopus pattern of its glaciers may be seen in the collection of Marianne Moore's papers at the Rosenbach Museum as may a

photograph" of her and her brother, John Warner Moore, during their ascent of the mountain on her visit to Bremerton, Washington, where he was stationed in 1920.[12] Much, but not all of the imagery, was stimulated by the outing on a remembered holiday.

The poem begins with the title "An Octopus" and continues

> of ice. Deceptively reserved and flat,
> it lies "in grandeur and in mass"
> beneath a sea of shifting snow-dunes;
>   . . . its clearly defined pseudo-podia
> made of glass that will bend—a much needed
>   invention—
> comprising twenty-eight ice fields from fifty to five
>   hundred feet thick,
> of unimagined delicacy.

The image is faithful to one of the poem's themes stated in the opening lines of the final passage: "Relentless accuracy is the nature of this octopus / with its capacity for fact." The massive, symmetrical, truncated summit of Mount Rainier, covered with ice and snow, is at the approximate center of the glaciers (twenty-eight in 1920, twenty-six by 1970) that cling to the flanks of the flat "dome" and radiate from it. The glaciers themselves, even though continuous with the summit ice, originate either in the summit névé or in cirques that are about four thousand feet below the top and are principally fed with the tremendous snows of winter, the wind sweepings, and the avalanches from the summit over fourteen thousand feet above sea level. "Imagining ourselves looking down from an airplane, we can think of it," Robert Sterling Yard wrote, "as an enormous frozen octopus sprawling upon the grass, for its curving arms of ice, reaching

out in all directions, penetrate" the dense forests which edge the flowering meadows that carry right up to the glaciers. Moore, without having noted his name, is indebted for the image to Yard's description of "Mount Rainier, Icy Octopus."[13]

Yard, who became executive secretary of the National Parks Association when it was founded in 1919, was one of a group of people—writers, academics, government officials, philanthropists, and private citizens—working to contravene the fact that "this glorious country was being rapidly marred." They saw that Americans, having for generations thought it necessary to fight against and conquer nature, have been infused not only with a spirit of exploration but also with a drive to tame and exploit the resources of a continental wilderness. In contrast to their energies and codes of conduct in the biotic community, the consequences of the enormous destructive power of humankind became a public issue at the beginning of the twentieth century. Mount Rainier National Park, for instance, was established by an act of Congress in 1899; the National Park Service, with the objective of protecting the scenic beauty and historic sites of the United States, was established by Congress in 1916; but appropriations for these important achievements were meager and insufficient.

From 1900 to 1920, the national parks were neglected; the conservation policy makers, at the height of their power, had no real interest in preserving nature at all costs. When cattlemen in the vicinity of Mount Rainier and other glacier parks demanded the right of pasturage on the alpine meadows, the popular view was that "wild posies," though beautiful, were hardly "as vital as mutton." The "aesthetic conservationists," who disagreed with the dominant utilitarian

conservationists and their arguments for efficiency in giant multipurpose development programs to take advantage of the natural resources, were accused of "sentimental nonsense."[14] Decades of hard political fighting have not yet resolved the conflicts between those interested in economic benefits, utilitarian conservation, ecology, and aesthetics. It was in 1921, however, that official interest in a "wilderness concept" was aroused to oppose increasing incursion into the national parks. Aldo Leopold, of the University of Wisconsin, is remembered as the first eloquent advocate of wilderness preservation; Yard was, nonetheless, the first of the idealists whose avid work for "appreciation of scenery" in the national parks reached large numbers of people. Marianne Moore must have been among them.

Yard, writing of the forests of the western slopes of the Pacific region, for example, uses figures such as "the court of King Sequoia," "here assembled in everlasting attendance, millions of his nobles. . . . Chief among the courtiers of the king is the sugar pine . . . largest and most magnificent of the Pacific pines, reaching sometimes 600 years of age. . . . Next in rank and scarcely less in majesty is the massive white fir. . . . The King of Trees is of royal lineage. The patient searchers in the rocks of old have traced his ancestry unknown millions of years. . . . His was Viking stock from Arctic Zones."[15] The poet, enthusiastic as she was about trees, could hardly help being amused by Yard's conceit, which she cuts back for the trace of humor when she describes how "The fir-trees in 'the magnitude of their root systems,' / rise aloof . . . , / austere specimens of our American royal families, / 'each like the shadow of the one beside it. / The rock seems frail compared with their dark energy of life

[.]' " (Even though Moore sometimes takes liberties with her snippets, she customarily gives credit for them; it is, perhaps, the mischievous pruning of Yard's figures that accounts for her not mentioning him in the company of John Muir and Ruskin, who also contribute to the cause of the poem.)

The accuracy with which Moore depicts what she saw as she climbed around in Mount Rainier park makes it possible for a reader who checks a guidebook to identify the trails she took. She lingers over the rock's "vermillion and onyx and manganese-blue exterior expensiveness, / left at the mercy of the weather," or under "the polite needles of the larches / 'hung to filter not to intercept the sunlight,'" or alongside the "dumps of gold and silver ore enclosing The Goat's Mirror" lake, "that lady-finger-like depression in the shape of the left human foot, / which prejudices you in favor of itself / . . . its indigo, pea-green, blue-green, and turquoise, / from a hundred to two hundred feet deep[.]"

She gives a sense of the topography, the myriad beauties, and the wildlife of the park. She lovingly names the animals: bears, elk, deer, wolves, ducks, and the exacting porcupine. She sights the " 'rat slipping along to its burrow in the swamp, / or pausing on high ground to smell the heather' "; the " 'thoughtful beavers / making drains which seem the work of careful men with shovels' "; and farther up, a "fragment" of the "terrible stalagmites," a goat, "its eye fixed on the waterfall which never seems to fall—" or a "special antelope" standing its ground "on cliffs the color of clouds, of petrified white vapor," a "crystal peak," "a mountain with those graceful lines which prove it a volcano[.]" She describes the mountain guide in worn-out trousers, the agile chipmunk, the water ou-

zel, the white-tailed ptarmigan, the buckwheat of the alpine meadows, and the eleven eagles of the west perched "on treacherous lava and pumice— / those unadjusted chimney-pots and cleavers[.]" One knows the height to which she has ascended as she notes the roar of water "winding slowly through the cliffs, / the road 'climbing like the thread / which forms the groove around a snail-shell, / doubling back and forth until where snow begins, it ends.' "

Remarking in a letter about the poem's length and "undesirable expansiveness" when she was at work on it, Moore said, "I am most impetuous and perilously summary in anything which is to me, so vital a matter."[16] Stopping to take bearings, the reader asks what beyond the poet's pleasure in the wilderness is "so vital a matter"? One considers the poem's first question: "What spot could have merits of equal importance" for the animals she names and describes? The porcupine, the rat, the beavers, the bears are on property "pre-empted by their ancestors." The goat stands "in stag-at-bay position," the antelope "stands its ground." The eagles are "used to the unegoistic action of the glaciers." "No 'deliberate wide-eyed wistfulness' is here[.]" The marmot is "the victim . . . of a 'struggle between curiosity and caution,' / inquiring what has scared it[.]" Sentimental nonsense? Endangered species?

The marmot, Moore observes with deceptive casualness, may have been scared by the Indian ponies, the first domesticated animals on the scene. She recognizes them as calico, or spotted, even though they are "hard to discern among the birch-trees, ferns, and lily-pads, / avalanche lilies, Indian paint-brushes, / bears' ears and kittentails, / and miniature cavalcades of chlorophylless fungi / magnified in profile on the

moss-beds like moonstones in water[.]" The cavalcade of ponies, she says, competes "with the original American menagerie of styles" and has been instructed—"none knows how"—"by business men who require for recreation / three hundred and sixty-five holidays in the year."

The poet, probably worried that the poem was too heavy with minutiae, excised thirty-two lines when she edited her work for *Collected Poems* (1951). Among the lines are those remarking that "this treacherous glass mountain" is "inimical to 'bristling, puny, swearing men / equipped with saws and axes.' " As hostile as the frozen cliffs and wooded heights are, there are still men who will be hostile in their attack on them. Marianne Moore was troubled by the encroachment of "puny men" in that extraordinary wilderness. This is a "vital matter." The knowledge that Big Snow Mountain is distinguished "by a beauty / of which 'the visitor dare never fully speak at home / for fear of being thought an imposter' " collides, moreover, with the awareness that any human presence is threatening to the natural beauty there. She herself enjoyed the holiday but had made a rash intrusion into that pristine world. One returns to the passage describing the antelope, "acclimated to 'grottoes from which issue penetrating draughts / which make you wonder why you came.' " Is the doubt more than a response to the cold? And what business have businessmen—"totemic scenery" that they are—in that park three hundred and sixty-five days a year? Yet they, too, may need to contemplate the "unegocentric action of the glaciers" —at least now and again.

There is, in the final versions of the poem, an abrupt break almost immediately after the sly humor at the expense of the businessmen and their "con-

spicuously spotted little horses." They are emblematic
—the poet's word is "totemic"—of a new subject: the
insight spurred by the pleasure in "beholding" the
"incredible" variety of natural life in a landscape like
that of which John Locke must have been thinking
when he said, "In the beginning, all the world was
America." Marianne Moore's vision of the radiance of
that world is disturbed by the children of Adam. Hers
is the "problem of an aesthetic conservationist" in the
public garden.

The change of subject provokes a change of style:

> "Like happy souls in Hell," enjoying mental
>   difficulties,
> the grasshoppers of Greece
> amused themselves with delicate behavior
> because it was "so noble and so fair";
> not practiced in adapting their intelligence
> to eagle-traps and snow-shoes,
> to alpenstocks and other toys contrived by those
> "alive to the advantage of invigorating pleasures."[17]

The Greeks, lively as grasshoppers, serve as a measure
by which the poet will ridicule in quick time American
laxity and excess. Resolving "with benevolent conclu-
siveness, / 'complexities which still will be complexities / as long as the world lasts,' " the poets and
philosophers of Greece believed in the reality of "a
spiritual substance or the soul itself." Although they
distrusted what was back of what could not be clearly
seen, and although the essence of the soul was hidden,
they thought it was manifest and phenomenally visible
in human actions, attitudes, habits, and power, a
power which the poet says Adam had and of which "we
are still devoid." But, the poem implies, that was in
another country, and besides, the Greeks are dead—

happily in Hell. What about Adam? Oh, he sinned—
long ago and far away; Americans, adaptable and vigorous, are new people in a new country where the
resources and beauty stimulate the moral character.
No need for the restraint to which the Greek soul had
been persuaded; remember Henry James, " 'damned
by the public for decorum'; / not decorum, but restraint[.]" Another example of "sacrosanct remote-
ness," like Mount Tacoma itself! We need roads and
parking lots; we've got the other equipment.

Back of the poet's mimicry are the platitudes
about the influence of God's Nature sonorously in-
voked to argue for the use of the parks. Those Greeks?
"Emotionally sensitive," yes; "their hearts," however,
"were hard." (Read the objection: Those delicate
Greeks—they were sentimentalists; they even owned
slaves.[18] This is a free country of free men.) Then the
restrained irony turns around once again. The remote
wisdom of the Greeks is not required by citizens who
can read "these odd oracles of cool official sarcasm /
upon this game preserve / where 'guns, nets, seines,
traps and explosives, / hired vehicles, gambling and
intoxicants are prohibited[.]' " It is, of course, "the
love of doing hard things" that has worn the public
out and made it necessary for people to be told, like
children, that they must do as they are told if they
would conquer Mount Tacoma. That is self-evident.
Back of the Swiftian satire was the indifference of a
nation, and its Congress, to the need for more than a
manual of regulations if the parks were to be preserved. Not the least of the difficulties in the struggle
was the lack of self-discipline among both the "attend-
ants," or guides, and the "visitors," or intruders in the
public domain. So much, then, for this landscape of
the American soul. After all of the poet's excessive

attention to the beauty of the place, the Romantic ode has deteriorated to a paltry criticism of the behavior of free men, "out of sympathy with neatness." Must be a woman writing.

But the poet, who prefers neatness of finish, hard as it is, appreciates vigor at the same time that she stands valiantly in awe of it. She finishes the ode with a music of the planet earth, the cadences of the explosive action of the almost forgotten, deceptively reserved octopus:

> "Creeping slowly as with meditated stealth,
> its arms seeming to approach from all directions,"
> it receives one under winds that "tear the snow to
> bits
> and hurl it like a sandblast
> shearing off twigs and loose bark from the trees."
> Is "tree" the word for these things
> "Flat on the ground like vines"?
> some "bent in a half circle with branches on one
> side
> suggesting dust-brushes, not trees;
> some finding strength in union, forming little
> stunted groves,
> their flattened mats of branches shrunk in trying to
> escape"
> from the hard mountain "planed by ice and polished
> by the wind"—
> the white volcano with no weather side;
> the lightning flashing as its base,
> rain falling in the valleys, and snow falling
> on the peak—
> the glassy octopus symmetrically pointed,
> its claw cut by the avalanche
> "with a sound like the crack of a rifle,
> in a curtain of powdered snow launched like a
> waterfall."

The heightened consciousness and gusto with which
the poet receives the austere vision are underscored
by the witty image of noble trees reduced to a cleaning
woman's ineffectual "dust-brushes." And since
Moore's is a moral intelligence, her exactitude and
controlled intensity are a modest but appropriate
confirmation of the grandeur, majesty, and indomita-
ble reality of Big Snow Mountain. The poem, after all,
is a landscape of the soul, and it leaves no doubt that
humankind is at the mercy of the fatal, sovereign
power of nature. Back of Marianne Moore's knowledge of that power is an Old Testament voice: "Then
the Lord answered Job out of the whirlwind, and said,
Who *is* this that darkeneth counsel by words without
knowledge? . . . Hast thou entered into the treasures
of the snow? . . . Out of whose womb came the ice?"[19]

III

The authority of the poet who had written "An Octopus" returned with new restraints in the verse she
published after an interim of several years. Having
since 1920 contributed "England," "The Labors of
Hercules," "The Monkey Puzzle," "An Octopus," and
other poems as well as reviews to *The Dial,* Moore was
asked to take the job of acting editor in the summer
of 1925. She became editor the next year and continued to write reviews, but the work left no time for
writing poetry. The magazine ceased publication in
July of 1929, just before the stock market collapsed.
The poet's issues changed as the Depression and the
human suffering that it brought became increasingly
severe in the early thirties.

Since a third of all personal income had gone to

5 percent of the population during the decade of the twenties, the inequalities in the possession of goods hardly prepared the nation for the steadily worsening crisis. By 1933, one American out of four was unemployed, and many workers could hardly maintain a bare subsistence for their families; a high percentage of businesses went into bankruptcy; a quarter of the country's farmers lost their land; crops were burned and cattle slaughtered to reduce food supplies and increase prices at the same time that there were thousands of people hungry on the public roads and city streets. The events stimulated a resurgence of fiction by writers who were primarily social realists or literary naturalists; there was a dearth of poetry. As Wallace Stevens wrote in "A Fading of the Sun" (1933), "Who can think of the sun costuming clouds / When all the people are shaken / Or of night endazzled, proud / When people awaken / And cry and cry for help?" Or Dylan Thomas: "I see the boys of summer in their ruin" (1934).

Moore herself must have considered writing fiction, but three poems under the collective title "Part of a Novel, Part of a Play, and Part of a Poem" (1932) constitute the extent of this inclination. Attention to the topical, experience in the acute rendering of actualities without idealizing the world around her, and courage in speaking out on substantive issues, however, had prepared her to write poetry in a period rather uncongenial to any serious literature but that with a sense of the historical moment.

One wonders whether or not it was the poems exemplifying the extreme conditions of the period that stimulated Moore's rejection of her famous definition of poetry as " 'imaginary gardens with real toads in them' " ("Poetry" [1921]). It did not, of

course, pertain to any of the poems in the public garden. The success that the definition has enjoyed seems
ironic after one has recovered from the shock of
Moore's later decision to cut it away, along with almost
all of "Poetry" itself. Although she has often been
thought capricious for having pruned the flourishing
metaphor, the "gardens" the poems transfigure are
equally as "real" and as "unreal" as the critters in
them. Imaginative metamorphosis of the pressures of
reality in her poems, therefore, may explain her willingness to sacrifice the misleading phrase. Both "The
Jerboa" (1932) and "Camellia Sabina" (1933) are
written for a disturbed society and in support of people crying for help.

"The Jerboa" is a finely wrought poem in two
parts, the first of which is entitled "Too Much." Fif-
teen of the seventeen stanzas of "Too Much" are devoted to detailed observations of the conspicuous
consumption of the Pompeys, the Popes, the Pha-
raohs, Princes, Queens, and royal households. Conspicuous consumption always raises matters of taste,
the commission of art works, and the freedom of the
artist. So a primary subject of this Depression poem is
art.

Moore begins by talking about a huge bronze
sculpture. "A Roman [not an American, surely] had
an / artist, a freedman, / contrive a cone / . . . with
holes for a fountain. Placed on / the Prison of St.
Angelo, this cone / . . . passed for art." If the rich have
bad taste, they have the money to prove it and display
it. In case one missed the point, the cone "looks like
a work of art made to give / to a Pompey. . . ." To
obtain favor or express gratitude or pay tribute? "Others could / build, and understood / making colossi
and / how to use slaves[.]" Architectural monuments

express the dynamics of economic power. But the cunning with which the powerful command exotic goods and the servitude of labor is obvious in the mock regard the poet gives to the possession by the privileged of whatever runs, swims, flies, or grows on earth. "They [baronial Americans?] had their men"; "They looked on as theirs . . ."; "and there were gardens . . . / combining planes, dates, limes, and pomegranates, / in avenues—with square / pools of pink flowers, tame fish, and small frogs." The scene and the extravagant life lived in it, however, are not without their beauty: "It was a picture with a fine distance[.]" Or "Dwarfs here and there, lent / to an evident poetry of frog grays, / duck-egg greens, and eggplant blues, a fantasy / and a verisimilitude that were / right to those with, everywhere, / power over the poor." Yes, there was time for poetry, too. One does not need to know that dwarfs were traditionally court jesters (fools), or wonder whether the fantasy might have been "escapist," or ask if the verisimilitude was appreciated for its truth or not. The dwarfs knew how to please; the patrons knew what they liked, and it could hardly be social realism.

Moore's documentary of the ancient world, with its implication of parallels to the United States, is reminiscent of allusions to the Roman empire by critics of the American republic during the thirties. If one required a vista from which to contemplate extravagant wealth, exploitation, and a slave economy, the poet knew the value of a picture with "a fine distance." There was Gibbon's study of the rise, decline, and fall of the empire at hand for the historical perspective.[20]

Suddenly, there is a change in point of view, which, as Moore would say, "is not inadvertent." She shifts, in stanza 12, from talking about the privileged

"them" to direct address: "The bees' food is your /
food." Your food? Whose food? No answer. She returns immediately to the perspective of the observer:
"Those who tended flower- / beds and stables were
like the king's cane / in the form of a hand, or the
folding bedroom / made for his mother of whom /
he was fond." (The names of the king and queen
are relegated to the notes for the poem.) "They"—
nameless—"made / basalt serpents and portraits of
beetles; the / king gave his name to them and he was
named / for them. He feared snakes, and tamed /
Pharaoh's rat. . . ." Moore identifies it as the rust-back
mongoose, and observes that no bust was made of it,
"but there / was pleasure for the rat. / Its restlessness
was / its excellence; it was praised for its wit. . . ."
Then, at last, the jerboa slips into the poem and will
not be denied. While there is no change in stanzaic
form and only slight variation in the syllabic count, the
movement becomes more straightforward:

> a small desert rat,
> and not famous, that
>   lives without water, has
>   happiness. Abroad seeking food, or at home
>   in its burrow, the Sahara field-mouse
>   has a shining silver house
>
> of sand. O rest and
> joy, the boundless sand,
>   the stupendous sand-spout,
>   no water, no palm trees, no ivory bed,
>   tiny cactus; but one would not be he
>   who has nothing but plenty.

The economy of language, the negatives, and the ironic understatement of these stanzas are fine counters to

"nothing but plenty," which has received copious attention for so long, perhaps too long, in the poem.

Noting the "obsession with luxury" in "Too Much," readers have been divided, seeing the emphasis on the vulgar display of wealth, or on the devoted craftsmanship. There is in the poet herself a tension between self-denial as spiritual discipline and the love of beautiful things, which, as Jean Dutourd observed, "doesn't mean one has a beautiful soul but that one has a taste for luxury."[21] The conflict is subsumed in "The Jerboa." The second part of the poem is titled "Abundance," and in it the poet's sympathies for the jerboa are further quickened.

The "desert rat" Moore describes is the common Egyptian or African jerboa (which she had observed at the American Museum of Natural History). Knowledge of the genera is pertinent to the initial lines of "Abundance": "Africanus meant / the conqueror sent / from Rome. It should mean the / untouched: the sand-brown jumping rat—free; / and the blacks. . . ." Becoming more openly didactic, the poet uses "Africanus" to connect the extremes and the inferences that abound within the extremes of "The Jerboa." The Romans, for example, even took possession of the word "Africanus." It was given in honor to Scipio, who turned the verdict of history toward Rome by defeating Hannibal in 202 B.C. and granting comparatively lenient terms to Carthage; thereafter, Scipio's adoptive grandson, a philosophical Stoic, destroyed the city, enslaved the survivors, established the province of Africa, and also assumed the name of Africanus. The poet, however, prefers the word's unsullied meaning, by which she draws a quick moral from the analogy between the jerboa and blacks: "that choice race with an elegance / ignored by one's igno-

rance." If the jerboa, as W. H. Auden has said, is "the emblem of true freedom," what of the blacks? Moore refrains from talking about what everyone should know—the consequences of the historical denial of true freedom to them by both pre-Christian and post-Christian societies in periods of expansion or rapacity.

After the judgment against Rome and America, Moore recalls the Biblical story of Jacob's ladder. As Jacob slept on a pillow of stones in the desert, he dreamed of beholding a ladder that reached from earth to heaven and of receiving a promise that all the families of the earth would be blessed.[22] Moore writes: "Part terrestrial, / and part celestial, / Jacob saw . . . steps of air and air angels; his / friends were the stones. The translucent mistake / of the desert does not make / hardship. . . ." She will say by contrast, later in the poem, "Course / the jerboa, or plunder its food store, / and you will be cursed." You must be warned: a people whose food has been plundered are not free. Although Marianne Moore was not a Marxist, she understood the tenet that freedom is the recognition of economic necessity. In a dire time, abundance is not affluence, abundance is enough.

The complexities of the poem, however, are not resolved by the obvious satirical contrast between "all those things" in "Too Much" and sanguine acceptance of a minimal existence. They are resolved by acknowledgment of the seductiveness of money and privilege, its costs to the human spirit, and the risks one runs in the effort to survive if one is as vulnerable as a jerboa. The strains of hunger are clear in what has been read as a dance of self-sufficiency and an acceptance of the conditions of "ordinary life." The jerboa

  honors the sand by assuming its color;

> closed upper paws seeming one with the fur
> in its flight from a danger.
>
> By fifths and sevenths,
> in leaps of two lengths,
>   like the uneven notes
>   of the Bedouin flute, it stops its gleaning
>   on little wheel castors, and makes fern-seed
>   foot-prints with kangaroo speed.
>
> Its leaps should be set
> to the flageolet. . . .

Praised for its precisely patterned movement, the skill in its rhythms, and the subtleties of its rhymes, the poem is also justly celebrated for the fact that the jerboa is a creature living from its own center of being. Like all common creatures, it should—the word is the poet's—be not only untouched, secure, free from want but also the subject of art and the source of music, albeit a desert music, haunting, solitary, delicate, melodic, and clear: part terrestrial and part celestial.

When Moore arranged the *Selected Poems* (1935), she chose to place "Camellia Sabina" immediately after "The Jerboa." The two share the poet's affection for mice—common jerboa, wild mouse, woodland rat, meadow mouse—and her pertinent criticism of society in a period of economic injustice. "Camellia Sabina" has not, however, been as well received as "The Jerboa," which is richer thematically and visually. The "compensatory" humor of "Sabina born under glass" has been interpreted as if it were the enigmatic verse of a hot-house gardener; but the poem has also seemed too straight-laced to readers who, in a time of plenty, have taken it to be a criticism of the taste for

vintage wines. It could as easily be read as a vegetari-
an's cookbook.

Although the image of the camellia is responsible
for the title, the images of food are pervasive: the
plum, juice of a cucumber, a meal broiled on vine
shoots, a mushroom, "the sliver from a beet root
carved into a rose," "wild parsnip- or sunflower- or /
morning-glory-seed, with an occasional / grape"—"a
food grape." And meat? Perhaps a little "blackthorn
pigeon's-blood" or "a flurry / of eels, scallops, serpents, / and other shadows[.]" One reaches for a comparison. The only one that comes to mind is "No
Possom, No Sop, No Taters" (1943), in which Wallace
Stevens writes of a hard time: "It is here, in this bad,
that we reach / The last purity of the knowledge of
good." During the harvest season of 1932, a thousand
Iowa farmers had picketed the roads to prevent deliv-
ery of grains, milk, and animals at prices that did not
pay for their production; mills and factories were
closed across the country; thousands of veterans
marched on Washington to demand immediate pay-
ment of bonuses for war-time service, and the Army
dispersed with tear gas the men who refused to go
home when Congress failed to act. The winter was
grim and desolate. A poet could not be oblivious to
the fear.

"I have been finishing a poem on the camellia and
the prune," Moore wrote to her brother (February 6,
1933). "Sounds something like Will Rogers but it is
serious."[23] All Rogers knew was just what he read in
the papers: "The Senate," he said, "passed a bill ap-
propriating $15 million for food, but the House of
Representatives has not approved it. They must think
it would encourage hunger." It is possible that people

who were still reading poetry in 1933 were not baffled at all by "Camellia Sabina."

The poet's free associations are neatly packaged in two sections of three stanzas each. Moore initially describes in droll tones the plum "from Marmade (France) in parenthesis" and the glass jar handmade for it. Fancy preserves? No, a "graft-grown briar-black bloom / on blackthorn pigeon's-blood"—but the curiosity is really the jar, unevenly blown, with a bubble that is green when held up to the light, and a screw top "sealed with foil" like Certosa. If one is persnickety, the reference is to the Certosino liqueur, green or yellow in pale reflection of the original Grande Chartreuse. (Certosino was a distillation of 130 herbs gathered in the mountains of Dauphiné by Certosa monks who added to the brew "carnations, absinthium, and the young buds of pine trees.") But anyone who has to say "Marmade (France) in parenthesis" would not know the difference between a prune and a pedantic gourmet. And French cuisine? What's that again? What do they eat in France? Well, the "French are a cruel race"; they not only seal flowers up in glass jars, they even "squeeze the diner's cucumber or broil a / meal on vine-shoots." Wait, though, till you see the "camellia-house"! If the poem sounds something like Will Rogers, he would add "it says here" that you have to " 'Dry the windows with a cloth fastened to a staff.' " The directions specify that " 'there must be / no smoke from the stove, or dew on / the windows, lest the plants ail. . . .' " What's the point? "A scentless nosegay"—the poem begins to sound like an advertisement—"is thus formed in the midst of the bouquet" from millions of red and white wines "which Bordeaux merchants / and lawyers 'have spent a great deal of / trouble' to select[.]" The plum blossom and

the camellia were "preposterous," but the enormous quantities of wine—eighty-four million bottles, or was it casks?—stagger the imagination. Why not go to France for the harvest festival? With the brief "logic" of a daydreamer diverted from what is troubling the mind, the poem allows the real preoccupation to surface: "A / food grape, however, . . . / is true ground for the grape-holiday." One is not surprised; even the pale stripe of the camellia itself looked as if it were a sliver of beet-root laid on a mushroom. Flowers, wine, whatsoever momentarily claims the attention, food is the basic necessity, and there is no way of going without it. The subject at the true center of the poem itself is, in plain American, vittles.

Food is not only the terminal subject of the first part of the poem but also the unadorned subject opening the second section: "The food of a wild / mouse in some countries is wild parsnip- or sunflower- or / morning-glory-seed, with an occasional / grape." The tone of the poem has changed; the voice has grown smaller, drier. The imagery veers toward the pathetic, then regains a precarious poise in the lyrical whim: "Underneath the vines of the Bolzano / grape of Italy, the Prince of Tails / might stroll." If plums can become prunes, why not a little magic for the mouse? A fairy-tale mouse, a nursery rhyme Prince of Tails? He might sail to Italy, where he could stroll in the vineyards of Bolzano and eat his fill of grapes. Obviously mice like grapes. "Does yonder mouse with a / grape in its hand and its child / in its mouth, not portray / the Spanish fleece suspended by the neck?" (The insignia for the Order of the Golden Fleece, the principal order of knighthood in Spain, consists of a gold collar formed of double links, entwined with stone, surrounded by flames with azure enamel and

rays of heraldic red; a lambskin, decorated in gold and bound in the middle, hangs from the collar.) "Yonder mouse"—"child in mouth" because that is the way the young are carried (the mouse is no cannibal)— scrounging for food and running, on three feet, to safety, is no less fitting an emblem than the sacrificial lamb of Christ for chivalric honors. It might seem wanton sacrilege only to Christians who are indifferent to hunger; or worse, "preposterous" to the cynical —the poet admits in a note, doesn't she, that the mouse was a wood rat? Besides, she saw it in a picture in a magazine. ("Sounds something like Will Rogers but it is serious.") Then the grammatical poser—ambiguous pronouns—and the surreality of hallucination or mirage:

> In that well-piled
>
>> larder above your
>> head, the picture of what you will eat is
>> looked at from the end of the avenue. The wire cage
>>> is
>> locked. . . .

The revery, the nightmare is tantalizing:

>> . . . but by bending down and studying the
>> roof [of the cage], it is possible to see the
>> pantomime of Persian thought: the
>>> gilded, too tight undemure
>>> coat of gems unruined
>>> by the rain—each small pebble of jade that
>>>> refused to mature,
>>> plucked delicately
>> off. Off jewelry not meant to keep Tom
>> Thumb, the cavalry cadet, on his Italian upland
>> meadow mouse, from looking at the grapes beneath
>> the interrupted light from them. . . .

The grapes are too beautiful, too good to eat.
They are not for you, whoever you are. That pan-
tomime was a conspicuous waste of time. Fairy tales,
circuses, action are more to one's liking. Remember
Tom Thumb? Which one? Sir Tom Thumb, a poor
boy who became, according to one tale, a knight in
King Arthur's court—"a mouse for a horse he used to
ride"—or the real one, discovered when he was five
and called Tom Thumb by P. T. Barnum, who made
the midget a rich and famous star of the big top?
(Quadrilles and polkas were named for Tom; among
the two million women he claimed to have kissed were
the queens of England, Spain, France, and Belgium; a
restaurant was named for him in Paris; Louis Philippe
presented him with a diamond-set emerald stickpin.
The great Thumb, two feet, eleven inches tall, even
owned a dazzling yacht, a stable of fancy horses, car-
riages, and a mansion, with Lilliputian furniture, in
Connecticut. He had presented his wife diamonds and
jewels valued at $10,000. When the wedding took
place in the vaulted Gothic Grace Church on Broad-
way, police barely managed to contain the crowd.
President and Mrs. Lincoln could not attend, but they
sent presents, as did the Astors, the Vanderbilts, the
Belmonts, and the Livingstons. Barnum understood
the public's need for distractions in a time of disaster
—the Civil War—and the wedding pushed all news of
the conflict off the front pages of the papers. Barnum
promoted Thumb to the rank of honorary general; he
wore the regalia and sang "Yankee Doodle Dandy."
After his death, Mrs. Thumb eventually married an
Italian count.) Remember when Tom was a "cavalry
cadet, on his Italian upland / meadow mouse"? The
"jewelry" was not meant to keep him from "looking at
the grapes beneath / the interrupted light from them"

as he dashed around the circus rings. (He had Yankee spunk. Sensational. American ingenuity far surpasses the French.)

"The wine cellar? No, / it accomplishes nothing and makes the / soul heavy. The gleaning is more than the vintage. . . ." There, one also remembers, is that word again: The jerboa stopped "its gleanings" in the flight from danger. Is this ridiculous poet never going to stop making allusions? She could not possibly be thinking of Jean François Millet's famous picture of "The Gleaners" (1857)—those peasants stooped over to pick up leavings of grain after the reapers; she is obsessed with mice and grapes. An ascetic, too, she did not drink wine, although she was known to nibble cheese and serve sherry to guests. For fussbudgets, however, it is the wine cellar, not the wine, that makes the soul heavy. The poet mentions as a matter of record that the history of the vineyard and of wine places a *mirabelle,* a yellow variety of plum, "in the *bibliothèque unique depuis* seventeen-ninety-seven." Useless information except for the fact that the plum makes a sweet dessert wine. Camellias are indigestible.

William Carlos Williams comes right to the point in the poem "To a Poor Old Woman" (1934): "Comforted / a solace of ripe plums / seeming to fill the air / They taste good to her[.]" Moore should also say what she has to say. She does: "(Close the window, says the Abbé Berlèse [author of a monograph on the camellia], for Sabina born under glass.)" It might get cold? Putting the advice in parenthesis, the poet neglects to say that people in the thirties were cold as well as hungry. That also goes without saying. The poem ends with its only extravagance: "O generous Bolzano!" O to be in Italy and eat grapes now that the

Depression's here. Such is the recreation of despair in a time of poverty and want.

As E. B. White has said of the evasiveness and fragility of the humorist—struggling along with good will, enduring pain, laughing instead of crying—"beneath the sparkling surface, flows the strong current of human woe."[24] Having once called the view that all truth should be dark "a dismal fallacy" ("In the Days of Prismatic Color" [1919]), Moore never surrendered to despair or melancholy in the verse of the early thirties. The poem suggesting "Part of a Novel" is "The Steeple-Jack" (1932), which has the visual clarity of an etching and the ambience of an old-fashioned genre painting. In it, Moore describes the "tame excitement" of life on a summer day in a New England fishing town. "It is," she writes, "a pleasure to see so much confusion" when the "whirlwind fire-and-drum" of a storm "bends the salt / marsh grass, disturbs stars in the sky and the / star on the steeple." The town "would be a fit haven for / waifs, children, animals, prisoners, / and presidents who have repaid / sin-driven / senators by not thinking about them." It is a town where people immediately set about straightening up and repairing the damage after the storm:

> a man in scarlet lets
>   down a rope as a spider spins a thread;
>   . . . but on the sidewalk a
>   sign says C. J. Poole, Steeple-Jack,
>   in black and white; and one in red
>   and white says
>
>   Danger. . . .
>
>   It could not be dangerous to be living

in a town like this, of simple people,
who have a steeple-jack placing danger-signs by the
church
while he is gilding the solid-
pointed star, which on a steeple
stands for hope.

There is, Jean Garrigue felt, "in this local setting en-
deared the gusto of a very idiomatic, very home-grown
paradise, the only paradise that some of us can believe
in, the one that's found, when it is found, on earth,
when 'there is nothing ambition can buy or take
away.' "[25] If the poem seems like a picture postcard
from a quiet, clean little place on the seacoast where
one could go for a week's vacation in invigorating air,
and if "hope," the point of the poem, seems trite, as
it does to many recent college students who wouldn't
want to live there, it can be read with a companion
poem, "The Hero" (1932), suggesting "Part of a
Play." There Moore reminds her readers of Pilgrim,
"having to go slow / . . . tired but hopeful— / hope
not being hope / until all ground for hope / has vanished. . . ." She is no banal optimist. Nor did she balk
at hazards. The remarkable range of forms, from those
like "Camellia Sabina" rejected as puzzles to those like
"The Steeple-Jack" rejected as direct and accessible
commonplaces, challenges easy generalization. Believing as a Calvinist in mortal sin and weakness, she
sometimes covered that belief, as did Mark Twain
when he said that "every man is a moon and has his
dark side which he never shows to anybody." While
she did not, like Twain, grow blatantly pessimistic and
bitter about the human race, she was scarcely immune
to the need to restrain her rancor. She learned, however, to be subtle and tempered in her critical images
of human fallibility. She writes in "The Hero":

Where the ground is sour; where there are
    weeds of beanstalk height,
    snakes' hypodermic teeth, or
    the wind brings the "scarebabe voice"
    from the neglected yew set with
    the semi-precious cat's eyes of the owl—
awake, asleep, "raised ears extended to fine points,"
                                    and so
on—love won't grow.

Moore is no scarebaby, given to the bravado of a
small child saying "I dare you" when a companion has
hardly less nerve than the one who risks the taunt.
Moore's hero "shrinks / as what it is flies out on
muffled wings, with twin yellow / eyes—to and fro— /
with quavering water-whistle note, low, / high, in bas-
so-falsetto chirps / until the skin creeps." Neither
hope nor courage, neither heroism nor love are words
she is embarrassed to use. A willingness to place these
common abstractions, so often shunned by the modern writer, in familiar settings is a sign of an urgency
to cope with malignant motives that threaten the substance of life itself. Moore must renew the meaning of
these often hollow and ineffective abstractions. For
her, they become simplicities beyond complexities;
they speak of integrities; and they have spiritual resonance. If they give a slight transcendence to the poems, that is because they are grounded in "a sense of
human dignity and reverence for mystery" which she
appreciates in the decorous, frock-coated Negro
"standing like the shadow / of the willow" beside the
tomb of "Gen-ral Washington and his lady" in "The
Hero." The funereal yew is not to be neglected; nor
are the ironies of the image of a black caretaker at the
shrine of a national hero and his wife, who once owned
slaves. The poet turns, as she did in "The Jerboa," to

the Old Testament: "Moses would not be grandson to Pharaoh." One hears between the lines the strong echoes of voices singing "Go down Moses, way down in Egypt land. Tell ole Pharaoh to let my people go." Then Moore: "It is not what I eat that is / my natural meat, / the hero says. / He is not out / seeing a sight but the rock / crystal thing to see . . . / brimming with inner light. . . ." As Elizabeth Bishop wrote in "Invitation to Marianne Moore" (1948): "With dynasties of negative constructions / darkening and dying around you, / with grammar that suddenly turns and shines / like flocks of sandpipers flying, please come flying."

IV

The nineteen-thirties, characterized by Auden in "September 1, 1939" as "a low dishonest decade," saw the collapse of democracies and the rise of totalitarianism subsequent to the political and social conflicts of economic depression in Europe. September 1, 1939, was the day Germany invaded Poland and World War II began. In June 1940, the German army moved across France, rapidly overcame French resistance, and seized Paris. Thus began four years of Nazi occupation, the acceptance of fascism by the radical right, and collaboration by the Vichy government, for which Marshal Philippe Pétain was chief of state in France. Moore's "Light Is Speech" (1941) is a tribute to the French people, whose historical ideals have been freedom, enlightenment, reason, and resoluteness of language to sustain them.

"One can say more of sunlight / than of speech; but speech / and light, each aiding each—when French / —have not disgraced that still / unextirpated

adjective," the poet writes. Although, as Auden said ("In Memory of W. B. Yeats" [1940]), "poetry makes nothing happen," it is a "way of happening, a mouth," in a time of "intellectual disgrace." Light and speech, Moore believes, can aid a people disgraced but not destroyed completely if the habits of mind and the intellectual heritage of France are still honored. The poem also associates the French traditions with English and American ideals: "Ironic points of light / Flash out," Auden noted in the September poem, "wherever the Just / Exchange messages."

The points of light recall the determination that "the lights must never go out," frequently repeated during both World War I and World War II. Viscount Grey of Fallodon, British Foreign Secretary, was reported to have said in 1914, "The Lamps are going out all over Europe; we shall not see them lit again in our lifetime," but the refutation became the cliché that was remembered. Moore's poem assumes common knowledge of the slogan, and enlarges it by attention to the power of light itself.

It is, of course, not possible to say what light is, since it is essentially more primitive than any of the terms that might be used to explain it; the nature of light is described either by mathematical forms or by enumerating its properties as well as proposing analogies and models. The poet, therefore, writes: "Free frank / impartial sunlight, moonlight, / starlight, light-house light, / are language." Having spoken of its qualities, she then makes an analogy: light is speech. Model number one is the Creech'h d'Ouessant light-house, the first visible to ships and planes approaching the European continent from North America. The aeromaritime lighthouse on its defenseless dot of rock off the coast of France is, according to the poem, in

direct line of descent from Voltaire, Montaigne, and Emile Littré, three great masters of language who are also models of light. These men occupy the center of the poem; Moore's admiration for their character and wisdom is central to themes of the verse. Voltaire, having vindicated a man wrongly accused of murdering a son, represents flaming justice. Montaigne, captured and then released by bandits, "was told" that he owed his deliverance to the balanced way he behaved and spoke (he "was too good a fellow to hold up"). He "lit remorse's saving / spark." Littré, whose dictionary of the French language is one of the outstanding lexicographic accomplishments of all time and required almost thirty years of work, and whose translation of Hippocrates' writings was so important to the history of medicine, stands for determination and ardor as well as love of words. To him, the poet gives the fullest attention, perhaps to suggest that freedom of thought has been also penalized in French society. "A man of fire, a scientist of / freedoms," she says of him in reference to the fact that because he was the chief philosophical materialist he was long opposed for membership in the Academie Française, guardians of the language itself. The poet's word play is free but lucid: "England / guarded by the sea, / we with re-enforced Bartholdi's / Liberty holding up her / torch beside the port, hear France / demand, 'Tell me the truth, / especially when it is / unpleasant.' " These are also ironic points of light. England, the poet is too diplomatic to mention, was guarded by more than the sea; the English were fighting determinedly and at first almost alone against the Nazis. The Free French, however, organized to fight from England and to resist in France. America was sending aid and mobilizing, but had not yet entered the war. The nation's Statue of

Liberty corresponds to the Ouessant pole of light. The poem also fuses them with history and popular sentiment, since the statue, paid for by contributions of the French people and presented to the United States in 1885, commemorates the birth of this nation as well as the friendship between the two democracies "in full liberty enlightening the world." Counterpointing the exchanges are the words of Pétain: "Tell me the truth," which the poet attributes to France and thereby heightens the ironies. If one values "Free frank impartial" light, the reply must be "The word France means / enfranchisement; means one who can / 'animate whoever thinks of her.' "

The poet may not be a statue of liberty—"A mighty woman with a torch, whose flame / Is the impassioned lightning," as Emma Lazarus wrote of it; but France, which Moore had praised long ago as " 'the chrysalis of the nocturnal butterfly' " in the poem "England," deserved to be free, and all that a poet could do was say so in the most spirited language she could command. Moore revives the root meanings of words as well as the memory of the past and common symbols for actions that were primary in the struggle for humane enlightenment. Thus, the play with words—"free," "frank," "enfranchisement," "France," "liberty," "fraternity," "generosity," "sincerity"—*lux et veritas* which animate the poem—might prove the poet's lively sympathies for a people to whom she paid the compliment of speech that was light.

The war, which the United States entered openly on December 7, 1941, tried the conscience of Marianne Moore as it did that of untold numbers of people relatively safe in the tumultuous time. The consciousness of the profound crises of one's genera-

tion or of one's era, as Wallace Stevens wrote in *Notes Toward a Supreme Fiction* (1942), is "the war that never ends." A violence from within, Stevens had said, "protects us from a violence without." The imagination, he observed, presses back against the pressures and the "immense reality of war." Stevens, praising the soldier, "the large, the solitary figure" who must bear "heroic fortunes" ("Examination of the Hero in Time of War" [1942]), comforted himself with the belief that "The soldier is poor without the poet's lines, / His petty syllabi, the sounds that stick, / Inevitably modulating, in the blood" *(Supreme Fiction).* He therefore wrote, as the conclusion to that major work: "How simply the fictive hero becomes the real; / How gladly with proper words the soldier dies, / If he must, or lives on the bread of faithful speech." Moore, reviewing the book in 1943, says in language indicative of the moral issue she had to confront: "In the final poem . . . the violence without is summarized—the soldier who is preserving that freedom of soul which gives rise to the violence within."

For Moore, the pressures of war caused a breach in one's self-defense, a violence within, the subject of her own spiritual examination, "In Distrust of Merits" (1943). Freedom of soul is a luxury for one who knows "I inwardly did nothing." Having done nothing becomes a burden of guilt. Compounding the guilt is the hatred one feels for the enemy and knowledge that one is susceptible to the same blind arrogance as the enemy. Yet even guilt is loose and immodest, a petty syllable, the privilege of those who benefit from the ultimate sacrifice of others for one's freedom of soul. Such struggles with a rigorous conscience do not, in fact, save one soldier from being blown to smithereens or one child from being buried in rubble. Freedom of

the soul, then, can be a scourge, not a solace. War, Moore wrote to her brother, shakes life into perspective.

Moore's poem begins with a question: "Strengthened to live, strengthened to die for / medals and positioned victories?" "They"—those lost "at sea before they fought," "some we love whom we know, / some we love but know not" are fighting in deserts, in caves, in snow, on crags, in quicksands—fighting that "hearts may feel and not be numb." The world has become "an orphan's home"; one hears "pleas of the dying for / help that won't come"; one sees a "quiet form upon the dust" at which one "cannot / look" but "must." There can be no peace without sorrow, without the shared confession that there never was a war that was not inward. Suffering the disease of the self— "We are / not competent to / make our vows"—the poet allows herself no false comfort when she states that "I must / fight till I have conquered in myself what / causes war, but I would not believe it." Such self-revelation seems close to self-indulgence. She was not capable of what she asked from the soldier.

She believed, as did most of the American people, that the war against the totalitarian powers was necessary. When the soldier "holds his ground" without anger and in patience, she writes, "that is action or / beauty," the soldier's defense and hardest armor. If the "great patient dyings," "the agonies / and wound bearings and bloodshed / can teach us how to live," they "were not wasted." How often one grasps for that reassurance without believing it, for no other reason than that "I inwardly did nothing." The poet's exclamation consequent to that betrayal—"O Iscariot-like crime!"—is a near mockery, saved only by its honest self-hatred. The poem's final words, "Beauty is ever-

lasting / and dust is for a time," are less forceful than terse; the poet's conflict is preempted by the facile assertion that beauty is everlasting and the obtrusive rhyme—"crime" / "time"—as questionable as the assertion.

"In Distrust of Merits" has been one of Moore's most popular poems. It has been called the greatest poem of World War II. It has also been the subject of severe critical debate. When Donald Hall asked Moore in 1960 for her judgment of it, she said she thought it sincere and truthful, "a testimony—to the fact that war is intolerable, and unjust." But it was "haphazard." As to form, she continued, "What has it? It is just a protest, disjointed, exclamatory. Emotion overpowered me." Referring to it again in 1966, she said she disliked the poem because of its didacticism. It was not customary for her to disapprove of poems in which she made moral observations. The sense that she failed to discipline her emotion, however, can be attributed to her concern with confessing it rather than holding fast to a point she had made in 1941. Having written, in an essay on Louise Bogan's poetry, that "there are no substitutes for the dead," Moore knew that no one acted in place of those who died in the war and that no one could ever replace them. Neither guilt nor distrust of merits (and meritorious words) of those who survive compensates for the absolute sacrifice of life.

That is, I think, one reason she came back to the immense reality of war in "Keeping Their World Large" (1944). The final version of the poem says of the dead "whose spirits and whose bodies / all too literally were our shield, / are still our shield":

All laid like animals for sacrifice—

    like Isaac on the mount,
               were their own sacrifice.

This is faithful speech, which it may not have been possible for the poet to write without having confessed her faithlessness.

"The Mind Is an Enchanting Thing" (1943) is not explicitly a war poem, but the edge that violates the "regnant certainty" of the mind is the last line of the first stanza: "Like Gieseking playing Scarlatti[.]" One of the characteristics of the mind that the poet contemplates is its inconsistencies—its nettings, like those of Moore's poetry, "are legion"—and one of the shocks of the period was the awareness of the "inconsistency" between the traditions of high culture and the barbarism of the totalitarian state that commanded that culture to validate the state. The name of Walter Gieseking (1895–1956) evokes the argument that the virtuoso pianist, as one of the great musicians willing to perform at the time in Germany, betrayed the humane spirit of art itself. The old romantic supposition that a civilized people would not countenance or commit the atrocities of the Nazi regime was a serious casualty of the ideological war. (Gieseking, for example, was not invited to return for concerts in the United States or France until 1953.) Moore's claim for art is only that it is "an expression of needs." As a poet, she knew the contradictions between art's inviolateness and its powerlessness to redeem humankind, even though the mind itself was "not a Herod's oath that cannot change." In 1951 she said: "One doesn't get through with the fact that Herod . . . 'for his oath's sake' " beheaded John the Baptist, "as one doesn't, I feel, get through with the injustice of the deaths died in the war, and in the first world war."

Among the revulsions the poet experienced as she witnessed the menace of totalitarianism to human freedoms was the effort to exterminate the Jews of Europe. In an essay on "Feeling and Precision" (1944), Moore writes that Professor Jacques Maritain, the French moral philosopher,

> when lecturing on scholasticism and immortality, spoke of those suffering in concentration camps, "unseen by any star, unheard by any ear," and the almost terrifying solicitude with which he spoke made one know that belief is stronger even than the struggle to survive. And what he said so unconsciously was poetry.

She had written stubbornly about intolerance and prejudice since "The Labors of Hercules," but by the time of the emotional outpouring of "In Distrust of Merits," Moore had become critical of her own self-righteousness. Exclaiming in that poem, "O / star of David, star of Bethlehem, / O black imperial lion of the Lord—emblem / of a risen world—be joined at last, be / joined," she turned on herself by declaring "it's a promise—'We'll / never hate black, white, red, yellow, Jew, / Gentile, Untouchable.' We are / not competent to / make our vows."

In "A Carriage from Sweden" (1944), she writes of a country cart, "a vein / of resined straightness" from "Sweden's once-opposed-to- / compromise archipelago of rocks." The ironies of the poem are deft and subtle. She begins: "They say there is a sweeter air / where it was made, than we have here; / a Hamlet's castle atmosphere." The fine cart is put away where no one may see it, in a museum in Brooklyn. Brooklyn—and by inference New York—is a city of "freckled / integrity," but the allusion to Hamlet's castle (and its bloody questions) suggests, even before

the phrase "once-opposed-to-compromise," that
Sweden's integrity is also in question. Ostensibly neu-
tral during the war, Sweden had made concessions to
the Germans from the time of the fall of Norway in
June 1940 until late summer of 1943. Despite the
precarious position of Sweden, there was sharp criticism and bitterness as well as protest because of its
cooperation with "the new order." The poet invokes
the names of two heroes of wars, Washington and
Gustavus Adolphus, and asks that they "forgive our
decay." The poem is clearly about more than "the
unannoying romance" of a cart lovingly and honestly
made in contrast to the shoddy merchandise of war.
(Washington lent the prestige of his office to religious
freedom, for example, by attending the first Jewish
synagogue in Newport, Rhode Island; Gustavus Adolphus was remembered for his wisdom and restraint,
religious toleration, hospitality to foreign artisans,
and educational reform.) "A Carriage" is so close to
the furor over Sweden's neutrality that Moore insert-
ed, after the poem's acceptance for publication, a brief
line referring to "Denmark's sanctuaried Jews!" in acknowledgment of King Gustav V's decision to open
Sweden on March 1, 1944, to Jewish refugees from
Denmark. She could hardly have been unaware of the
attractiveness of a free country as shelter for many
others of all nationalities who had already escaped
there from German oppression. In historical context
the poem is also not the simple travel poster it seems
to resemble, and when Moore asks, "Sweden, / what
makes . . . / those who see you wish to stay?" the
images of "the table / spread as for a banquet," a
"Dalén light-house, self-lit," "moated white castles"
or a "bed of white flowers" signify safety and relief.
The air is indeed sweeter there. The poem's final

words, "carts are my trade," modest and light in tone, express both nostalgia for a more peaceful time and a sense of the burdens to be carried in the midst of violence, destruction, and the strategies of survival.

The delicacy with which Moore treats the evil for which there have never been words of sufficient power may be thought to be inconsistent with the imperatives of conscience that she struggled to articulate. She does not write about atrocities in concentration camps or the mass murders of the holocaust. She writes, instead, about extinct birds—the roc known only from its remains and legend, the flightless moa, the harmless great auk—and the flightless ostrich, exploited, threatened, and nearly extinct, in "He 'Digesteth Harde Yron' " (1941). For Moore, the ostrich "was and is / a symbol of justice." The poem, like that on the emblematic jerboa, fuses observation with interpretation. Citing the historical fact that "six hundred ostrich-brains [were] served / at one banquet," as well as use of the eggshells as goblets, the plumes for decorative purposes, and eight pairs of the birds harnessed to draw carts, she says the birds "dramatize a meaning / always missed by the externalist." She then rises to the statement confirmed by her work: "The power of the visible / is the invisible"—a statement followed by the words: "as even where / no tree of freedom grows, / so-called brute courage knows." Moore's tribute to "the almost terrifying solicitude" with which Professor Maritain spoke of those suffering in concentration camps is anticipated in the last stanzas of "He 'Digesteth Harde Yron' ":

> Heroism is exhausting, yet
> it contradicts a greed that did not wisely spare
> the harmless solitaire

or great auk in its grandeur;
  unsolicitude having swallowed up
all giant birds but an alert gargantuan
      little-winged, magnificently speedy running-bird.
This one remaining rebel. . . .

"He 'Digesteth Harde Yron' " is also read as
an ecologist's poem, and with good reason, as is
"Rigorists" (1940), whose subject is the action of one
man to save a people whose survival was threatened.
The rigorists are Siberian reindeer, which can live on
scant pasture and were introduced into Alaska in the
1890s when sources of food were difficult to replenish.
"And / this candelabrum-headed ornament / for a
place where ornaments are scarce / . . . was a gift
preventing the extinction / of the Eskimo." The
poem's preceding six stanzas are devoted to the handsome reindeer, "Santa Claus' reindeer," but the poet's
appreciation of them is itself rigorous and without
sentimentality. The final three stanzas, which state the
moral, are so unsensational as to seem dull to many
readers. One is apt also to think the language of the
conclusion unusually trite: "The battle was won /
by a quiet man, / Sheldon Jackson, evangel to that
race / whose reprieve he read in the reindeer's face."
Jackson, who was General Agent for the U. S. Education Bureau in Alaska, was the uncle of girlhood
friends of Marianne Moore in Carlisle, Pennsylvania,
and she remembered him once again in "Education of
a Poet," which she wrote for *Writer's Digest* (1963). The
choice of Jackson as a heroic figure in a bureaucratic
battle won fifty years before she published "Rigorists"
is hardly an accident if one also reflects upon the implied contrast between the "evangel" and what
Moore, in a letter of 1939, called "the wrongful tyran-

ny" of the Germans "in persecuting and being subject
to Hitler." The reading of the word "reprieve" in the
reindeer's face suggests, if nothing else does, a rigo-
rist's habit of mind. As Randall Jarrell wrote in
"Losses" (1945), "It was not dying: everybody died."
It was the engineering of the mass extermination of
another people that appalled and that Moore's poem
quietly, perhaps too quietly, opposed. The wish for
another deliverance is, nonetheless, benevolent. And
the voice of benevolence is never strident or loud. As
Auden said, "whenever a modern poet raises his voice,
he sounds phony."

The losses of war, the destruction of defenseless
people everywhere, and the uses of power are impetus
for Moore's dream of peace, "Elephants" (1943). "As
if, as if, it is all as ifs; we are at / much unease," she
writes in the poem. Elephants, characterized by massive size and great physical strength, are alleged to
have a high order of intelligence, although their brains
are not unusually well-developed. Amenable to training and normally timid, even placid, elephants can be
dangerous when aroused. (As a trainer of circus animals said in comparing animals: "Elephants are the
smartest, but they like to take it easy.") The poet is
obviously fascinated by the "alliance" between the
powerful elephants and their "gnat trustees"—human
beings—who may lack the wisdom to use the power
entrusted to them to effect peace.

The dissonant opening lines of the poem describe
the "matched intensities" of two elephants, their
trunks in a "deadlock of dyke-enforced massiveness.
It's a / knock-down drag-out fight that asks no quarter?" No, the struggle is happily "Just / a pastime."
The elephants are, also as a matter of fact, "templars
of the Tooth"; knights, not of the religious and mili-

tary order established in the early twelfth century for
the protection of pilgrims to the Holy Sepulcher in
Jerusalem, but of the tooth that serves the elephant
both for digging food and as a weapon. The poet
comments on the elephants' showering, foraging for
food, taking "master care of / master tools," and one
is described as "sleeping with the calm of youth, /
at full length in the half-dry sun-flecked stream-bed,"
its hunting-horn-curled trunk at rest on shallowed
stone. Moore then humorously observes that "the
sleeper's body / cradles the gently breathing emi-
nence's prone / mahout, asleep like a lifeless six-foot
/ frog, so feather light the elephant's stiff / ear's unconscious of the crossed feet's weight." The elephant's keeper-driver, a "defenseless human thing
sleeps as sound as if / incised with hard wrinkles,
embossed with wide ears, / invincibly tusked, made
safe by magic hairs!" The poet's imagining that the
protected mahout has assumed the impressive power
of the elephant is, of course, an "as if." "But magic's
masterpiece is theirs,— / Houdini's serenity quelling
his fears." Having witnessed the elephants at play, at
work, and in repose, and having permitted herself a
moment of imaginative fantasy, she is tempted to the
resounding chorales appreciated by the hard-of-hear-
ing (the elephant's sense of hearing is poorly developed), but she lowers her voice to rephrase the
poignant statement of "as if": "Elephant-ear-wit-
nesses-to-be of hymns / and glorias, these ministrants
all gray or / gray with white on legs or trunks, are a
pilgrims' / pattern of revery not reverence. . . ." The
poem is not, then, "like daydreaming to Scarlatti,"
even though Cyril Connolly said that was his experience in reading Moore.

When Moore remarked that T. S. Eliot "pays us

the compliment of expecting our reading to be more thorough than it is," she could have been talking about herself; she also expects us to know what she knows. Following the pleasures of observing the "ordinary" elephants, she celebrates them in their less familiar service to the Buddhist pilgrims who gather in Kandy, Ceylon, for the Perahera, the annual torchlit procession to the Temple of the Tooth. The sanctuary was erected to house the treasured relic, the Buddha's sacred tooth; a material trace of a life that embodied higher verities, the treasure makes faith more real for the common person who would emulate the Buddha's teachings. She accurately describes the Perahera as "a religious procession without any priests, / the centuries-old carefullest unrehearsed / play" in which the elephants, obedient beasts, bless the streets. The amenable white elephant, the sacred elephant of Kandy, augustly and slowly carries the white-canopied, blue-cushioned Tooth to the shrine. He is, she says, not there "to worship and he is too wise / to mourn,—a life prisoner but reconciled." The poem has become gravely meditative. The elephant's "trunk tucked up compactly" is a "sign of defeat—he resisted, but is the child / of reason now. His straight trunk seems to say: when / what we hoped for came to nothing, we revived." Neither a seeming invincibility nor magic could save him from captivity, despite the fact that he could have crushed his "gnat trustees." Having accepted his destiny, like Socrates, he is the embodiment of tranquility. Representing "the brotherhood / of creatures to man the encroacher," the elephant is also an ideal ministrant, wise in service and the knowledge of that service well-performed; but as significant as the service is the restraint he exemplifies in the use of his great strength. "These knowers [the obedient

beasts blessing the streets] 'arouse the feeling that they are / allied to man' and can change roles with their trustees."

The mutual trust is reassuring; but the balance of power between the commanders and the commanded is a precarious one and can be a source of profound anxiety. The poet almost takes a leap of faith: "Hardship makes the soldier; then teachableness / makes him the philosopher—as Socrates, / prudently testing the suspicious thing, knew / the wisest is he who's not sure that he knows." The dream of peace depends finally on the soldiers' equanimity, their restraint in the exercise of enormous power. One cannot, however, be certain that when their energies are unleashed they will restrain and use them reasonably: "Who rides on a tiger can never dismount; / asleep on an elephant, that is repose." Neither the enlightenment of Buddha nor the prudence of Socrates is a guarantee of the right relationship between power and the trustees or "keepers" of it. The poem once again is an "As if, as if, it is all as ifs; we are at / much unease."

"Those who have power to renounce life are those who have it," Moore had written in 1936; "one who attains equilibrium in spite of opposition to himself from within, is stronger than if there had been no opposition to overcome; and in art, freedom evolving from a liberated constraint is more significant than if it had not by nature been cramped."[26] In war, in art, one would not be he who has nothing but destructive power.

V

The poems of the war years brought increasing recognition of Moore as a public figure. She gave interviews to a number of younger writers for national magazines. She made lists of books she remembered from childhood or had liked during the last ten years. She replied tersely to questions on the language of American and English poetry (1950), religion and the intellectuals (1950), women and the machine civilization (1963), and the war in Vietnam (1967). She entertained readers with her unsuccessful trials at naming a new automobile (1957) for the Ford Motor Company. She read a prosaic poem, "Blessed Is the Man" (1957) for Class Day ceremonies of the Phi Beta Kappa chapter at Columbia University. She wrote, by request, on topics such as "If I Were Sixteen Today" (1958), or "About Age: Random Thoughts Apropos Our Aging Population" (1960), and contributed commonplace reminiscences about the past. She made zany comments on fashion: She was the recipient of a "donated French brocade emerald jacket and purple velvet skirt of papal quality. . . . Sir Winston Churchill had nine hats!" She did not say how many she owned. But "the New Guinea Tari tribesman's bunch of leaves at the back, steadied by a vine string, is perhaps the least hampering concession to fashion." Something like Will Rogers, again, she kept the flair for social criticism.

Moore's penchant for humor and the topical made her a celebrity among readers who would otherwise never have heard of her. Among the most popular of the light verses were those stimulated by her enthusiasm for horses and for baseball. Her opposition to betting on the races did not keep her from

admiring the horses and riders or from writing skillful, intricate minor poems on "Tom Fool at Jamaica" (1953), a "handy horse," and "Blue Bug" (1963), a limber polo pony with "pitchfork-pronged ears stiffly parallel." And while no one heeded her disapproval of trading those "miracles of dexterity," baseball players, the poem "Hometown Piece for Messers. Alston and Reese"—manager and captain of the Brooklyn Dodgers—to the tune "Mama goin' buy you a mocking-bird," put Moore on the front page of a New York newspaper for the opening day of the World Series (1956). The poem was said, over-enthusiastically, to excel the tributes she paid to poets, "Yeats, Eliot, Shakespeare, and the like." (She had written one early poem, "To William Butler Yeats on Tagore" [1915]; her essays on Eliot are among the most perspicacious she wrote; and when she referred to Shakespeare it was to praise the effect of "helpless naturalness" in the poetry.) The light verse is pleasingly offhand, like improvised music, spontaneous and immediate.

As a public poet, Moore not only responded graciously to invitations for "pieces" if she thought she could say something appropriate, but she continued to write poems on crucial issues in which she had long been interested or about which—as she said—she was roused. Some, although not all of the work, demonstrates diminishing vitality. She repudiated none of it. The subject might be more important than reputation.

"The Staff of Aesculapius" (1954), appearing in a publication of the Abbott Laboratories and an anthology titled *Imagination's Other Places: Poems of Science and Mathematics,* lends support to medical research in the effort to prevent poliomyelitis and treat cancer. Although the miracles of healing by the priests of Aesculapius—for whom the staff with a serpent coiled

around it was the emblem—are evoked by the title, the
poem moves quickly to suggest the protracted history
of rational and scientific medicine from the time of the
"experiments such as Hippocrates made / and sub-
stituted for vague / speculation" to stay "the ravages
of a plague" in the fifth century B.C. The immediate
issue of the poem, however, was the work against in-
fantile paralysis, which had reached epidemic proportions in the United States, Northern Europe, and Asia
in the period from 1942 to 1953. The major controversy regarding control of the acute infectious disease
centered around the relative merits of two vaccines,
the attenuated (live) oral polio virus and the inactivated (killed) virus. The poet gives approval to the
efforts of the virologist Dr. Jonas Edward Salk at the
time he was testing the inactivated virus vaccine; the
effectiveness of Salk's arduous work, including his
program early in 1954 to innoculate 5,000 children in
little more than five weeks, was in doubt. Although the
poem has been thought in retrospect to be obvious,
it was written at a time when news reports were saying: "It is still too early to answer the question, 'Is this
the year of victory over polio?' " Whether the vaccine
would give "lifelong immunity" or not, the poet
writes, "suppose" it is at least "effective / say tem-
porarily— / for even a year[.]" Furthermore, "knowledge has been gained for another attack." The tone is
reasonable and speculative. (Salk greatly reduced the
incidence of paralytic polio after the vaccine was em-
ployed throughout the world beginning in 1955). Another gain over destructive illness, the controlled
attack on cancer cells, resectioning of the lung and
implanting a plastic sponge so that "cells following /
fluid, adhere, and what / was inert becomes living"
was to Moore like the master-physician's Sumerian

rod, "a sign of renewal." Granted the public's interest in these subjects, the poem itself is closer to document than to the powerful transformations of "Elephants" or "The Jerboa." The fact that Moore chose to write on the experimental research is more worthy of note than the dull intensity with which she writes.

She commemorated "Carnegie Hall: Rescued" (1960) after the success of the "campaign" led by "Saint Diogenes / supreme commander," alias "Mr. Star," Isaac Stern, the violinist, to save the musicians' "old brown home" "menaced by the 'cannibal of real estate'—bulldozing potentate, / land-grabber, the human crab. . . ." The clichés are unfortunate, the poem just plain bad, even if the cause was good. "Rescue with Yul Brynner" (1961) is lean but right in praise of the work of the actor as special consultant of the United Nations Commission for Refugees, 1959–1960: "There were thirty million; there are thirteen still— / healthy to begin with, kept waiting till they're ill. / . . . 'Have a home?' a boy asks. 'Shall we live in a tent?' / 'In a house,' Yul answers. . . . 'You'll have plenty of space.' "

In addition to volunteering such topical verses, Moore accepted requests to write poems consonant with the habitual attention she gave to the American experience. "Enough: Jamestown, 1607–1957" was comissioned by the *Virginia Quarterly Review* for the tercentenary observances of the first permanent settlement by the English in North America. The work is subsequent to a companion poem, "Virginia Britannia" (1935), for which, as Marie Boroff has pointed out, the unspoken theme is "E pluribus unum." Moore "made her country's aspiring motto come true imaginatively in her vision of genuineness: the perceived authenticity of aspect or action that can 'unite'

the deer-fur crown of the Indian chief with the coat of arms of the English colonist, and the singing of the hedge-sparrow with the affirmation of human rights in the Preamble to the Declaration of Independence."[27] "Enough" is structurally and thematically a poem of contrasts in octosyllablic rhymed couplets with the parenthetical reminder "Don't speak in rhyme / of maddened men in starving-time." The past and present are joined by collocation of the three sailing ships in which the settlers came and three "namesake" jet planes traversing the sky on May 15, the anniversary of the settlers' arrival at Jamestown. There is no idealization of the past in the "too earthly paradise" where the "communistic" plan with the "same reward for best and worst" failed but where with initiative "they could live" on three acres each. The rivalries, "unnatural" cannibalism, lawlessness, and slavery contrast with the romance of John Rolfe and the Indian princess Pocahontas, love flowering in marriage, deliverance, and liberty. The futile search for gold is contrasted with the profitable cultivation of the golden weed, "controversial" tobacco, in the yellow soil. The pests and pestilence of the marshy land are contrasted with the fragrance of the verdure, the "artlessly perfect French effect," and the emblematic presence of "the feeble tower / to mark the site that did not flower." The old uncertainties, "Who knows what is good!" or "could the most ardent have been sure / that they had done what would endure?" are softened by the faith that the partial proof from America's past generates in the poet. The present, however, depends for Moore on an "if": a pivotal word in the conclusion —"enough . . . if . . . proof" is mended. She is not talking about revisionist history. (She would have enjoyed the bicentennial debate over the bones of Poca-

hontas, who died in England where she went with her husband, was introduced to "society," and became a sensation. The princess "is on record as being very reluctant to return to Virginia," according to the Rev. Colin Pilgram, guardian of the common grave in which she is buried. Virginians have contended that she died in England as she was about to return to America.) Moore simply says the princess was "in rank / above what she became—renounced her name / yet found her status not too tame." Both the serious history and the humor of "Enough" are homegrown.

The down-to-earth poem "Enough" has been less appreciated than "In the Public Garden," which Moore wrote in response to an invitation to read at the Boston Arts Festival in 1958. She views the cultural, political, and religious heritage as well as the secular life of Boston less critically than the painful beginnings at Jamestown. She feels legitimate pride and affection for a city where "intellect is habitual" and "legend can be factual." Relying on the authority of an "exceptional" taxi-driver, she quotes him as saying, "They / make some fine young men at Harvard." Boston's "cupolas of learning / (crimson, blue, and gold)," she says, "have made education individual." Recognizing that, like silence, freedom of the individual or a people is unattainable, she nevertheless asks, "what is freedom for?" The answer is tempered with humor: " 'for self-discipline,' as our / hardest-working citizen [the president of the United States, then Eisenhower for whom she had voted] had said—a school," and "for 'freedom to toil' / with a feel for the tool." (A poet whose father was named John Milton Moore surely knew that Adam and Eve "toiled" in the Puritan garden of Eden, but by 1958 "the Puritan work ethic" had become a pejorative phrase.) The

poem is not, however, a right-to-work manifesto. Rather, there are people who work without freedom. "In the Public Garden," as George Nitchie has observed, "finds its unemphatic focus in the situation of 'those in the trans-shipment camps,' whose circumstances modify, change, even give the lie"[28] to the aura of a festival. For those who are denied freedom, their only hope of release is if they have "a skill" and stay well so they can "work" and "buy" their way out.

Allied with the theme of political freedom are the themes of religious and artistic freedom. Moore is mindful of Boston's Protestant origins: "let me enter King's Chapel / to hear them sing [a traditional Southern tune] 'My work be praise while / others go and come.' " She feels "like a child" at home there, and comments that both a place for worship and a festival for the arts mean "giving what is mutual, / even if irrational. . . ." Her poem, she asserts, "is no madrigal— / no medieval gradual"; it is an expression of grateful praise. The mention of the medieval lyric and liturgical music may be plain English "that dogs and cats can read" but is hardly obvious. It seems to refer teasingly to the question of whether the use of language in American poetry differs notably from that of English poetry. Horace Gregory, along with Moore, had responded to the question. "Perhaps the most important difference in 'sensibility,' " he said "is that in both a cultural and historical sense those who have spent their childhood in the United States lack a European concept of the Middle Ages. This . . . shows its presence in a great variety of ways." Moore finessed her answer and talked about illiteracy or ignorance of work other than one's own, which she did not care to concede as "typically American."[29] Acknowledging her distance from European experience and discount-

ing an anonymous criticism of her poetry, Moore says humorously in historical Boston that although she is "without that radiance which poets / are supposed to have," she can wish poetry well all the same. She is glad that "the Muses have a home and swans— / that legend can be factual," and is "happy that Art, admired in general, / is always actually personal." If she lacks a concept of the Middle Ages, she has an American "sensibility" or mind that is "incapable of the shut door" on the paradoxes of freedom. If she is "without radiance," the poem's single rhyme, which recurs forty times beginning with "festival" and ending with "personal," suggests a prolonged pealing of bells in joyous celebration. One is reminded simultaneously of two different poems in English—Thomas Hardy's comic verse, "The Respectable Burger," thirty-six lines composed on a single rhyme; and W. H. Auden's elegy, "In Memory of W. B. Yeats (1940): "In the prison of his days / Teach the free man how to praise." Moore was a congenial pupil.

Praise with a little Yankee salt is evident in "Combat Cultural," whose subject is the appearance of the Moiseyev Dance Company during its 1958 American season at New York's Metropolitan Opera House. Formed originally with dancers from the Bolshoi Ballet School, the spirited ensemble represented the sophistication of art (politically well-defined) for the people. There was little in the work presented in the United States that touched openly upon social or political questions, but there was much written about "terpsichorean diplomacy." In accordance with the new cultural exchange between the United States and the Soviet Union, the Moiseyev troupe was the first from the U.S.S.R. to come to the United States after "the door had been shut" for forty years. In 1955, the

Russians had received the American musical "Porgy and Bess," but difficulties in negotiations, requiring congressional waiver of fingerprinting regulations, were finally resolved, and the reception given by the American people to the Soviet company was exuberant. Not only were programs sold out in major cities across the country, but the Ed Sullivan show "spent a fortune" so that the folk ballets could be seen nationally on TV. "The enthusiasm includes more than *interest* in seeing the dancers," according to an editorial in *Dance Magazine.* "It heightens at performance, where over and over one hears, 'This does more good than all the diplomats put together.' . . . We have known Soviet citizens only by hearsay. The impact of having these dancers immediately before us . . . evokes emotion like that of meeting a member of the family who has been away for a long time. . . . If there must be a cold war, we think the best possible weapons are those of the arts." A news story editorialized: "We have found a common language. If we want to understand each other, let us dance together more often." The dancers learned the Virginia reel and took it back to Russia; Igor Moiseyev returned with praises for American music and general cultural life—the *New York Times* headline reported that he "glowed" (January 19, 1959); but a talk he was scheduled to give at the House of Journalists was canceled—and the *Times* headline read, "Moiseyev Is Censured By Soviets" (April 16, 1959). Moore's "Cultural Combat" was published in June of 1959.

The poem is a *jeu d'esprit* on seeing and seeming. The first words are "One likes to see," after which there is a description of "a visual fugue" with "a mist / of swords that seemed to sever / heads from bodies," followed by "Let me see . . ." in a ruminating

tone, and a final account of a skillful deception of the
eyes. Images of "a laggard rook's high speed" outfly-
ing "the dark," a horse—a mount—trained for jumping barriers, and a "team of leapers turned aerial"
express the acrobatics and simple choreography of the
Moiseyev dances. (A review of the performance describes, for example, the final Hopak, in which a young
man suddenly "flew over the heads of a close line of
girls extended across the stage, and landed before
them to continue his dancing unruffled," or the dancers "jumping higher than we had ever dreamed possible," the "whole troupe seemingly . . . on invisible
horses," or "a huge circle of leaping men.")[30] Moore's
adjective "laggard" for the common, gregarious, old-
world bird (related to the American crow), the phrase
"to outfly the dark," and the term "barrier" double as
commentary on political issues. One, understandably,
likes to see the spectacular actions of ballet. Recalling
a documentary of Cossacks "stepping as though
through / harpstrings in a scherzo," the poet says,
"However, / the quadrille of Old Russia for me" in
reference to another of the Moiseyev pieces, "City
Quadrille," humorously depicting instances of life in
prerevolutionary Russia. Continuing to play with
words, the poet corrects herself, "Old Russia, I said?
Cold Russia / this time," and signals the description
of a dance indigenous to the frozen north of Russia at
the same time that she puns on the cold war. The
dance, "Two Boys in a Fight," according to Doris
Herring's review, "had the playfulness of children."
Performed in a special costume—the poet calls it a
rug—by one man, the dance "juxtaposed two tiny
boys, kicking, scrimmaging, even pressing each other
against the proscenium. . . . a circus trick, . . . danced
with extreme artistry." Moore, still punning, speaks of

it as a "platform-piece," "trip-and-slug," and "flip-flop." The conceit is as witty as John Donne's metaphysical image for the souls of lovers: "If they be two, they are two so / As stiff twin compasses are two." Moore writes: "Some art, because of high quality, / is unlikely to command high sales; / yes, yes; but here, oh no," not the "tight touch-and-go" of these battlers who, "dressed identically— / just one person—may, by seeming twins, / point a moral, should I confess." The revelation of the trick in the poem is surprising; the "moral" is not unexpected: We see them first as two boys, when they are in fact one; even if they are in combat, we must see that the two are one, and so forth. Moore leaves these formulations for the reader to make. She puts the moral differently: "we must cement the parts of any / objective symbolic of *sagesse.*" The worst of her puns, in "we must cement the parts," is not quite rescued by the poet's good intentions, although the ambiguities of "sagesse"—wisdom? discretion? prudence? the good behavior of children?—save the cliché. She must have enjoyed "every minute of it"—the plummeting clear across the stage, the bolting into the air, the tricks played on the eye, the hoopla, and the clichés—if only there were not the trans-shipment camps.

"Granite and Steel" (1966) is a poem of antiphonal voices, "O path amid the stars / crossed by the seagull's wing!" / and "O radiance that doth inherit me!" affirming threatened American ideals. The poem's ironic "ornaments" are the Brooklyn Bridge and the Statue of Liberty, which dominate the bay of New York City. In an early poem titled "New York" (1921), prompted by a statement that the city had become "the center of the wholesale fur trade," as Harry Levin pointed out, Moore's "imagery trans-

forms the metropolis back into a predatory forest."[31]
In "Granite and Steel" New York, one of "our cities /
in the sea," is remembered as an open city where the
chains of tyranny lie broken at the feet of the Statue
of Liberty, but there are now obstructions to "acquies-
cent feet / about to step ashore." She therefore celebrates the bridge: "way out; way in; romantic
passageway," and "composite span," "enfranchis-
ing cable," a "double rainbow." The bridge—a monu-
ment to the German immigrant engineer John Roebling, who devised a method of making light and
strong suspension cable from woven steel wire in a
catenary curve—is "implacable enemy of the mind's
deformity." The beautiful arc of a perfectly flexible,
resilient cord hanging freely from two fixed points—
tower and pier—is Moore's metaphor for liberated
constraint, which she valued in art and all human activities. Only by such constraint could freedom be
maintained. The mind's deformity is "man's uncom-
punctious greed, / his crass love of crass priority."
(Greed, she said, "seems to me the vice of our century.
. . . We must not want something from another so
much that we steal it; cannot kill another and benefit."
She was writing for *Seventeen* magazine, but "Granite
and Steel" is for all who might read it.) Without apology for her willingness to use old-fashioned abstractions and to write about "Topics," she makes an
old-fashioned criticism of a society in which gross
profit takes priority over values she believes should
transcend greed. "To the bonanza, the legacy, the
professional hit," she also wrote in "Profit Is a Dead
Weight" (1963), "it would be well if our attitude were
that of the Brazilian dazzled by unearthing a . . . cluster
of diamonds: 'My Lord and Heavenly Father, if this
wealth endangers my soul, let it vanish.' It is what
every poem is about, as Robert Frost writes, 'the tri-

umph of the spirit over materialism by which we are
being smothered.' " In "Granite and Steel," freedom
is threatened by the vice of greed, in itself a tyranny
when a people seem unable to place limits on their
acquisitive behavior. The subject of America's betrayal of itself is mediant between "Cultural Combat" and
"Tippoo's Tiger."

Although she called it a ballad, "Tippoo's Tiger"
(1967) is a modern fable in which Moore describes the
Indian Tipu Sultan of eighteenth-century Mysore and
the accoutrements of power he enjoys. If he were not
a historical figure, one could believe she made him up,
yet one knows the type. The wealth, a palace with
silver stairs leading to the throne; obeisant subjects
who kiss the meadow-green velvet carpet under the
sultan's feet; finely dressed soldiers and guards; hunt-
ing cats; the "vast toy," an efficient mechanical contrivance that repeatedly enacts the macabre episode of
a man killed by a tiger and automatically plays the
ironic music of death for the ruler's delectation: all of
these images are the ultimate conclusion of "Too
Much" in "The Jerboa." Tippoo's fable anticipates
that this "master" for whom the tiger was prototype
is doomed to destruction ("Who rides on a tiger can
never dismount"). Despite the sultan's possession of
weapons "engraved with tiger claws and teeth /
in spiral characters that said the conqueror is God," the
enemy—"the infidel"—"claimed Tipu's helmet and
cuirasse" and the "curious automaton." (The facts,
given in the poet's note, confirm that in 1799 the
"toy" was captured when Tipu was defeated and killed
by the British at Seringapatan. She had seen the automaton when it was exhibited in New York in 1955.)[32]
The poem says that "This ballad still awaits a tiger-
hearted bard."

Marianne Moore was not that bard, nor was John
Keats, to whom she alludes in "Tippoo." "The Cap
and Bells: A Faery Tale—Unfinished," Keats's last
work, is credited as a source in the notes. She is indebted to Keats for a description of the Emperor Elfinan, whose subjects "kiss'd nine times the carpet's
velvet face . . . of meadow green" and feared him
"when he play'd on his Man-Tiger Organ," "prettiest
of his toys," "play-thing of the Emperor's choice." But
Elfinan's organ made a "little buzzing noise," whereas
Moore describes Tipu's automaton "with organ pipes
inside / from which blood-curdling cries merged with
inhuman groans." Elfinan, sharing the sultan's obsession with tigers, prompted a homespun sampler
"whereon were broider'd tigers with black eyes"; the
forefeet of Tipu's throne were "tiger's feet." "The
Cap and Bells" is about jealousies, the taste for ven-
geance, and the illicit passion of an Emperor, an
oblique sketch of George IV; Moore's poem is a succinct account of the lust for violence and the brutality
of which the human species is capable.

   The fusion of borrowings—from a poem satirizing an English monarch with images of an Indian ruler
defeated by the British—implies, if a reader is not
overly cautious, the unstated history of many peoples
whose exploitation by both their own and colonial
rulers continues to cause widespread disruptions and
revolution in the twentieth century. The discrepancy
between the use of the original form of the sultan's
name, "Tippoo," in the title and the use of "Tipu, the
accepted modern form" (as Moore explains in a note)
for the text of the poem may also imply that the
themes of the fable are as contemporaneous as were
those in Keats's satire. In any event, she must be saying that there are Tippoo-Tipus in many cultures.

   Moore's concluding lines—the moral which was

for La Fontaine "the soul of the fable"—suggest a general application. "Great losses for the enemy / can't make the owner's loss less hard." The abrupt turn of those final words and the impact of Tipu's man-eating tiger machine on the consciousness argue for the poem as an antiwar apologue. It is, I think, related to the Vietnam war and the moral as well as political dilemma over which Americans agonized but spent their spirit in a waste of shame.

History, as Eliot wrote, has many cunning passages and guides us by its vanities. Following direct military participation by the United States in the Vietnam conflict from March of 1965, the sustained aerial bombardment of North Vietnam thereafter, and the Buddhist protests that reached near rebellion against the government of South Vietnam in the spring of 1966, Moore expressed equivocal opinions. She replied, in the autumn of 1966, to two questions: "Are you for, or against, the intervention of the United States in Vietnam? How, in your opinion, should the conflict in Vietnam be resolved?" She responded to the first question with another: "Does it have to be 'Give me death or liberty'?" She did not say that the choice between death and liberty was an American revolutionary war choice, hardly one for the South Vietnamese under either communist or republican governments. The answer to the second question seems muddled: "It is short-sightedly irresponsible, I think, to permit communist domination and acquiesce in the crushing of the weak by the strong. *Can* negotiations be imposed by force? Winston Churchill thought appeasement solved nothing." Fiercely anti-communist, she does not make clear who she believes to be the weak or the strong; one infers that for Moore the anti-communists were the weak, but one cannot be certain. The question of whether negotiations could

be "imposed by force" seems antiwar, but invoking the authority of Churchill, she seems to take back the opposition to use of force.[33]

By midsummer of the next year, there were 450,-000 American troops, in addition to the Republic of Vietnam armed force estimated at over 700,000, committed to a war they were not to win. The opposition of Americans to the war had so intensified that the commencement speaker at New York University, for example, warned graduates "on rigid war attitudes" in exercises June 14, 1967, at which time Moore received an honorary doctor of letters degree. The poem on the tiger-machine was published on September 25 of that year.

The poet who had said sanguinely in 1960 that "war is intolerable and unjust" was once again confronted with the atrocities of war and the emotional necessity of finding effective words for questions that had always troubled her. "Tippoo's Tiger" is, I think, an attempt to symbolize the complex issues of an intolerable war and the fact that people were trapped in a "man-made" tiger machine. A "liberal conservative" —she was said, whether accurately or not, to have been the only serious poet in the country to vote for Nixon in 1960—Moore was adamant against political repression and economic injustice. Tippoo-Tipu is a composite figure for both tyrannical government and self-aggrandizing economic power, for both the mentality and the resources directed toward the perfection of monstrous "toys" that automatically kill people caught in the machine: "The tiger moved its tail as the man moved his arm." The poem may be a paper tiger, but the tiger cage is a reality.

Tipu, of course, suffers the loss of the cruel machine. The poet catches him just after the loss and just before he is to be killed, which for him is the moment

of truth from which the lesson of the fable is derived. It is a matter-of-fact lesson on the self-defeating arrogance of the will to power, the exercise of brute force, and the blood-dimmed tide that is loosed upon the world. The tiger-hearted may take satisfaction in the losses (great losses) of the enemy, but when the loss is to oneself—even for the privileged human being whose murders are performed by automatons—there is no consolation.

"Tippoo's Tiger" is Moore's last poem on a crisis of such magnitude. As the poet observes in "The Labors of Hercules," published in 1922, "one detects creative peor by its capacity to conquer one's detachment[.]" From the beginning of Moore's career as a writer, then, the character of her work is signally influenced by her responses to the events of her era. The fact that controversial issues often provoked disruptions within Moore herself accounts for the vigor with which she sought to resolve the conflicts as well as for the difficulties and nuances of many of the poems. It is to her credit that she risked so much of the energy of her imagination to express the turmoil of her epoch, that she rarely became propagandistic, and that she even more rarely resorted to simplistic views. She hoped against hope for a "common understanding—some sincerity about 'justice for all.'" She was not one of those escapist "women poets" against whom Theodore Roethke brought the charge that they hid "from the agonies of the spirit" and refused "to face up to what existence is," even though he spoke disparagingly of her "lapsing into a sententiousness that implies the author has reinvented integrity."[34] She is usually modest, sometimes amused and sometimes mortally enraged, always pertinent, and frequently wise.

6

Conclusion:
Piercing Glances into the Life of Things

Marianne Moore was an unaccommodating woman who wanted to be accommodating. With an alertness to the spirit of her own times, she went confidently about the pleasures and the work of writing poetry that is unmistakably individual. The style is so idiosyncratic that it has had no poor imitators, and, unlike many singular writers, she is difficult to parody. Taking part in the modernist movement, she created radically new forms that share in the reality that is the substance of the verse but also are integral to its significance. She was, like her contemporaries, Eliot and Pound, an avid student of both well-known and obscure or nearly-forgotten works of the past; selective and pronounced in her tastes, she wrote poems that are transformations of the old forms or texts with the freedom of one who has discovered them for herself, made them her own, and given them new life. There is about much that she wrote the air of private, personal enthusiasms as well as devotion to nuances and snippets of learning inseparable from her enthusiasms. These qualities combine to give her poems a density or opacity often requiring a care comparable to her own if one is to enjoy them. Many readers are, nonetheless, irritated or discouraged, while those who are over-serious and dedicated in the pursuit of the poem may learn that they have misplaced their care and lost the poem. Yet by attending to her forms, her discriminations, and her sensibility, we find that she is often also a powerfully lucid, even translucent poet, and the poem "a rock crystal thing to see." (One hears Moore saying wittily about her characteristic use of details she collected and assembled in the verse: "they are like flies in amber.") She objected to the work's being dulled by generalization or bisected without re-

gard to continuities and to "the principle that is hid." In her writing, the literal and factual give point to the figurative. Style is an act of compression, but the truth of the whole poem cannot deny the truth of the particulars. Words are an act of faith, and their value for the reader depends on the genuine value they had for her.

One of the glories of the poet and the person is that she insisted on the divine right to be herself. For that reason, attention to her affinities is entertaining, gratifying, and invigorating, like a visit to a person who is seldom boring. There is no poet who remarks as frequently as Moore about what she likes and dislikes. The cat's alligator eye, a porcupine quill, a bird's squeak, silence, a parenthesis of wit, a hero, a virile word, an elegant word, or quirks of the mind are important to her. The disciplines she set for herself, her honest tongue, the righteously cruel ridicule of others, and then the ridicule of herself, her humor, her good humor, pluckiness, and the wish for self-realization when it was not one's conscious aim, her tough and resilient spirit, the scrupulous observations of others (including the animals) and of her own mind at work— the resources for survival—meant that she lived in the reality which belonged to her. It was, fortunately for her poetry and its readers, a large reality. It was neither bleak nor glossy; it was splendid.

Moore's confident determination to be herself and to find words for her vision of the world's splendor was sustained by a profound faith in God as the center and source of light, the mysteries of grace, beatitude, love as "the only fortress strong enough to trust to," hope, and fear. She believed in spiritual necessity and the spiritual forces that make words, like the poetry of the Old Testament, "piercing glances

into the life of things." She also believed in the reality of sin—"existence is flawed; transcendence, conditional; / 'the journey from sin to redemption, perpetual.' "

It is within the structure of Christian belief that she was a person of moral passion: intensely concerned about virtuous behavior and traditions of civility as well as openly sensitive to questions of right and wrong. As a person who wanted ideally to live and work according to spiritual values, she was never indifferent to public issues and conflicts in which human dignity, rights and needs, perhaps civilization itself, were at stake. She not only wanted to survive herself, but she wanted good to survive. She became, therefore, a public poet, even though she insisted that she wrote for herself and her inner happiness.

"Victory," she said, "won't come / to me unless I go to it." She took responsibility for herself. And she spoke her own mind with a poetic intelligence reinforced by all that she could learn from newspapers, photography, sports, documentaries, history, fashions, biography, nature, travel, museums, society, music, art, television and recordings, or theologians, taxi drivers, dancers, scientists, authors of hymns, fairy tales and literary criticism, to say nothing of other writers, enemies, friends, and family during a long life in which she practiced what she modestly called her trade. We admire her achievement; it is ironic that her work has been commended for being a "triumph of limitations."

She was once referred to as the greatest woman poet of the century—Langston Hughes quipped, "Negro woman poet." Generally appreciated by fellow poets, she also influenced the generation that followed them. She was an early mentor of Elizabeth

Bishop, Jean Garrigue, and May Swenson; W. H. Auden, Donald Hall, W. D. Snodgrass, and Thom Gunn turned from traditional metrics to the syllabic verse for which Moore is noted; Charles Tomlinson, Denise Levertov, Robert Duncan, and Richard Wilbur also have benefited from her example; but all of them paid her the compliment of refusing to imitate her. She became New York City's unofficial poet laureate. She should have been, and in retrospect was, America's poet laureate.

Notes

1. Marianne Moore

1. Winthrop Sargeant, "Humility, Concentration, and Gusto," *The New Yorker,* 32 (February 16, 1957), p. 52.
2. Sargeant, p. 44.
3. Donald Hall, "An Interview with Marianne Moore," *McCall's,* 93 (December 1965), pp. 188, 184.
4. Sargeant, pp. 47–48; Hall, pp. 186–188.
5. Monroe Wheeler, "Reminiscence," in Tambimuttu, ed., *Festschrift for Marianne Moore's Seventy-Seventh Birthday by Various Hands* (New York: Tambimuttu & Mass, 1964), pp. 128–129.
6. Marianne Moore, "Idiosyncrasy and Technique," *A Marianne Moore Reader* (New York: Viking Press, 1961), p. 169.
7. Sargeant, p. 44.
8. Marianne Moore, "Ten Answers: Letter from an October Afternoon, Part II," *Harper's,* 229 (November 1964), pp. 98, 95.
9. Hall, p. 185.
10. Hall, p. 186.
11. Marianne Moore, "Things Others Never Notice,"

Predilections (New York: Viking Press, 1955), p. 137. She quotes William Carlos Williams.

12. "Marianne Moore by Marianne Moore," *Esquire*, 58 (July 1962), p. 99.
13. Sargeant, p. 76.
14. Sargeant, p. 56.
15. Sargeant, p. 52.
16. Sargeant, p. 68.
17. Donald Hall, "Marianne Moore," in *Writers at Work, Second Series* (New York: Viking Press, 1963), p. 75.
18. Moore, "Idiosyncrasy and Technique," p. 181.
19. Laurence Stapleton, *Marianne Moore: The Poet's Advance* (Princeton: Princeton Univ. Press, 1978), p. 250, n. 4.
20. Stapleton, p. 93.
21. Moore, "Ten Answers," p. 92.
22. Marianne Moore, "Education of a Poet," *Writer's Digest*, 43 (October 1963), p. 72.
23. Holly Stevens, ed., *The Letters of Wallace Stevens* (New York: Knopf, 1966), p. 715.
24. Jean Garrigue, "Emily Dickinson, Marianne Moore," in Tambimuttu, *Festschrift*, p. 52.
25. Moore, "Education of a Poet," p. 72.
26. Stapleton, p. 148.
27. *The Fables of La Fontaine* (New York: Viking Press, 1954), p. x.
28. Sargeant, p. 58.
29. Sargeant, p. 58; Stapleton, pp. 4, 129–130.
30. George Plimpton, "The World Series with Marianne Moore: Letter from an October Afternoon," *Harper's*, 229 (October 1964), p. 55.
31. Moore, "Education of a Poet," p. 72.
32. Sargeant, p. 59.
33. Moore, "Ten Answers," p. 91.
34. Hall, "An Interview," p. 182.
35. "Ashes of Marianne Moore, Famed New York Poet, Are Interred in Evergreen Plot," *Gettysburg Times*, April 8, 1972, p. 1.
36. Stapleton, p. 243, n. 5, p. 69, p. 242, n. 1.

37. Hall, "Marianne Moore," p. 64; Robert Sencourt, *T. S. Eliot: A Memoir,* ed. Donald Adamson (New York: Dodd, Mead, 1971), p. 131.
38. Hall, "An Interview," p. 182.
39. Hall, p. 74.
40. Hall, pp. 182, 185.
41. Marianne Moore, "If I Were Sixteen Today," in *A Marianne Moore Reader,* p. 195; "Education of a Poet," 72.
42. See selections from correspondence in Stapleton.
43. Hall, "An Interview," p. 190. See also Moore, "If I Were Sixteen Today," pp. 195–196.
44. See Moore, "Ten Answers," p. 91.
45. Stapleton, p. 188.
46. See Stapleton, p. 188; Hall, "An Interview," p. 182; and Ruth Limmer, ed., *What the Woman Lived: Selected Letters of Louise Bogan* (New York: Harcourt Brace Jovanovich, 1973), pp. 236, 336, 338.
47. May Swenson, "A Matter of Diction," in Tambimuttu, *Festschrift,* p. 48.
48. Moore, "Education of a Poet," p. 35.
49. Hall, "An Interview," p. 182.
50. Marguerite Young, "An Afternoon with Marianne Moore," reprinted in Tambimuttu, *Festschrift,* p. 70.
51. Moore, "Education of a Poet," p. 35; Hall, "An Interview," pp. 182–183.
52. Moore, "Education of a Poet," p. 35.
53. Moore, "Education of a Poet," p. 35; and "M. Carey Thomas of Bryn Mawr," in *A Marianne Moore Reader,* pp. 245–249. For a more critical assessment, see Helen Vendler, "Carey Thomas of Bryn Mawr," *The New York Times Book Review,* February 24, 1980.
54. Stapleton, p. 14.
55. The remark, she pointed out, was from an essay by a schoolboy quoted in a French newspaper. See Hall, "An Interview," p. 182.
56. Hall, "An Interview," p. 185.
57. Hall, "Marianne Moore," pp. 79–80; Moore, "*The Dial:* A Retrospect," *Predilections,* pp. 103–114.

58. Stapleton, pp. 110–111.
59. Craig Abbott, *Marianne Moore: A Reference Guide* (Boston: G. K. Hall, 1978), p. 38.
60. Marianne Moore, "Sweeney Agonistes," *Poetry*, 42 (May 1933), p. 107.
61. Marianne Moore, "Ezra Pound," *Predilections*, p. 69.
62. Marianne Moore, "Paul Rosenfeld (1890–1946)," in *A Marianne Moore Reader*, p. 208.
63. Marianne Moore, in "Presenza Della Donna Nella Civiltà Attuale," *Civilta delle machine*, 11 (Luglio-Agosto 1963), p. 32.
64. "A Letter from Kathleen Raine," in Tambimuttu, *Festschrift*, p. 111.
65. An account of the episodes with Beaton was given to me by Marguerite Young in a conversation (June 5, 1979).
66. "Marianne Moore, Poet, Dies at 84," New York Times News Service (February 6, 1972).
67. The prayer printed in the *Gettysburg Times* (April 8, 1972) will be found in Chapter 3, pp. 142–143.
68. Donald Hall, *Remembering Poets* (New York: Harper & Row, 1979), p. 190.

2. *The Art of Singular Forms*

1. Laurence Stapleton, *Marianne Moore: The Poet's Advance* (Princeton: Princeton University Press, 1978), p. 6. The course was in "imitative writing" and was based on texts by Bishop Andrewes, Francis Bacon, Jeremy Taylor, John Milton, and others. Moore once remarked: "People say, 'How terrible.' It wasn't at all, the very thing for me. Somewhat as Mr. Churchill acquired a love of well-shaped sentences from Gibbon and Macaulay. I was really fond of those sermons and the antique sentence structure." See Donald Hall, "An Interview with Marianne Moore," *McCall's*, 93 (December 1965), p. 182.

2. Stapleton, p. 7.
3. Oscar W. Larkin, *Art and Life in America,* (New York: Holt, Rinehart & Winston, 1960), pp. 354, 357.
4. William Pratt, ed., *The Imagist Poem: Modern Poetry in Miniature* (New York: Dutton, 1963), pp. 108, 109–110.
5. In the essay "Feeling and Precision," Moore observed: "When writing with maximum impact, the writer seems under compulsion to set down an unbearable accuracy; and in connection with precision . . . I think of Gerard Hopkins . . . his saying about some lambs he had seen frolicking in the field, 'It was as though it was the ground that tossed them'; at all events, precision is a thing of the imagination; and it is a matter of diction, of diction that is virile because galvanized against inertia." See *Predilections* (New York: Viking Press, 1961), p. 4.
6. Stapleton, p. 75.
7. Grace Shulman, "Conversation with Marianne Moore," *Quarterly Review of Literature,* 16 (1969), pp. 159–160. Other comments on *Marriage* appear in the Foreword, to *A Marianne Moore Reader,* p. xv.
8. Shulman, p. 157.
9. Shulman, p. 156.
10. Balanchandra Rajan, ed., *Modern American Poetry* (New York: Roy Publishers, 1953), p. 182.
11. Donald Hall, "Marianne Moore," in *Writers at Work,* Second Series (New York: Viking Press, 1963), p. 17. The additional poems were "Statecraft Embalmed" and "Critics and Connoisseurs," which are discussed in Chapter 3. Kreymborg also published "Portrait of a Lady," by Eliot; "Oread," by H. D.; "Tract," by Williams; and "Peter Quince at the Clavier," "Domination of Black," "The Worm at Heaven's Gate," and "Le Monocle de Mon Oncle," by Stevens. See *Others: A Magazine of the New Verse,* 1–5 (1915–1919).
12. From the paper, "Humility, Concentration, and Gusto," which Moore read at the Grolier Club (December 21, 1948). See *Predilections,* pp. 12, 20.

13. "A Letter to Ezra Pound," in Charles Tomlinson, ed., *Marianne Moore, A Collection of Critical Essays* (Englewood Cliffs, N. J.: Prentice-Hall, 1969), p. 17.
14. Shulman, pp. 155–156.
15. Shulman, p. 158.
16. Shulman, p. 162.
17. John Ashberry, "Straight Lines Over Rough Terrain," *The New York Times Book Review* (November 26, 1967), p. 1.

3. Art Is Always Actually Personal

1. Thomas H. Johnson, ed., *The Letters of Emily Dickinson* (Cambridge, Mass.: The Belknap Press of Harvard University Press, 1958), Vol. 2, p. 412.
2. See Pound's "Praefatio Ad Lectorem Electum" to *The Spirit of Romance* (London: J. M. Dent and Sons, 1910).
3. Donald Hall, "Marianne Moore," in *Writers at Work*, Second Series (New York: Viking Press, 1963), p. 86. The interview took place in November, 1960.
4. See "Sir Herbert Read," in Tambimuttu, ed., *Festschrift for Marianne Moore's Seventy-Seventh Birthday by Various Hands* (New York: Tambimuttu & Mass, 1964), pp. 28–29.
5. Laurence Stapleton, *Marianne Moore, The Poet's Advance* (Princeton: Princeton University Press, 1978), p. 255, n. 7.
6. Stapleton, p. 99.
7. John Unterecker, *A Reader's Guide to William Butler Yeats* (New York: Noonday Press, 1959), p. 261; see also Yeats's "Lapis Lazuli."
8. "The Proper Plenitude of Fact," in Charles Tomlinson, ed., *Marianne Moore: A Collection of Essays* (Englewood Cliffs, N.J.: Prentice Hall, 1969), p. 168.
9. "Poet, Witty and Wispy, Belittles Her Own Verse," New York Times News Service, April 21, 1967.

4. *The Spiritual Forces*

1. Richard Chase, *Emily Dickinson* (New York: Dell Publishing Co., 1951), p. 135.
2. Howard Nemerov, *Poets on Poetry* (New York: Basic Books, 1966), pp. 11–12.
3. "Religion and the Intellectuals," *Partisan Review*, 17 (February 1950), 137–138.
4. Laurence Stapleton, *Marianne Moore: The Poet's Advance* (Princeton: Princeton University Press, 1978), pp. 210, 257.
5. Joan Evans, *Magical Jewels of the Middle Ages and the Renaissance* (Oxford: Clarendon Press, 1922), pp. 35, 23, 146, 47–48. The topaz was also ascribed to Mercury; rosemary was the herb associated with the gem.
6. *The Presbyterian Hymnal*, No. 402, n. p.
7. "Introduction: Marianne Moore, Her Poetry and Her Critics," in Tomlinson, ed., *Marianne Moore: A Collection of Critical Essays* (Englewood Cliffs, N. J.: Prentice Hall, 1969), p. 6.
8. She wrote of Paul Rosenfeld (1890–1946): "He cared what becomes of us. 'America,' he said, 'must learn to subordinate itself to a religious feeling, a sense of the whole of life, or be dragged down into the slime.' " See *A Marianne Moore Reader* (New York: Viking Press, 1961), p. 209.
9. Randall Jarrell, *Poetry and the Age* (New York: Knopf, 1953), p. 164.
10. *A Marianne Moore Reader* pp. 197–198.
11. Stapleton, p. 150.
12. *The Presbyterian Hymnal*, Nos. 19 and 308, n. p.
13. Donald Hall, *Marianne Moore: The Cage and the Animal* (New York: Pegasus, 1970), p. 146.
14. Harry Torczyner, *Magritte: Ideas and Images* (New York: Harry N. Abrams, 1977), trans. Richard Miller, pp. 58, 75, 55, 215, 179, 25, 186–187, 71.

5. *In the Public Garden*

1. Laurence Stapleton, *Marianne Moore: The Poet's Advance* (Princeton: Princeton University Press, 1978), pp. 4, 233.
2. Moore, *Tell Me, Tell Me,* p. 46. The Nineteenth Amendment to the Constitution, forbidding denial of the abridgment of the right to vote on account of sex, was ratified in 1920.
3. Moore, p. 6. Moore quotes Lord Birkett, a British judge, who, when he was asked why he left his father's business to study law, said, "I think it was the fascination of using words in a way that would be effective."
4. Frederick W. Dupree, ed., *Henry James: Autobiography* (New York: Criterion Books, 1956), p. 480. Moore, in "Henry James as a Characteristic American," refers to the discussion of the point by James. See *Predilections* (New York: Viking Press, 1955), pp. 21–22.
5. William Carlos Williams, *Selected Essays* (New York: Random House, 1954), p. 29.
6. Enid Starkie, *Flaubert, the Master* (New York: Atheneum, 1971) Vol. 2, pp. 56, 85. *Salammbô* has been described as an archaeological novel of the highest pretension.
7. Peter Thornton, *Baroque and Rococo Silks* (New York: Taplinger Publishing Co., 1965), p. 168.
8. In the newspaper cartoon "Herman," by Ungar (February 26, 1980), a disgruntled man peers into the monkey cage at a zoo. The woman behind him says, "Don't stand too close; you'll make them homesick!"
9. The *Araucaria* is located in the subtropical forests of Los Paraguas and Nahuelbuta.
10. John Ashberry, "Straight Lines Over Rough Terrain," *New York Times Book Review* (November 26, 1967). The poem, he says, is "a miracle." In discussing the poem, I use the versions from *Selected Poems* (1935) and *Collected Poems* (1951).
11. A. Kingsley Weatherhead, *The Edge of the Image* (Seattle:

University of Washington Press, 1967), p. 69; and Stapleton, pp. 44–45.

12. Stapleton, pp. 85, 240, 243.

13. Robert Sterling Yard, "Mt. Rainier, Icy Octopus," in *The Book of National Parks*, pp. 159–180, 410. Yard, formerly editor of *Century Magazine* and journalist on the *New York Sun* and the *New York Herald*, became publicity director for the parks in 1915. He made a map that shows "the octopus pattern" of Mount Rainier and that is reproduced in *The Book of National Parks*; he also wrote *The National Parks Portfolio*. Both were published by Scribners in 1919. Paid for mostly by the Western Railroads, *The Portfolio* (which I have not seen) was mailed free of charge to more than a half million people (carefully selected) by volunteers from the General Federation of Women's Clubs and corps of clerks from the Office of Interior. Among those who joined Yard's efforts to boost the park movement were writers for *The New York Times*, the *Saturday Evening Post*, *National Geographic*, and the Hearst chain of newspapers, as well as members of the Sierra Club, the American Civic Association, and individuals such as H. V. Kaltenborn, Thomas Cochran, William Pierce Hamilton, Solomon R. Guggenheim, J. D. Rockefeller, and Sweden's Crown Prince Gustaf.

14. Donald C. Swain, *Wilderness Defender: Harold M. Albright and Conservation* (Chicago: University of Chicago Press, 1970), pp. 39–40, 57, 320, passim.

15. Yard, pp. 87–92. When "An Octopus" appeared in *Observations* (1924), Moore's note read: "Quoted descriptions of scenery and animals, of which the source is not given, have been taken from government pamphlets on our national parks." She adapted or "used" rather than quoted Yard's figures of speech.

16. Quoted in Stapleton, pp. 35–36.

17. The phrase, "Like happy souls in Hell," is from Richard Baxter, *The Saints' Everlasting Rest*, (Boston: Gould, Kendall, and Lincoln, 1841), abridged edition, p. 61. Baxter, a controversial but politically influential Prot-

estant in seventeenth-century England, described himself "as a dying man preaching to dying men." "Saints in heaven," he writes of the excellence of their rest, would be miserable should they be dispossessed "after the age of a million worlds," and "souls in hell" happy should they "but escape after millions of ages!" Moore's use of the phrase to describe the Greeks is probably a reference to Plato's *Apology*, in which it is asked if it would not be "unimaginable happiness" to talk and argue with "the thousands" of the dead "to find out who is really wise among them, and who only thinks that he is" (40e–41c). But why "grasshoppers of Greece"? The Greek equivalent of grasshopper is the cicada, which first appears in the *Iliad* (3:151) as a simile to describe the clear voices of the old men of Troy. In Plato's *Phaedrus*, Socrates says that the cicadas "once upon a time" were men "so thrilled with the pleasure of music" that they went on singing until they actually died without noticing it. They tell "of those who live a life of philosophy and so do honor to the music" of the Muses, "whose theme is the heavens and all the story of gods and men, and whose song is the noblest of them all" (258e–259d). Translation is from Edith Hamilton and Huntington Cairns, eds., *The Collected Dialogues of Plato* (Princeton: Princeton University Press, 1961), pp. 25, 504–505.

18. W. D. Hyde, *The Five Great Philosophies of Life* (New York: Macmillan, 1904, 1911): "It is because Christianity has introduced a Love so much higher, and deeper, and broader than anything of which the profoundest Greeks [Plato and Aristotle] had dreamed, that it has made what was permissible to their hard hearts forever impossible for all the more sensitive souls in whom the Love of Christ has come to dwell" (p. 232); "The Christian will forego many pleasures which Epicurus and even Aristotle would permit, because he is infinitely more sensitive than they. . . ." (p. 255); and "What was the end which Aristotle set before himself and his disciples? Citizenship in a city state half free and half

enslaved, with leisure for philosophic contemplation of the learned few, bought by the constrained toil of the ignorant, degraded many; the refined companionship of choice congenial spirits for which it was expected that the multitude would be forever incapacitated and from which they would be forcibly excluded. Over against this aristocracy of birth, opportunity, leisure, training, and intelligence, Jesus sets the wide democracy of virtue, service, Love" (p. 285). Moore, who was less sanguine about the virtues of the children of Adam, must have deliberately changed Hyde's analyses (to which the poet's notes refer) for purposes of satirizing the American desecration of the park.

19. Job 38:1–2, 22, 29. "My favorite poem?" Moore wrote, "The Book of Job, I have sometimes thought—for the verity of its agony and a fidelity that contrives glory for ashes." See "Foreword," *A Marianne Moore Reader*, pp. xvii–xviii.

20. As students encouraged by our professors during the thirties, we talked about America in relation to Gibbon's work. Stapleton points out (p. 69) that "Moore's reading diary of 1916–21 includes pages of notes on the taste for luxury."

21. Jean Dutourd, *The Horrors of Love*, trans. Robin Chancellor (Garden City, New York: Doubleday, 1967), p. 665.

22. Genesis 28: 10–16.

23. Stapleton, p. 74.

24. E. B. and Katharine S. White, eds., *A Subtreasury of American Humor* (New York: Coward-McCann, Inc., 1941), p. 147.

25. *Marianne Moore* (Minneapolis: University of Minnesota Press, 1965), pp. 41–42.

26. Moore, "It Is Not Forbidden To Think," *Predilections* (New York: Viking Press, 1955), p. 50.

27. Marie Boroff, *Language and the Poet* (Chicago: University of Chicago Press, 1979), pp. 134–135.

28. George Nitchie, *Marianne Moore* (New York: Columbia University Press, 1969), pp. 159–160.

29. Balachandra Rajan, ed., *Modern American Poetry* (New York: Roy Publishers, 1955), pp. 184–185.

30. Doris Herring, "Reviews," *Dance Magazine*, (June 1958), pp. 34–35. See also "The Moiseyev Dance Company: What Is It? What Is Its Appeal? What Is Its Lesson?" in same issue, pp. 33, 57, 74.

31. Harry Levin, "A Note on Her French Aspect," in Tambimuttu, ed., *Festschrift for Marianne Moore's Seventy-Seventh Birthday by Various Hands* (New York: Tambimuttu & Mass, 1964), pp. 42–43.

32. Moore recalled ("Crossing Brooklyn Bridge at Twilight," *New York Times*, August 8, 1967, p. 22) that "Tippoo's Tiger with victim" had been exhibited "some time ago" in New York. In a monograph prepared for the Victoria and Albert Museum, Mildred Archer gives the date as 1955. Moore cites the monograph, "Tippoo's Tiger" (London: Her Majesty's Stationery Office, 1959) in her notes for the poem. Like many matters in Moore's verse, the automaton had obviously caught her imagination and been remembered over a number of years before the poet was able to write about it as she wished.

33. Cecil Woolf and John Baggueley, *Authors Take Sides on Vietnam* (New York: Simon and Schuster, 1967), pp. x, 139.

34. Ralph J. Mills, Jr., ed., *On The Poet and His Craft: Selected Prose of Theodore Roethke* (Seattle: University of Washington Press, 1965), pp. 133–134. See also p. 141 for Roethke's comparison of Louise Bogan, Emily Dickinson, and Marianne Moore: "The final experience, however vivid and exact the imagery" of their poems "comes to us obliquely. . . . None quails before the eye of eternity; their world is their own, sharply defined. If others enter it, the arrival, the meeting, is on their terms."

Bibliography

I. WORK BY MARIANNE MOORE

POETRY

Poems. London: Egoist Press, 1921

Marriage. New York: Manikin Number Three, Monroe Wheeler, 1923.

Observations. New York: Dial Press, 1924.

Selected Poems. New York: Macmillan; London: Faber & Faber, 1935.

The Pangolin and Other Verse. London: Brendin, 1936.

What Are Years? New York: Macmillan, 1941.

Nevertheless. New York: Macmillan, 1944.

Collected Poems. New York: Macmillan; London: Faber & Faber, 1951.

Like a Bulwark. New York: Viking Press, 1956. (London: Faber & Faber, 1957).

O To Be a Dragon. New York: Viking Press, 1959.

The Arctic Ox. London: Faber & Faber, 1964.

Tell Me, Tell Me: Granite, Steele, and Other Topics. New York: Viking Press, 1966.

The Complete Poems of Marianne Moore. New York: Macmillan/Viking Press, 1967.

Selected Poems. London: Faber & Faber, 1969.

Unfinished Poems by Marianne Moore. Philadelphia: The Philip H. and A.S.W. Rosenbach Foundation, 1972.

The Complete Poems of Marianne Moore. New York: Macmillan/Viking Press, 1981.

COMEDY

The Absentee. A Comedy in Four Acts Based on Maria Edgeworth's Novel of the Same Name. New York: House of Books, 1962.

TRANSLATIONS

Adalbert Stifter, Rock Crystal, A Christmas Tale. New York: Pantheon Books, 1945. (With Elizabeth Mayer.)

The Fables of La Fontaine. New York: Viking Press, 1954.

Puss in Boots, The Sleeping Beauty & Cinderella. Based on the French of Charles Perrault. New York: Macmillan, 1963.

Selected Fables of La Fontaine. London: Faber & Faber, 1955.

CRITICAL AND MISCELLANEOUS (SELECTED FROM OVER THREE HUNDRED CONTRIBUTIONS TO PERIODICALS)

Predilections. New York: Viking Press; London: Faber & Faber, 1955.

A Marianne Moore Reader (includes fifty-three of the poems). New York: Viking Press, 1961.

"Well Moused, Lion," and "The World Imagined . . . Since We Are Poor," in *The Achievement of Wallace Stevens,* ed. Ashley Brown and Robert S. Haller. Philadelphia: J. B. Lippincott Company, 1962.

"The Knife," in *These Simple Things,* ed. Harriet Burket. New York: Simon & Schuster, 1962.

"Education of a Poet," *Writer's Digest,* 43 (October 1963).

"Ten Answers: Letter from an October Afternoon, Part II," *Harper's,* 229, No. 1374 (November 1964).

"Some Answers to Questions Posed by Howard Nemerov," in *Poets on Poetry,* ed. Howard Nemerov. New York: Basic Books, 1966.

"Three Essays on Williams," in *William Carlos Williams,* ed. J. Hillis Miller. Englewood Cliffs, N. J.: Prentice-Hall, 1966.

"In Fashion Yesterday, Today and Tomorrow," "Crossing Brooklyn Bridge at Twilight," and "The Library Down the Street in the Village," in *America at Random,* ed. Herbert Mitgang. New York: Coward-McCann, 1969.

II. BOOKS ON MOORE

Boroff, Marie. *Language and the Poet: Verbal Artistry in Frost, Stevens, and Moore.* Chicago and London: The University of Chicago Press, 1979.

Engel, Bernard. *Marianne Moore.* New York: Twayne Publishers, 1964.

Garrigue, Jean. *Marianne Moore.* (University of Minnesota Pamphlets on American Writers, No. 50) Minneapolis: University of Minnesota Press, 1965.

Hadas, Pamela White. *Marianne Moore: Poet of Affection.* Syracuse: Syracuse University Press, 1977.

Hall, Donald. *Marianne Moore: The Cage and the Animal.* New York: Pegasus, 1970.

Nitchie, George W. *Marianne Moore: An Introduction to the Poetry.* New York and London: Columbia University Press, 1969.

Stapleton, Laurence. *Marianne Moore: The Poet's Advance.* Princeton: Princeton University Press, 1978.

Tambimuttu, [Thurairajah], ed., *Festschrift for Marianne Moore's Seventy-Seventh Birthday by Various Hands.* New York: Tambimuttu & Mass, 1964.

Tomlinson, Charles, ed. *Marianne Moore: A Collection of Critical Essays.* Englewood Cliffs, N. J.: Prentice-Hall, 1969.

Therese, Sister M[ary]. *Marianne Moore: A Critical Essay.* Grand Rapids, Mich.: William Eerdmans, 1969.

Weatherhead, A. Kingsley. *The Edge of the Image: Marianne Moore, William Carlos Williams, and Some Other Poets.* Seattle and London: University of Washington Press, 1967.

III. BIBLIOGRAPHIES

Abbott, Craig S. *Marianne Moore: A Descriptive Bibliography.* Pittsburgh: University of Pittsburgh Press, 1977.
_____. *Marianne Moore: A Reference Guide.* Boston: G. K. Hall & Co., 1978. (Includes useful notes on writings about Moore, 1916–1976.)

Sheehy, Eugene P., and Kenneth A. Lohf. *The Achievement of Marianne Moore: A Bibliography 1907–1957.* New York: The New York Public Library, 1958.

Index

"About Age: Random Thoughts Apropos Our Aging Population," 209
"Abraham Lincoln and the Art of the Word," 135
"Abundance," 181–83
"Afternoon with Marianne Moore (1946), An" (Young), 18
"Apparition of Splendor," 96
"Appellate Jurisdiction," 123
Apollinaire, 26
Arcadia (Sidney), 99, 101
"Artic Ox (or Goat), The," 103, 111
Ascham, Roger, 17
Ashberry, John, 68, 165
"At Rest in the Blast," 145
Auden, W. H., 60, 91, 181, 193–94, 205, 216, 231

"Ballad of the Mermaid of Zennor, The" (Watkins), 113
Barchester Towers (Trollope), 49
Barnum, P. T., 188
Baudelaire, Charles, 57
Baxter, Richard, 47, 48
Beaton, Cecil, 18
"Bird-Witted," 91–93
Bishop, Elizabeth, 193, 231
"Bison, The," 37
"Blessed Is the Man," 209
"Blue Bug," 209
Bogan, Louise, 10, 144,199
"Bold Virtuoso, A," 71, 73
Book of Moments (Burke), 37
Boroff, Marie, 212
Browne, Francis F., 14
Bryn Mawr College, 10–12, 22

"Buffalo, The," 33–37
Burke, Kenneth, 37
"Burning Desire to Be Explicit, A," 53, 106
"By Disposition of Angels," 143–46

Calligrammes, 26, 30
"Camellia Sabina," 178, 183–89
  food and drink in, 184–86, 188–89
  free association in, 184–85
  Tom Thumb in, 187–88
Cantos (Pound), 17, 40
"Cap and Bells: A Faery Tale—Unfinished, The" (Keats), 221
"Cardinal Ideograms" (Swenson), 121
Carlisle Commercial College, 12
Carlisle Evening Sentinel (newspaper), 156
"Carnegie Hall: Rescued," 211
"Carriage from Sweden, A," 70, 201–3
Carson, Rachel, 16
Carta Marina (Olaus Magnus), 129
Cavendish, Thomas, 129
"Chambered Nautilus, The" (Holmes), 138
"Charity Overcoming Envy," 128, 149–51
Chase, Richard, 116
Cinderella (Perrault), 16
"City in the Sea, The" (Poe), 58
collage, 46, 50
Collected Poems 16, 118, 172
Collingwood, R. G., 91

Colum, Llewelyn, 73
"Combat Cultural,"
    216–19
Complete Poems, The, 18, 63,
    68, 75, 123
Connolly, Cyril, 206
"Counseil to a Bachelor,"
    44
conservationism, 168–69,
    174
content, artistic form and,
    25, 30, 58
Coolidge, Calvin, 35
Counter-Statement (Burke), 37
Craig, Gordon, 12
Crane, Stephen, 12
"Critics and
    Connoisseurs," 77–79
cubism, 23, 24, 36
cummings, e. e., 15, 73
Curry, John S., 34

Dadaism, 76
Dante, 11
da Vinci, Leonardo, 8, 109,
    110
*Decline and Fall of the Roman
    Empire* (Gibbon), 8, 179
Depression of 1929,
    176–77, 184
Dial, The (periodical), 14,
    22, 94, 176
Dial Press, 14
Dickinson, Emily, 5–6, 59,
    71, 72, 79
    Chase's comments on,
    116
    as Moore's predecessor,
    159
Donne, John, 218
Donoghue, Denis, 112
Doolittle, Hilda, 13, 22
Dudek, Louis, 25
Duncan, Robert, 231
Dürer, Albrecht, 96, 101

"Education of a Poet," 204
Egoist (periodical), 12
"Egyptian Pulled Glass
    Bottle in the Shape of
    a Fish, An," 31
"Elephants," 128, 205–8
Eliot, T. S., 6, 15, 17, 22,
    31, 159
    combative sincerity of, 76
    comments of, 148, 223
    Moore's references to,
    73, 80, 118, 206
    The Wasteland of, 44, 45
    in Watkin's "Ode," 86
Ellerman, Winifred
    (Bryher), 13
Ellis, Havelock, 108
Emerson, Ralph Waldo,
    14, 43, 66, 96
Encyclopaedia Brittanica, 7
"England," 157–59
"Enough," 212–14
"Enough Jamestown,
    1607–1957," 212
essays by Moore, 70, 89,
    91, 144, 157, 199
    on Louise Bogan, 199
"Examinations of the Hero
    in Time of War"
    (Stevens), 197
"Expedient—Leonardo da
    Vinci's—and a Query,
    An," 108–11
Expositor's Bible (Smith), 51

Fables of La Fontaine, The, 4,
    6, 16
"Fading of the Sun, A,"
    (Stevens), 177
Faerie Queene, The (Spenser),
    129
"Feed Me, Also, River
    God," 74
"Feeling and Precision,"
    200–201
feminism, 6, 17

Filles et Garçons (France), 48
"Fish, The," 27–28, 63, 72
Flaubert, Gustave, 163
Flood, The (Stravinsky), 9
"For February 14th," 148–49
form, artistic, 25, 30, 37, 38, 58
France, Anatole, 48
freedom, artistic, 59–60, 70
free verse, 33, 44, 61
"Frigate Pelican, The," 88
From Here to Eternity (Jones), 16
Frost, Robert, 22, 220
Fuller, Margaret, 14

Garrigue, Jean, 5, 190, 231
Gates, Mrs. Merrill R., 121
Gibbon, Edward, 8, 179
Gieseking, Walter, 200
"Gleaners, The" (Millet), 189
Godwin, William, 48
"Gold Bug, The" (Poe), 57
"Granite and Steel," 219–20
"Grave, A," 32–33, 58
Gregory, Horace, 215
Grosz, George, 76
Gunn, Thom, 231
Gustavus Adolphus, 202

Hall, Donald, 6, 40, 60, 61, 72, 94, 102, 199, 231
on a poem by Moore, 146
Handel, George Frederick, 90
Hardy, Thomas, 26, 216
Hartley, Marsden, 23, 24
Hawkins, Sir John, 129
Hawthorne, Nathaniel, 156
Hazlitt, William, 48
H. D. (Hilda Doolittle), 13, 22
"He 'Digesteth Harde Yron,'" 203

"Henry James as a Characteristic American," 157
"Hero, The," 137, 191–93
Herring, Doris, 218
Higginson, T. W., 71
"His Shield," 94–96
Historia Animalum (von Gesner), 34
History of Rasselas, The (Johnson), 89
Holmes, Oliver Wendell, 138
"Hometown Piece for Messers. Alston and Reese," 209–10
Hopkins, Gerard Manley, 36
Hughes, Langston, 230
"Hugh Selwyn Mauberly" (Pound), 159
Hugo, Victor, 57
humor, 67, 81, 87, 136, 189

"If I Were Sixteen Today," 209
Imaginary Conversations (Landor), 108
Imaginations Other Places: Poems of Science and Mathematics (anthology), 210
Imagists, the, 27, 30
Imami, 102, 103
"I May, I Might, I Must," 62
"In the Days of Prismatic Color," 81, 190
"In Distrust of Merits," 197–99
"In Memory of W. B. Yeats" (Auden), 193, 216
"In the Public Garden," 71, 159, 214–16
"Invitation to Marianne Moore" (Bishop), 193

Jackson, Sheldon, 204
James, Henry, 73, 89, 103,
  105, 130
  on Hawthorne, 156
James, William, 103
Jarrell, Randall, 135, 204
"Jerboa, The," 178–83
Jones, James, 16
Joyce, James, 12

Keats, John, 221–22
"Keeping Their World
  Large," 199
Kenner, Hugh, 35
King, Georgiana Goddard,
  22–23
Kirstein, Lincoln, 56
Kreymbourg, Alfred, 59

"Labors of Hercules, The,"
  68, 159–60
Lachaise, Gaston, 56
La Fontaine, Jean, 4, 16,
  51, 222
Lapidary of Alfonso X, 119
Lawrence, D. H., 74
Lazarus, Emma, 196
Leavis, F. R., 44
lectures by Moore, 95
Leopold, Aldo, 169
"Le Salon de Dieu"
  (Magritte), 152
Levin, Harry, 219
Levertov, Denise, 231
"Light Is Speech," 193–96
Lincoln, Abraham, 135–36
Like a Bulwark, 145
"Like a Bulwark" (poem),
  145, 146
"Literature the Noblest of
  the Arts" (Saintsbury),
  70
Littré, Emile, 190, 195
"Losses" (Jarrell), 204
"Love and Folly" (La
  Fontaine), 51
Luhan, Mabel Dodge, 74

Luther, Martin, 120, 145

McCall's (periodical), 72
"Magician's Retreat, The,"
  151
Magnus, Olaus, 129
Magritte, René, 147, 152,
  153
Mallarmé, Stephane, 26, 57
Maritain, Jacques, 200–201,
  203
Marriage, 44–52
  allusion to other authors
    in, 47–49
  collage structure of, 44,
    50
  divisions of, 46, 47–49,
    49–50, 50–52
  persona of, 46, 47, 49,
    50, 52, 72
  satire in, 51
  The Wasteland (Eliot) and,
    45
Mayer, Elizabeth, 16
Melanchthon, Philipp,
  127–28
"Melanchthon" ("Black
  Earth"), 71, 123–28,
  132
"Melchior Vulpius," 147
Mentor Book of Religious Verse
  (anthology), 118
"Mercifully," 147–48
"Mighty Fortress Is Our
  God, A" (Luther), 145
Millet, Jean François, 189
"Mind, Intractable Thing,
  The," 111–12
"Mind Is an Enchanting
  Thing, The," 66,
  199–200
"Mirror, The" (Picasso),126
"Mr. Apollinax" (Eliot), 83
modernism, 22, 24, 26
Moiseyev, Igor, 217
Moiseyev Dance Company,
  216–19

Molière, 81–82
"Monkey Puzzle, The,"
    161–65
"Monkeys, The," 83–84
Montaigne, Michel de,
    194–95
Moore, Clement, 7
Moore, John Milton
    (father), 7
Moore, John Warner
    (brother), 5, 9, 13, 166
Moore, Marianne
  appearance of, 2–3
  awards to, 16, 19
  brother and, 5, 9, 13
  childhood of, 6
  critics of, 16, 17, 27, 74,
    76
  death of, 18–20
  as *The Dial*'s editor,
    14–15, 176
  early poems of, 12–13
  education of, 5–6, 8–9,
    11–12
  as freelancer, 15
  grandparents of, 7–8
  habits of, 2
  influences on, 10–11,
    53–59
  Mount Rainier ascent by,
    166–67
  musical training of, 8–9
  as news personality, 18
  parents of, 6–8, 10
  post-war activities of,
    208–9
  in public appearances,
    18–19
  reviews by, 17, 197
  self-portrait of, 3–5
  as translator, 4, 6, 16
Moore, Mary Warner
    (mother), 6–8, 10, 13,
    142
Moore, William
    (grandfather), 7

Muir, John, 170
"My Apish Cousins," 83
"My Crow Pluto—A
    Fantasy," 53, 72

National Parks Service, 168
Nitchie, George, 214
Naumberg, Margaret, 17
"Nevertheless," 41–43, 230
New Yorker, The
    (periodical), 4
New York Times, The
    (newspaper), 2, 18, 39,
    102, 217
Norcross, George, 10
Norcross, Louise Jackson,
    10
"No Swan So Fine,"
    37–41, 143
*Notes Toward a Supreme
    Fiction* (Stevens),
    196–97
"Novices," 14, 33, 46, 76

Observations, 14
"Octopus, The," 165–76
  conclusion of, 175–76
  descriptiveness in,
    169–71
  glaciers in, 167, 175, 176
  Greek references in,
    173–74
  lengthiness of, 171, 172
  Mount Rainier and,
    166–68, 170
  octopus symbolism in,
    165–66
  trees in, 169, 175–76
"Ode" (Watkins), 86
One Times One (cummings),
    73
Others (periodical), 13
  "Our God, Our Help in
    Ages Past" (Watts), 145
"Overdrove Ox"
    (Rowlandson), 35

"Pangolin, The," 133–37
Panzini, Alfred, 111
"Paper Nautilus, The,"
    137–40, 229
Parker, Robert Andrew,
    139
"Part of a Novel, Part of a
    Play, and Part of a
    Poem," 177, 190, 191
patriotism, 6, 161–65
Perrault, Charles, 16
persona, 33, 46, 47, 49
    in "In the Public
        Garden," 71, 72
    in "Melanchthon," 124
    in "My Crow Pluto," 55,
        57
Pétain, Marshal Philippe,
    193, 196
"Peter," 87–88
Philip, Percy, 39
"Philosophy of
    Composition, The,"
    53, 55
phonetic qualities of
    Moore's poetry, 30, 54
Picabia, Francis, 23, 24
Picasso, Pablo, 23–24, 29,
    36, 46, 126
"Pied Beauty" (Hopkins),
    36
Pocohantas, 213
Poems, 13
Poems (Eliot), 159
Poe, Edgar Allan, 51, 53–59
"Poetry," 59, 72, 73, 177
Poetry (periodical), 13
poetry of Moore, 228–31
    artistic freedom and,
        59–60, 70
    form and content in, 25,
        30, 37, 38, 58
    free verse and, 33, 44,
        61
    imagery and, 26–30, 41
    imperious qualities in,

    74–77
    Moore's personal views
        and, 72
    objectivism and, 70
    rhythm and, 16, 63, 66
    savagery in, 79–80
    syllabic verse and,
        60–62, 64–66
    symbolism and, 36
poets, 12–13, 22–23, 51,
    68, 159, 210
Porgy and Bess (Gershwin),
    216
*Portrait of the Artist as a
    Young Man* (Joyce), 12
Potter, Beatrix, 105
Pound, Ezra, 17, 19, 22,
    40, 41
    Moore's communications
        with, 61, 123
    as poetic influence on
        Moore, 74
    satirized in *Marriage,* 51
"Profit Is a Dead Weight,"
    220
"Purloined Letter" (Poe),
    51
Puss in Boots (Perrault), 16

Raine, Kathleen, 17
"Raven, The" (Poe), 53,
    55, 57
Reade, Charles, 51
Read, Sir Herbert, 78
recordings by Moore,
    63–64
"Rescue with Yul
    Brynner," 212
"Respectable Burger, The"
    (Hardy), 216
reviews by Moore, 17, 197
rhythm, poetic, 61, 63, 66
"Rigorists," 204
Robert of Sorbon, 50
Rock Crystal (Stifter), 16
Roebling, John, 220

Roethke, Theodore, 225
Rogers, Will, 184, 185,
    187, 209
"Rosemary," 141–42, 148
Rosenbach Museum, 166
Rosenfeld, Paul, 17
"Roses Only," 75
Rowlandson, Thomas, 35
Ruskin, John, 11, 170

Saintsbury, George, 70, 84
Saint's Everlasting Rest, The
    (Baxter), 47
Salammbô (Flaubert), 163
Salk, Dr. Jonas E., 211
Santayana, George, 48
Sargeant, Winthrop, 19
satire, 51, 55–56, 76, 222
Scipio Africanus, 181
Scopes, John, trial of,
    161–62
Sea Around Us, The
    (Carson), 16
"Sea Unicorns and Land
    Unicorns," 128–33
Selected Poems, 15, 118, 183
"September 1, 1939"
    (Auden), 193, 194
Shaw, George Bernard, 76
Sidney, Sir Philip, 99, 101
"Silence," 49
Sleeping Beauty, The
    (Perrault), 16
Smith, George Adam, 51
"Smooth Gnarled Crape
    Myrtle," 126
"Snakes, Mongooses,
    Snake Charmers, and
    the Like," 85
Snodgrass, W. D., 231
"Song of Myself"
    (Whitman), 165
Spenser, Edmund, 60, 129
Spirit of Romance, The
    (Pound), 40
"Staff of Aesculapius,
    The," 210

Stapleton, Laurence, 34,
    58, 143
"Steeple-Jack, The," 137,
    190–91
Stein, Gertrude, 17, 22–23
Stein, Leo, 23
Stevens, Wallace, 5, 22, 68,
    71, 72
  works of, 177, 184,
    196–97
Stieglitz, Alfred, 23, 24
Stifter, Adalbert, 16
Stravinsky, Igor, 9, 62
"Subject, Predicate,
    Object," 70
"Sun" ("Fear Is Hope"),
    117–22
Sweeney Agonistes (Eliot), 17
Swenson, May, 10, 16, 121,
    231
"Sycamore, The," 12
syllabic verse, 60–62,
    64–66
symbolism, 36, 119, 122,
    124

Tailor of Gloucester, The
    (Potter), 105
"Talisman, A," 117,
    122–23
"Teach, Stir the Mind,
    Afford Enjoyment,"
    40, 41
Tell Me, Tell Me, 118
"Tell Me, Tell Me"
    (poem), 105–7
Thayer, Scofield, 14
"Then the Ermine,"
    99–100
Thomas, Dylan, 177
Thomas, Martha Carey, 12
"Those Various Scalpels,"
    79–80, 81
"Tippoo's Tiger," 220–22,
    224–25
"To a Chameleon," 26–27,
    63

"To Be Liked by You
    Would Be a Calamity,"
    74
"To an Intra-Mural Rat,"
    75
"To a Man Working His
    Way Through a
    Crowd," 12
"Tom Fool at Jamaica,"
    209
"To Military Progress," 12
Tomlinson, Charles, 124,
    231
"Too Much," 178–81, 221
"To a Giraffe," 230
"To the Peacock of
    France," 81–82
"To a Poor Old Woman"
    (Williams), 189
"To a Prize Bird," 76
"To a Snail," 140
"To the Soul of
    'Progress.'"
    See "To Military
    Progress"
"To Statecraft Embalmed,"
    75
"To a Steam Roller," 76
"To Victor Hugo of My
    Crow Pluto," 53
"To William Butler Yeats
    on Tagore," 210
trees, 169, 175–76
Trollope, Anthony, 4, 11,
    70
Twain, Mark, 7, 191
"291" (gallery), 23
"Two Songs from a Play"
    (Yeats), 140, 141

"Versailles Reborn: A
    Moonlight Drama"
    (Philip), 39
Vietnam War, 222–24

"Virginia Britannia," 212
"Visit from St. Nicholas,
    A" (Clement Moore),
    7
Voltaire, 194
von Gesner, Konrad, 34
"Voracities and Verities,"
    148
Voznesensky, Andrei, 19

Warner, Jennie Craig
    (grandmother), 8
Warner, John Riddle
    (grandfather), 7
Washington, George, 202
Wasteland, The (Eliot), 44
Watkins, Vernon, 86, 113
Watson, James Sibley, 14
Watts, Isaac, 145
Webster, Daniel, 52
"What Are Years?" 19,
    64–66, 93
"When I Buy Pictures,"
    116
White, E. B., 189
Whitman, Walt, 59, 160,
    165
Wilbur, Richard, 231
Williams, William Carlos,
    22, 30, 31, 37, 40
    Depression poem of, 189
    on Moore's poetry, 50,
    159
"W. S. Landor," 107–8

Yard, Robert Sterling,
    167–70
Yeats, William Butler, 15,
    104, 117, 140
Young, Marguerite, 18

Zulli, Floyd, 54

In the same series (*continued from page ii*)
FRANZ KAFKA   *Franz Baumer*
KEN KESEY   *Barry H. Leeds*
RING LARDNER   *Elizabeth Evans*
D. H. LAWRENCE   *George J. Becker*
C. S. LEWIS   *Margaret Patterson Hannay*
SINCLAIR LEWIS   *James Lundquist*
ROBERT LOWELL   *Burton Raffel*
GEORG LUKÁCS   *Ehrhard Bahr and Ruth Goldschmidt Kunzer*
NORMAN MAILER   *Philip H. Bufithis*
BERNARD MALAMUD   *Sheldon J. Hershinow*
ANDRÉ MALRAUX   *James Robert Hewitt*
THOMAS MANN   *Arnold Bauer*
MARY McCARTHY   *Willene Schaefer Hardy*
CARSON McCULLERS   *Richard M. Cook*
MARIANNE MOORE   *Elizabeth Phillips*
ALBERTO MORAVIA   *Jane E. Cottrell*
VLADIMIR NABOKOV   *Donald E. Morton*
ANAÏS NIN   *Bettina L. Knapp*
JOYCE CAROL OATES   *Ellen G. Friedman*
FLANNERY O'CONNOR   *Dorothy Tuck McFarland*
EUGENE O'NEILL   *Horst Frenz*
JOSÉ ORTEGA Y GASSET   *Franz Niedermayer*
GEORGE ORWELL   *Roberta Kalechofsky*
KATHERINE ANNE PORTER   *John Edward Hardy*
EZRA POUND   *Jeannette Lander*
MARCEL PROUST   *James Robert Hewitt*
RAINER MARIA RILKE   *Arnold Bauer*
PHILIP ROTH   *Judith Jones and Guinevera Nance*
J. D. SALINGER   *James Lundquist*
UPTON SINCLAIR   *Jon Yoder*
ISAAC BASHEVIS SINGER   *Irving Malin*
LINCOLN STEFFENS   *Robert Stinson*
JOHN STEINBECK   *Paul McCarthy*
TOM STOPPARD   *Felicia Hardison Londré*
J. R. R. TOLKIEN   *Katharyn F. Crabbe*
LIONEL TRILLING   *Edward Joseph Shoben, Jr.*
JOHN UPDIKE   *Suzanne Henning Uphaus*
GORE VIDAL   *Robert F. Kiernan*
KURT VONNEGUT   *James Lundquist*
PETER WEISS   *Otto F. Best*
EUDORA WELTY   *Elizabeth Evans*
EDITH WHARTON   *Richard H. Lawson*
ELIE WIESEL   *Ted L. Estess*
OSCAR WILDE   *Robert Keith Miller*
THORNTON WILDER   *Hermann Stresau*
VIRGINIA WOOLF   *Manly Johnson*
RICHARD WRIGHT   *David Bakish*
EMILE ZOLA   *Bettina L. Knapp*
CARL ZUCKMAYER   *Arnold Bauer*

MODERN LITERATURE SERIES

GENERAL EDITOR: Philip Winsor

In the same series:

S .Y. AGNON   *Harold Fisch*
SHERWOOD ANDERSON   *Welford Dunaway Taylor*
LEONID ANDREYEV   *Josephine M. Newcombe*
ISAAC BABEL   *R. W. Hallett*
JAMES BALDWIN   *Carolyn Wedin Sylvander*
SIMONE DE BEAUVOIR   *Robert Cottrell*
SAUL BELLOW   *Brigitte Scheer-Schäzler*
JORGE LUIS BORGES   *George R. McMurray*
BERTOLD BRECHT   *Willy Haas*
ANTHONY BURGESS   *Samuel Coale*
ALBERT CAMUS   *Carol Petersen*
TRUMAN CAPOTE   *Helen S. Garson*
WILLA CATHER   *Dorothy Tuck McFarland*
JOHN CHEEVER   *Samuel Coale*
COLETTE   *Robert Cottrell*
JOSEPH CONRAD   *Martin Tucker*
JULIO CORTÁZAR   *Evelyn Picon Garfield*
JOAN DIDION   *Katherine Usher Henderson*
JOHN DOS PASSOS   *George J. Becker*
THEODORE DREISER   *James Lundquist*
FRIEDRICH DÜRRENMATT   *Armin Arnold*
T. S. ELIOT   *Burton Raffel*
WILLIAM FAULKNER   *Joachim Seyppel*
F. SCOTT FITZGERALD   *Rose Adrienne Gallo*
FORD MADOX FORD   *Sondra J. Stang*
JOHN FOWLES   *Barry N. Olshen*
MAX FRISCH   *Carol Petersen*
ROBERT FROST   *Elaine Barry*
GABRIEL GARCÍA MÁRQUEZ   *George R. McMurray*
ELLEN GLASGOW   *Marcelle Thiébaux*
MAKSIM GORKI   *Gerhard Habermann*
GÜNTER GRASS   *Kurt Lothar Tank*
ROBERT GRAVES   *Katherine Snipes*
PETER HANDKE   *Nicholas Hern*
LILLIAN HELLMAN   *Doris V. Falk*
ERNEST HEMINGWAY   *Samuel Shaw*
HERMANN HESSE   *Franz Baumer*
CHESTER HIMES   *James Lundquist*
HUGO VON HOFMANNSTHAL   *Lowell W. Bangerter*
JOHN IRVING   *Gabriel Miller*
CHRISTOPHER ISHERWOOD   *Claude J. Summers*
SARAH ORNE JEWETT   *Josephine Donovan*
UWE JOHNSON   *Mark Boulby*
JAMES JOYCE   *Armin Arnold*

(*continued on last page of book*)

MARIANNE MOORE